D1276332

SAMUEL HEARNE AND THE NORTHWEST PASSAGE

Courtesy The Champlain Society, Toronto, Canada

SAMUEL HEARNE

Samuel Hearne and the Northwest Passage

By
GORDON SPECK

ILLUSTRATED WITH PHOTOGRAPHS

THE CAXTON PRINTERS, LTD.
CALDWELL, IDAHO
1963

Library of Congress Catalog Card No. 63-7445

Printed and bound in the United States of America by
The CAXTON PRINTERS, Ltd.
Caldwell, Idaho
94725

For
Jane and Jon

Acknowledgments

THIS interpretation of the life of Samuel Hearne and the myth of Anián could not have been written without the help of others both in North America and in the Old World. Many of them must remain nameless for they were the carriers of books and the copyists of ledgers and wills—and indispensable for all of that; but there are others to whom I can pay grateful tribute. To R. A. Reynolds, Secretary to the Governor and Committee of the Hudson's Bay Company, London, I am indebted for aid in clarifying many details of Hearne's life and for permission to search the archives of the Company for additional information; to Dr. William Kaye Lamb, Dominion Archivist, Ottawa, who so courteously expedited the quest for material; to Clifford P. Wilson, Editor, *The Beaver,* Winnipeg, for illustrative material and suggestions for further sources of information; to Miss Julia Jarvis, Champlain Society, Toronto, for data on the pre-Hearne voyages and many illustrations; to W. S. Chevalier, Clerk of the Board, Metropolitan Water Board, London, and N. F. Sharp, British Museum, London, for their laborious and gratuitous search of Board archives for previously unpublished data on the Hearne family; to Miss Helen Thacker, F.S.G., Record Agent, and the Public Record Office, London, for their help in outlining Hearne's naval career; to B. W. Waugh, P. E. Palmer, W. H. Miller, D. C. Carnochan, Department of Mines and Technical Surveys, and Fred Fraser, Department of Resources and Development, Ottawa, for their untiring aid and unfailing courtesy in supplying the several dozen detail maps and charts used in preparing this manuscript; to F. C. G. Smith, Department of Mines and Technical Surveys, for his assistance in delineating the navigational data on the Coppermine River; to K. J. Christie, Department of Northern Affairs and National Resources, Ottawa, for the latest evidence on the copper deposits along the Arctic coast; to W. Winston Mair, Department of Northern Affairs and National Resources; W. P. Daly, Geological Survey of Canada; N. G. Drolet, Royal Canadian Air Force; E. J. Meek, National Air Photo Library; J. D. Darling, National Museum of Canada, all of Ottawa, and all of whom went beyond the requirements of their respective positions to gather the many photographs herein; to Robert R. Payne, English Counties Periodicals, Derby, England, for his aid in obtaining the pictures and information on early Beaminster; to Miss M. Andress, B.Sc., Librarian, Beaminster, England, and H. W. Elliott, F.L.A., County Librarian, Dorchester, England, for their assistance in collecting the existing fragments of fact about Hearne's schooling and boyhood; to A. E. Davis, London Library, for his help in tracing the activities of the Bucks Club; to J. L. Johnston, Provincial Librarian, Winnipeg; Dr. Richard Glover, University of Manitoba, Winnipeg; Roy P. Basler, Library of Congress, Washington, D.C.; M. I. Foley, Public Library, San Francisco; Dr. N. S. Golding and Miss Velma Phillips, State College of Washington, Pullman; Dr. J. M. Dille, School of Medicine, University of Washington, Seattle; Edward J. Johnson, Department of Parks, Seattle; and Miss Beulah Russell, Ballard High School, Seattle, for valuable additions of minutiae without which no color is possible in a biography and also for their numerous suggestions regarding further sources of information; to Donald C. Holmes, Library of Congress; Robert E. Scudder, Free Library of Philadelphia; Christian Brun, Clements Library, University of Michigan, Ann Arbor; Henry Raup Wagner, San Marino, California; Clifford K. Shipton, American Antiquarian Society, Worcester, Massachusetts; Ronald Todd, Robert D. Monroe, and Mrs. Margaret McClure, University of Washington, Seattle, for their efforts in finding copies of the earliest maps of the New World from which it was possible to outline the story of Anián; to C. C. Uilar, British Museum, London, for his labor in searching out and photographing the piece of copper Hearne brought back from the Arctic; and to S. J. Gooding, Royal Ontario Museum of Archeology, Toronto, for supplying illustrative material and information on Company trade guns.

In addition to the above I wish to make special

acknowledgment to Miss Phoebe Harris, Miss Wanda Brockman, Mrs. M. M. Lowery, and Harold Wilson, Seattle Public Library, for their patience in answering innumerable questions and doing an infinite variety of errands far beyond the limits of their duties. Were it not for their friendly and helpful interest these chapters could never have been finished.

G. S.

Table of Contents

List of Illustrations

MAPS

Introduction

THE belief in a Northwest Passage through the American continent existed for three centuries. Staid governments and adventurous citizens expended vast fortunes and countless lives in the fruitless search and later historians have chronicled their doings many times. Hundreds of books have been written, and published, about the men who failed to find a nonexistent passage but no one has said much about Samuel Hearne, the first white man to reach the Arctic coast and thereby prove the whole business of a strait was a myth. This volume is his story.

In summarizing the history of the myth we have attempted to do only three things: enumerate some of the major steps in the search for the Strait of Anián, or Northwest Passage; place them in chronological order; and show how Hearne's work was the culmination of the search.

Scholars may criticize our omissions or inclusions, or the spellings of proper names, but it is quite impossible even to mention all the attempts to find the strait and, therefore, we have included only those which seemed to us best suited to forward our case. In the second instance, many of the explorers could neither read nor write and those who could sometimes used one name or spelling and sometimes another (especially true of the Spaniards, who were known either by their father's or mother's surname, or both), and it is important only that we have identified the man or place so there will be no mistake. In no case have we consciously used an unusual or unknown spelling or name.

Outside of Hudson's Bay Company and government circles one of the first known mentions of Samuel Hearne's trip to the Arctic was made in the introduction to Captain Cook's third expedition and Hearne's route was traced out on the Cook map. Thomas Pennant's *Arctic Zoology*, 1784, took cognizance of Hearne and the *Supplement* of 1787 and the edition of 1792 displayed his place names. These acknowledgments came before Hearne's journals were first published in England, 1795. Hearne had died in 1792 but his journals were almost certainly prepared in the major part by himself, although we know that Dr. John Douglas, Bishop of Salisbury, aided in the editing.

Hearne gave his field notes to the Hudson's Bay Company but they were already missing from the Company archives in 1819. Before his death, however, Hearne made, or had made for him, different copies of his journals because, he said, "Several learned and curious gentlemen are in possession of manuscript copies of, or extracts from, my Journals, as well as copies of the Charts." One of these copies, dated 1791, is now with the Stowe manuscripts in the British Museum. Hearne said there were some discrepancies in dates in these early copies but that later releases had been corrected from his original notes. He also said that he had added or expunged certain remarks as his larger experience had made it advisable.

These first copies and extracts evoked criticism of Hearne in the scientific world and he defended himself. It is from some of these exchanges that we get bits of information concerning what manner of man he was.

Sixteen pages of Indian vocabulary were lent by the Company to Mr. Hutchins, Corresponding Secretary for the Company, to be copied for use by Captain Duncan on his trip of 1790, but Mr. Hutchins' death intervened and the vocabulary and any marginal notes Hearne may have appended were lost.

The Hearne journals were immediately reprinted several times: Dublin 1796, a French translation by A. I. N. Lallemant, and other editions in Holland, Germany, and Sweden. Despite these widespread publications no further attention, beyond a terse paragraph in Company histories, was paid to Hearne until Mr. J. B. Tyrrell, engineer and explorer, working with the Canadian Geological Survey and aided by the Champlain Society, made an attempt to put Hearne's work before the North American public in the early years of the present century. But the Champlain Society issues only limited editions, mainly confined to the largest libraries, and Mr. Tyrrell was interested only in tracing Hearne's routes and editing his journals, not in an interpretation of the man or the significance of his work.

Every student of the North is grateful to Mr. Tyrrell for the perfection of his work and we shall make no attempt to go beyond it in so far as the several routes are concerned for our interest is in Hearne as a man and in what he did to disprove the existence of a strait through North America. Attached maps will offer the best presently available data on his probable tracks. Whether Hearne bedded down five miles this side of that, or that side of this, is of interest to a very small group and one with which we are neither qualified nor have any wish to debate. We are willing to accept their collective or individual opinions as the final word on any disputed path.

But we shall go beyond previously published volumes in an attempt to get acquainted with the man, Samuel Hearne, and appraise his relation to the search for a Northwest Passage.

The Champlain Society's copies of the Hearne journals were published in 1911 and 1934. The first deals with the three Coppermine expeditions and the 1934 volume with the establishment of Cumberland House.

The journals comprise three parts, sometimes intermixed, but generally separated: the routes and the happenings thereon; footnotes about allied or separate items of interest; and a summary of the plant and animal life as Hearne found it.

Unfortunately, Hearne's picturesque spelling

and grammar have been modernized in the Coppermine edition and much of the color of the original is lacking.

In addition to the journals there are the day books, ledgers, and other records kept by Hearne while he was in command at Fort Prince of Wales but these have never been released in their entirety by the Hudson's Bay Company. We have also used the journals of other Hudson's Bay Company men and such secondary sources as have offered pertinent data.

We have had a special search made in London of: the records of the London Water Works for information regarding the Hearne family; the files and letter books of the Company for details of Hearne's personal life and his relation with La Perouse; and the muster books of the British Admiralty for data on Hearne's naval service.

We have attempted to keep the chronology in order but we have, nevertheless, quoted Hearne out of time order in many instances where he was the only witness to a precedent or later act than that under general discussion.

Hearne returned from his Coppermine expeditions in 1772 and from then until Mr. Tyrrell went over the Barren Grounds in 1893, no white man had crossed them—only a few had hunted on their fringes. Even today there are no detailed and accurate maps of much of the area over which Hearne traveled. Official Canadian maps carry these warnings: "Caution, relief data incomplete"; "Highest elevation unknown"; "Caution, topography may be incomplete and inaccurate"; "Caution . . . other features may exist of which no information is available"; and for thousands of square miles no detailed maps exist at all, incomplete or otherwise.

In Hearne's day the Hudson's Bay Company was generally referred to as "the Company," with the upper case *C*, and we have adhered to that practice.

Unless specifically stated otherwise, all direct quotations are from the Tyrrell editions of the Hearne journals or other personal statements by Hearne.

SAMUEL HEARNE AND THE NORTHWEST PASSAGE

CHAPTER ONE

Samuel Hearne

TWO eminent explorers of modern times stand out as great and gentle men: Vitus Bering and Samuel Hearne. Each refused to use his position to save his life or drive his men to reach a goal. Each eschewed ruthless leadership for kindly persuasion and each reaped suffering and a shortened life for his consideration of others. But they were great and splendid voyagers for all of that. Bering died in a frozen, sand-filled cavern on the lonely Commander Islands but Hearne was denied so dramatic an exit. He died of dropsy in a bed in London. Bering well deserves his fame and Hearne deserves more than he has been accorded. He was the first white man to reach the American Arctic by land and thereby prove there is no Strait of Anián, or Northwest Passage, across our continent; he discovered Great Slave Lake; he established Cumberland House and saved the Hudson's Bay Company from financial difficulty if not disaster; and he presented a panorama of the North and its nomadic inhabitants, the Chipewyan Indians, now almost extinct, which has never been surpassed for truthfulness, sympathy, and color.

The family name, Hearne, is a place name, coming down from very early times in the British Isles and going through the usual corruptions but never losing its basic meaning—a nook, a corner, a bit of land in the turn of a fence, a hiding place. Bardsley's *English Surnames* says "any nook or corner of land was . . . a 'hearne.' "[1] Lacking evidence to the contrary we may assume that this was the origin of Samuel Hearne's family name.

Samuel Hearne, senior, a solid, prudent man from Somersetshire, was secretary and engineer to the London Bridge Water Works, a private business supplying almost two million gallons of water per day to nearly eight thousand homes. We can infer that Hearne, senior, knew the right people or he would not have gained a position coveted by many and certainly dependent in some degree on preferment from a source of authority.

The elder Hearne was a man of ability for while he was inventing and installing new waterwheels designed to eliminate the factor of human error, he also superintended the regular workmen, paid the bills, and still found time to write a detailed thesis on the waterworks, "a thing never attempted by any of my predecessors," he said. This manuscript is still in the possession of the Metropolitan Water Board, London, although most of the records were destroyed by fire in 1779.

In 1744, the year before young Samuel's birth (he had no middle name), the Board bought a house for the Hearnes between Thames Street and the river, and very close to the west side of the

[1] C. W. Bardsley, *English Surnames* (London: Chatto & Windus, 1898), p. 130.

Courtesy Metropolitan Water Board, London

THE WATER WORKS AT LONDON BRIDGE

There were five of these machines in use when Samuel Hearne's father was in charge of their operation. They supplied approximately 2,000,000 gallons of water per day to London residences.

bridge. Almost certainly the boy was born in the new home. The father could not have influenced his children to any great degree for he died of a fever in 1748, age forty, leaving his wife, the three-year-old Samuel, and a daughter, Sarah, age five years.

Almost all we know of Samuel Hearne's childhood comes from an obituary published in the *European Magazine and London Review* for June, 1797. The obituary says that after the death of the senior Hearne the family moved to "Bimmester in Dorsetshire," the native place of Mrs. Hearne, and that she settled down and lived the life of a respected gentlewoman. The choice of words would indicate that Mrs. Hearne — her Christian name was Diana, though we do not know her maiden surname—came from a social and economic stratum a little above the average.

Beaminster (the modern spelling) lies in a wide valley almost completely surrounded by rolling hills and watered by the Brit. Even now no railroad upsets the quiet of rural English ways but good roads lead to Dorchester and London, 133 miles to the northeast. Except for the inevitable changes of fire and time on timber and stone, riverbanks and fields, Beaminster is not too different from what it was in Samuel Hearne's boyhood. Thatched roofs have burned but solid stone houses still line the same streets; the sturdy shops still carry the same signs and similar good; the town crier still makes his rounds; the parish church,

Courtesy English Counties Periodicals, Limited, Derby, England

BEAMINSTER WELL DESERVES ITS REPUTATION AS ONE OF THE LOVELIEST OF OLD ENGLISH TOWNS

The Gothic spire dominates the valley and guards the burial grounds at its base

dating from 1503, still rises in soft brown stone one hundred feet into the sky.

More than sixty years before the Hearnes returned to Beaminster a spinster known as Mrs. Frances Tucker died and left a will which included the following paragraphs:

> For the maintenaunce of a Schoolemaster (sucessively to be chosen by my Exers or the major pte of them) I give twenty pounds p anum for ever wch Schoolemaster shall have twentie of the poorest Boyes of the pish of Beaminster aforesaid comitted to his charge and shall bee bound to take care of their manners, To Catechise them, to teach them to read to write, and, in some competent measure to cast an account.

> Item My Will is that Thirty pounds p añum bee for ever ymployed by my Exrs for the bindeing out Apprentice to some honest calling three or more of the said Boyes yearly as farr as the money will reach whereof one at least if not two shall be evy yeare sent to sea when they are fitted for it and all the Boyes before menconed to bee successively appoynted and chosen by my said Exers

This bequest of 1682 was not, however, the very beginning of the Tucker school to which Samuel Hearne was sent, for it had carried on classwork for many years previously in a portion of the parish church. Nor was it the only school in town. There was the Netherbury Grammar School, one of the oldest in England and founded before Columbus. Today the two ancient schools are amalgamated but in Hearne's time there was a certain amount of rivalry.

We do not know why Hearne was sent to Tucker's instead of Netherbury. If the Hearnes

Courtesy English Counties Periodicals, Limited, Derby, England

THE MARKET CROSS, BEAMINSTER, WHERE SAMUEL HEARNE RECEIVED HIS SCHOOLING

were moderately well off, and there is inferential evidence to indicate they were, we might have expected the boy to attend the older school, particularly since the Reverend Samuel Hood, M.A., had been master there and when the time came young Hearne went to sea under the command of the master's son, Samuel Hood. Tucker's would seem to have carried the flavor of charity and, since Mrs. Hearne was a "gentlewoman," charity was not indicated, although a small "scholarship" may have been acceptable. Perhaps Tucker's was chosen because there was provision made in spinster Tucker's will for certain boys to go to sea each year and Samuel hankered for the sea. Anyhow, he was at Tucker's about 1753.

Samuel was tractable and generally acceded to the wishes of others but he did not enjoy school. Nevertheless, he studied; he was quick to learn; he excelled in sports; and he was facile with the drawing pencil.

His mother, true Britisher, wanted him to enter trade but he would have none of shops and invoices and balances. Ironically, he was fated to become an important figure in the greatest trading company of all time, the Hudson's Bay Company.

Whether it was his desire to go to sea or that Tucker's could offer nothing more, or that the family finances were strained, we do not know, but Mrs. Hearne gave in, left Beaminster, went to Portsmouth and stayed with Samuel until Hood, famous British naval commander, accepted him as midshipman in the Royal Navy, 1756.

Since he was about eight years old when he entered Tucker's and only eleven when he went with Hood, he could not have received much formal education, considering the short school terms of the times. His journals, written and published many years later, show a very commendable vocabulary but a deficient appreciation of the grammar and spelling of his mother tongue.

Midshipmen in the 1750's were commonly entered on the rolls at age fifteen. They expected to learn navigation and be ready for a berth as mate at seventeen. Obviously, then, Samuel Hearne had one or both of two attributes—either he was precocious or his mother had unusual political connections which accounted for his early appointment with the future Viscount Hood, who, incidentally, took a particular liking to the boy and is said to have promised Mrs. Hearne that he, personally, would look after her son.

The boy that Hood took under his protection was a shy, self-effacing lad, quite incapable of enjoying the cruder pleasures of the seamen. Bear-baiting, drunkness, and brawling were not amusing to him—attributes sometimes mistaken for weakness by his more earthy companions.

The sight of suffering made him ill. Tears came more easily than to most and he had not yet learned how to cover his real feeling with a veneer of unconcern when he was thrust, at the age of eleven, into the blood and violence of the Seven Years' War.

The muster books in the Admiralty records,

London, leave some doubts as to the exact status of Hearne's connection with Hood and the Navy. Hood was shifted from ship to ship with possibly more than normal frequency, and he held several temporary commands. He was on the *Jamaica* for some of the months, during which time Hearne was presumably his servant, but Hearne's name does not appear on the *Jamaica's* muster books. Then Hood was transferred to the *Bideford,* which he commanded from July 3 to October 31, 1757, and Hearne is then listed as his servant. We know, however, that Hood was also captain on the *Bideford* in 1756, and Hearne was presumably with him then although the records are incomplete or confused. Some authorities place Hood in temporary command of the *Antelope,* fifty guns, some time in 1757, and he is credited with driving a French ship ashore in Audierne Bay and with the capture of two privateers.

In 1758 Hood became captain on the *Vestal* and the muster rolls indicate that young Hearne was transferred from the *Bideford* to the *Vestal,* thirty-two guns, at the same time.[2]

The log of the *Vestal* records some exciting names and events: she captured the *Bellona* off Cape Finisterre after a sharp three-hour fight; on March 4, 1759, she was in Portsmouth harbor where she "sent all French prisoners on shore"; she served under the great Rodney in destroying

[2] Also listed on the rolls of the *Vestal* was another "Saml Hearne. Quality Ordy." This common seaman was always listed in addition to the "Captain's servant" so could not have been the same person.

the French transports intended for the invasion of England; she touched at or passed "the Isle of Dieu, Cape Ortagal, Hamouze, Cape Clear, Ushant, Barfleur, Gilbraltar Hill, Milo, Mallacha, Matapan" and the southern Greek city of "Vatticha." Very definitely not a dull itinerary for an eleven- or twelve-year-old boy!

There is a story to the effect that Hood mentioned sharing the prize money with his young recruit and Hearne is supposed to have said to give any such reward to his mother as she would know best how to use it. If this carries a certain overfamiliar I-owe-everything-to-Mother tinge, nevertheless there are several references in the Company records of payments being made to Hearne's mother long after he reached maturity. On August 8, 1772, he wrote from Fort Prince of Wales and asked the Company to "pay to Mrs. Diana Paine [his mother had remarried] the Balance of my last 3 Years Wages; and as Your Honours Mentioned that a gratewaty would be granted me at my return from the Inland Journey: that also Please pay to Mrs. Paine all of which she is to put out for my Benifett, and her receipt shall be your full discharge. . . ."[3] Almost a full nine months later the Company answered the above request as follows:

. . . Being desirous that you should hereafter enjoy the benefit of your Labours in the early Stage of Life We did not comply with your Order in paying your Balance of Wages and the

[3] H. B. C. Arch. A. 11/14 fo. 175. Published by permission of the Governor and Committee of the Hudson's Bay Company.

Gratuity to be allowed you but as the whole sum due to you is £272. 16. 6 We have placed £258. part thereof in the purchase of £300 Bank Consolidated 3 per Cent Annuities which will produce you £9 a year until such time as you shall chuse to alter the Mode of the present Investment. . . .[4]

The above refusal to comply with Hearne's request may indicate a distrust of family judgment, especially the mother's; or, was the Company playing the benevolent despot and exercising the best tenets of paternalism?

From his days with Hood, while little more than a child, almost to the end of his life the gentle Samuel Hearne was entrusting or giving his earnings to someone else—and they were often handsome sums: £48 to his mother, £150 to his married sister, Sarah Le Petit, and a baffling £4. 4s. to one Richard Hearne,[5] of whom there is no record beyond the entry of disbursement in the Company books.

The Treaty of Paris, 1763, closed the Seven Years' War and apparently ended Hearne's naval career.[6] He had served seven years. The timid boy of eleven had grown into a tall, powerful, and handsome young man of eighteen. His courage had been tested through seven years of war but he was still a gentle man, preferring persuasion to force and hating violence and suffering

[4] H. B. C. Arch. A. 5/1, fo. 152. Published by permission of the Governor and Committee of the Hudson's Bay Company.

[5] Published by permission of the Governor and Committee of the Hudson's Bay Company.

[6] Research in the Admiralty records finds no reference to Samuel Hearne after April 30, 1763.

Courtesy The Champlain Society, Toronto, Canada

HEARNE'S NAME CARVED IN THE GLACIATED ROCK OF SLOOP'S COVE

and bloodshed, against which he could lash out in verbal fury. And if he had learned that he could not always escape violence and death, he had also learned to forgive those who were responsible for them. Despite these Christian attributes he was not a religious man; in fact, he professed a nonbelief.

He loved good food but could go long days without it; he was fond of the colorful clothes of the Revolutionary period but he was no fop; he enjoyed companions but they must have content to their thinking; he took pleasure in social events but never forgot they were only social events; and he was possessed of a stubborn determination to "make a name" for himself, to use his own phrase.

But most of all he was endowed with an intense curiosity. Nothing escaped his attention: animals, topography, and flowers, tribal customs, primitive philosophies, and mankind, either individual or collective, were never-ending sources of interest.

He was not without faults. His meekness often led to indecision and inaction while he secretly nursed a good opinion of his own ability; he tolerated action in others, which endangered his own objectives and the lives of those who trusted his leadership; and he seldom inspired his subordinates, particularly those of his own race, with a blind devotion to his command.

Nevertheless, his qualities far outweighed his faults and he stands unchallenged among New

World explorers for the risks he took to win his goal.

Why Samuel Hearne left the Royal Navy we do not know but on February 12, 1766, he entered the employ of the Hudson's Bay Company at a salary of £25 per annum. He arrived at the Company post, Fort Prince of Wales, at the mouth of the Churchill River on the west side of Hudson Bay, in August.

Hearne's life is full of gaps about which nothing is known. He left no personal record of his experiences with Hood, or where he was or what he did between April 30, 1763, when he presumably quitted the Royal Navy, and February 12, 1766, when he joined the Company; and from August of 1766, when he arrived at Churchill, until he began his explorations to the Arctic there is but the scantiest data. He was assigned to the sloop *Churchill,* a Company ship trading about the mouth of the river; two years later he was on the *Charlotte* under Joseph Stevens, with whom he was not notably happy; he is seen, often by inference, carving his name on a rock, hunting wild geese to supply the winter larder, repairing equipment or tending the Company store—but essentially he was preparing himself, quietly but with determination, to make the first overland journey to the American Arctic and either find the supposed Strait of Anián or prove its nonexistence.

It was a dream of mighty achievement and worthy of the myth of Anián.

C H A P T E R T W O

The Myth of the Strait of Anian

SAMUEL HEARNE and the Strait of Anián! Excepting the Crusades and the search for the Holy Grail, more fortunes and lives were spent in seeking the Strait of Anián, or the Northwest Passage, than for any other myth in history. It was a great chimera and the man who proved the myth was but a myth shares in its greatness.

In the beginning the mythical strait was thought to separate the Old World from the New but before that assumption could be adequately tested Pope Alexander VI drew the Line of Demarcation, dividing the New World between Spain and Portugal, and thereby forced other European powers to seek a route to the Orient which would, in effect, nullify the edict.

Any one of three possibilities would do: a seaway north of Russia, a northwest passage across the top of North America—or a strait through it.

How the latter two possibilities became fused into the myth of Anián no one knows, but in less than a generation after Columbus the cartographers and sailors had created the myth—there was a Strait of Anián somewhere across North America, although there was no agreement on either its nature or location.

For two hundred and seventy years they sought the myth by land and sea and when Samuel Hearne proved there is no landward passage they concentrated on the Arctic sea and searched another one hundred and seventy-five years until Roald Amundsen put his little ship, the *Gjoa,*[1] through the Arctic floes in 1903-6 and charted a maritime route from the Atlantic to the Pacific.

There is no satisfactory record of the beginnings of either the name, or the idea, of the Strait of Anián. Some say the name was a corruption of names and stories from the days of Marco Polo and an unknown Anus Cortereal; some believe the name, the idea of a strait, and its location, were all pure fabrication; some think the myth should be identified with early rumors of Bering Strait. In any event, the four centuries of seeking were the work of royal courts, the great city and commercial companies, and the dedicated scientists in every branch of human knowledge and in every land. And they spent vast fortunes and unnumbered lives in the search.

Certain known facts are pertinent: South America was recognized as a continent long before North America was so accepted; Marco Polo reported a strait from China to India; and, since Columbus believed the West Indies to be Japan and the mainland of America to be Asia, it was, therefore, logical to seek Polo's strait.

The earliest known map of the New World by

---

[1] The *Gjoa,* thoroughly reconditioned, is now in Golden Gate Park, San Francisco.

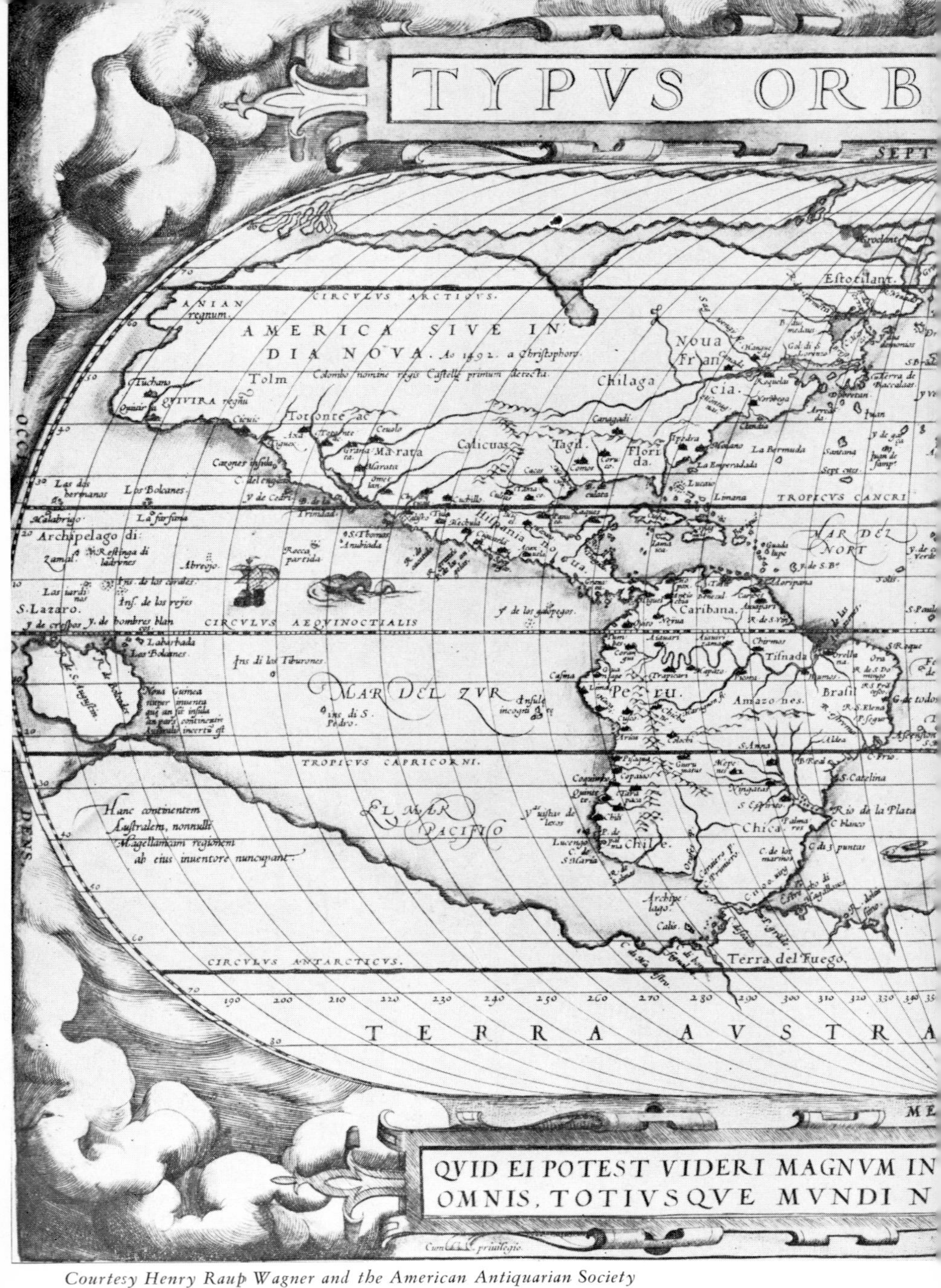

Courtesy Henry Raup Wagner and the American Antiquarian Society

ORTELIU

It places Anián on the mainland of North America a

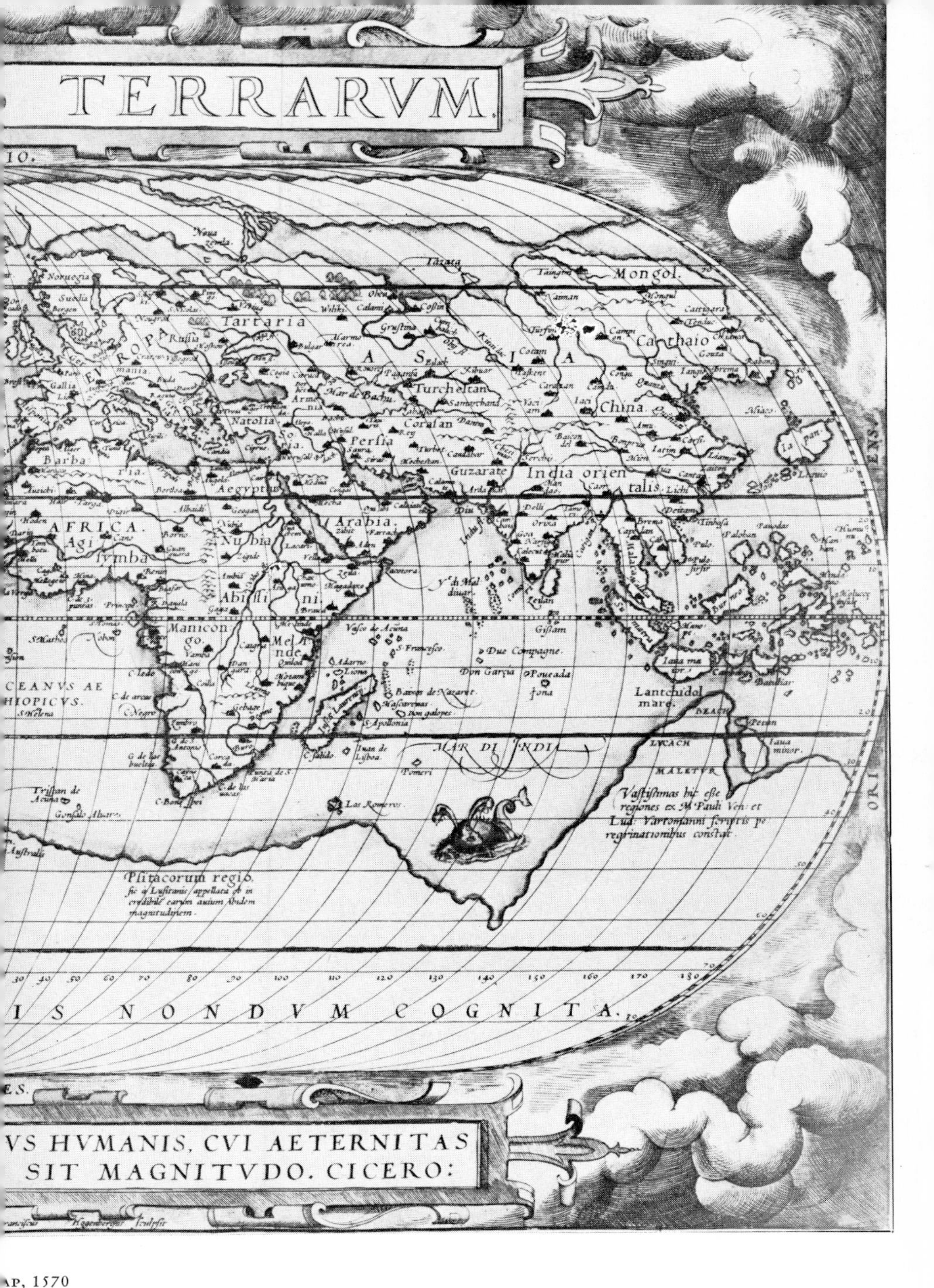

ᴀᴘ, 1570
phasizes the Four Polar Islands and the Polar Strait

Juan de la Cosa, 1500, showed a passage below the equator in South America. From that time until Samuel Hearne proved no such waterway existed almost every map maker included Anián somewhere in his work.

The myth of Anián was perpetuated by three categories of participants: the cartographers, who included it on their maps; the frauds, who reported fantastic discoveries; and the actual expeditions sent out by the great commercial houses and courts—expeditions whose commanders honestly believed they had found evidence to support their hopes.

In this volume it is permissable to cite only such examples as will give perspective to the work of Samuel Hearne.

The Cartographers

Here we may sample, somewhat by geographic distribution and in chronological order, a few of the map makers whose repetition of old errors and their own fresh imaginations kept the myth alive.

Johan Schöner, the German, separated his "Cuba" from Japan with a strait; and Sebastian Münster and Gemma Frisius drew a strait across North America. Previous to Elizabeth I much of the hope for a route, north of Columbus' landfall, was across the top of Russia. Here was a known land mass; here were at least semi-Christian peoples; here was the beginning of a known way, the ice-strewn track from the North Sea to the river Ob. But, when the Zeno brothers, 1558, placed Greenland squarely across such a route the emphasis returned to the New World.

By 1561 the Venetian, Giocomo Gastaldi, whose charts were widely used by the best mariners, pushed the coastline of Asia as far north as 50°, where he located Anián. Then Abraham Ortelius, of Antwerp, 1564, followed Gastaldi's lead and added Cartier's discovery of the St. Lawrence. Bolognino Zaltieri, of Venice, and the great Gerard Mercator used the name Anián and projected a strait across the New World.

About 1582 two Englishmen, Michael Lok and Dr. John Dee, compared the charts they had drawn. Lok was a successful London merchant with a deep and sincere interest in exploration. He was a chief promoter of the Davis and Frobisher voyages and enjoyed a reputation as a serious cartographer.[2]

Dr. Dee was an established authority. He was a Cambridge mathematician; he had studied under Frisius and Mercator and he was instructor in navigation and astronomy to "almost all the Arctic captains and pilots of his day."[3] Yet he, too, embraced the myth of Anián.

Lok had one strait in the approximate latitude of Juan de Fuca but Dr. Dee had a northeast pas-

---

[2] H. H. Bancroft, *History of the Northwest Coast* (New York: The Bancroft Company, n.d.), I, 64, 101; also Dorothy O. Johansen and Charles M. Gates, *Empire of the Columbia* (New York: Harper & Brothers, 1957), p. 23.

[3] L. P. Kirwan, *A History of Polar Exploration* (New York: W. W. Norton & Co., 1959), p. 16.

IL Disegno del discoperto della noua Franza, ilquale s'è hauuto ultimamente dalla nouissima nauigatione de Franzesi in quel luogo: Nel quale si uedono tutti l'Isole, Porti, Capi, et luoghi fra terra che in quella sono.
Venetijs æneis formis Bolognini Zaltery
Anno . M . D . LXVI .
MARE SETENT
IN COGN
TERRA
IN COGNITA
AVACAL
APALCHEN
PAR
TE
DI
QVINCIT
AS
I
A
Cuanzu
STRETO DE ANIAN
Pangin
Almaro
Sinaua
Sinzu
Tingui
Caman
Vnque
Quinsay
Quelinfu
Zaitò
Sacrat
Vguin
Zangia
P. de zaiton
Tinzu
Brema
P. Campu
GOLFO
CHINAN
Galera
Sierra Neuada
Tuchano
QVIVIRA
PRO:
Quiuira
P. Primo
C. Neua
P. d. Fuogo
Chichuich
P. de S. Michel
Axa
R. Axa
C. de Crus
Tiguas
Ancoras
CIVOLA
GRANATA
Granata
Iguas
Comos
R. Tontonteac
Chucho
Coacos
Culiaz
Vachus
Meschite
Coloaton
Tontonteac
S. Michel
Panuco
Chicana
Chamariá
Villaricca
Colima
Tinistitam
Apusalca
Mistecai
Tacantepech
Crux Santo
Camola
Guatusco
Cumat
Nicara
Granada
P. Serado
C. del Cortese
MARE DE MANGI
GIAPAN
Mezacar
Cazones
Isola di ripara
P. d' Lea
P. Ascòdido
C. de lingano
Y. di Cedri
P. d' Canoas
P. de Labbate
P. Canoas
C. delle Corente
Y. delle Perle
C. S. +
MARE DEL SVR
S. Bortolamio
Rocha Partida
S. Tomaso
PONENTE
TRAMON

Courtesy Library of Congress, Washington, D.C.

Bolognino Zaltieri Believed An

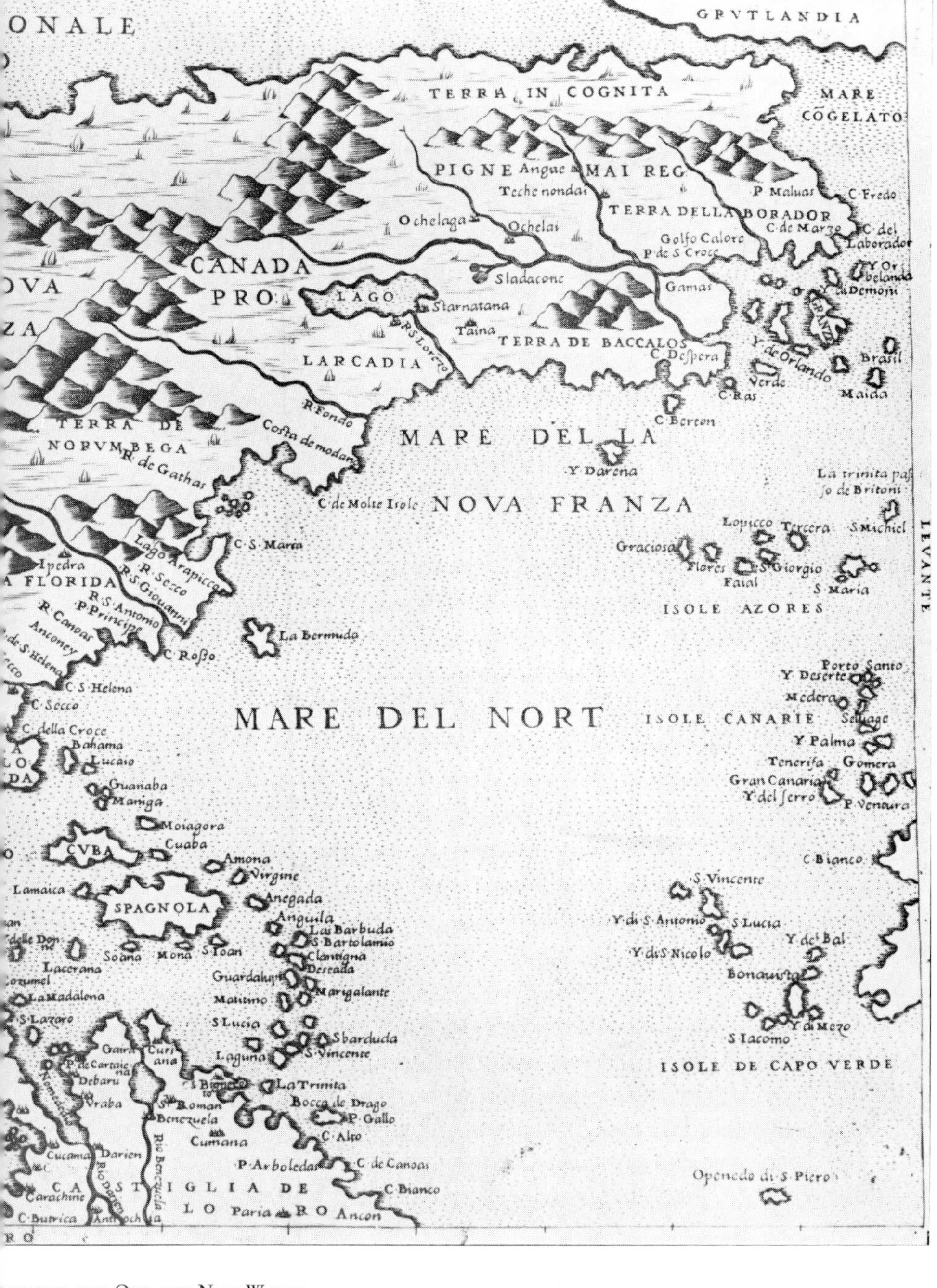

ARATED THE OLD AND NEW WORLD

sage and a northwest passage; another followed up the St. Lawrence and via several rivers and lakes debouched into northern California; still another ran north and south to the "Verazana Sea." Supplementing these were an intricate series of lesser waterways — the whole bearing no resemblance whatever to the truth.

More sedate cartographers such as Peter Plancius, of Amsterdam; Joannes Martines, of Spain; Gabriel Tatton, of England; and the noted Flemish engraver, Jodocus Hondius, all believed in a maritime passage somewhere in the New World. Even the renowned Richard Hakluyt, English journalist, sponsored a large lake in Nevada and three huge rivers heading up in Yellowstone Park and flowing gently off to the Arctic!

And five years after the *Mayflower*, 1625, *Purchas His Pilgrimes* said there was a "faire entrance to the nearest and most temporate passage to Japan and China" from "North Fretum Hudson and Button's baye."

Now it might reasonably be assumed that as time went on the charts would become less fanciful and the myth of Anián be accepted for the legend it was—but such was not the case. If the early explorers failed to find Anián they also failed to prove its nonexistence and by this very failure kept the myth alive. Between the landing of the Pilgrims and Samuel Hearne, one hundred and fifty years later, the Strait of Anián, under one guise or another, was included on most charts and globes.

When Hearne was a boy of seven years the

famous Delisle map, 1752, was published.[4] It included all the old myths and some new ones. "Aguilar's River" and the "Entree de Juan de Fuca" were there; the "Mer de l'Ouest," a large inland sea connected to the Pacific by "Aguilar's River" and "de Fuca" were there; north of these waterways were "Lac Belle," "Lac de Fonte," and others ending up in Hudson Bay.

After two and a half centuries Delisle produced a map containing as many or more fallacies as the very first charts after Columbus.

From de la Cosa, 1500, to Delisle, 1752, the map makers agreed on one thing: the myth of Anián.

The Frauds

No great cause escapes the frauds who fatten on the current daydream, and the search for Anián presented them with four centuries of opportunity.

Pedro Menendez de Aviles, colonizer of Florida, met a man in 1554 who had gone through a strait on a French vessel; it was common gossip that Drake had not really sailed around the world but had returned to England via Anián; a French version had one end of Anián in Germany; fabled Quivira was sometimes on Anián and Hakluyt has it that "there went from Europe three brethern through this passage; whereof it took the name

[4] Joseph Nicolas Delisle and his older brother, Guillaume, were both well-known cartographers. There were many editions and imitations of the 1752 map.

Courtesy Library of Congress, Washington, D.C.

ONE VERSION OF T

lisle-Buache Fantasy

of 'Fretum trium fratum,'" the Strait of the Three Brothers.[5]

By one hundred years after Columbus some very considerable prizes were offered for the discovery of Anián and Lorenzo Ferrer de Maldonado, who had actually made one trip to the New World, proposed to claim one of them and let others prove he lied.

In 1588, the year of the defeat of the Spanish Armada, Maldonado said he went to Iceland, thence to the "Strait of Labrador" which he followed to about 75° north. He turned "down from that latitude" to 60° "where the Strait of Anian is to be found." "The Strait of Anian is fifteen leagues long and you can easily pass through it with a tide." There were twenty-four hours of daylight but it was intensely cold, and ice formed on the rigging. Dried apples, plums, pears, and grapes were left over from the preceding summer; there were deer with large shovel-like horns and black and white spots on a grey pelt; there were several kinds of swine, one in particular which had the "umbilical cord on the back"; there were outsized fish; the uncivilized people were Christian Catholics; and, while he was anchored at the southern end of the strait a great ship of 800 tons (50 tons were common) carrying "Hanseatic" merchants "came to pass from the south sea into the Strait."

Then there was the legend of Juan de Fuca,

[5] Richard Hakluyt, *Voyagers' Tales and Voyages in Search of the North-West Passage* (London: Cassel and Company, Ltd.), p. 41.

1592, a Greek in the service of Spain. He met Michael Lok in Venice in 1596 and told him that four years previously he, Juan de Fuca, had found the Strait of Anián at approximately 49° north, very near the modern strait of Juan de Fuca. The Delisle map of 1752 still credited him with the discovery and Thomas Jeffreys, geographer to the English Crown, had a splendid map, 1768, showing the de Fuca voyage. Even today we cannot be positive that Juan de Fuca did not discover the strait which bears his name, even if it is not Anián.

The London *Monthly Miscellany, or Memoirs of the Curious* published certain letters in April and June of 1708 telling of the apocryphal voyage of Bartholomew de Fonte. According to the letters de Fonte "put to Sea the 3rd of April, 1640," traveled up the west coast of North America, surmised that California might be an island, reached de Fuca, turned northeast and sailed blithely across the Rockies and on through the wide central prairies until he met a Captain Shapley from Boston. De Fonte's narrative was taken so seriously that sixty years later Thomas Jeffreys (there is some disagreement as to his real name) showed the de Fonte voyage and said that the idea of a Northwest Passage "hath continued for more than two Centuries" and the rewards offered for its discovery so high that even those who doubted its existence nevertheless treated the idea "with a becoming Decency." This was on the very eve of the American Revolution! George Washington

Courtesy Henry Raup Wagner and the American Antiquarian Society

HENRY BRIGGS'S MAP SHOWI

ifornia As an Island

was a Virginia hero and old Ben Franklin an international celebrity!

Several years before the de Fonte letters were released, Thomas Peche, himself possibly only an English legend, told of a lurid voyage to the Moluccas. Having finished trading there he decided to go home via Anián but the current inside the strait was too strong; starvation was decimating his crew and in order to save something of the venture he threw 120 dead men overboard and tossed in 35 live ones for good measure. They had threatened mutiny, he said.

As late as April, 1790 (Washington was President), Aaron Arrowsmith published an English map hinting broadly of a strait across the continent just north of "Quivira." This was arrant nonsense for by 1790 the trappers had overrun all the headwaters of the St. Lawrence, Samuel Hearne had gone to the Arctic, and thousands had traveled the Mississippi to the Gulf. If any east-west strait existed these men would have crossed it.

CHAPTER THREE

Early Voyages

WHILE the cartographers were busy with their charts and the impostors with their lies, the actual search for the Northwest Passage, either through or around North America, was under way. Only five years after Columbus, John Cabot lost his life in the search but his son, Sebastian, "described this passage" and said, according to Hakluyt, "he might, and would have gone to Cataia [loosely our China or Orient] if the mutinie of the Master and Mariners had not been."

Hernando Cortez captured Mexico as a preliminary to the search for Anián; the Spaniard, Lucas Vasquez de Ayllon, examined the James River and Chesapeake Bay in 1524, seeking a way west; and in the same year the Italian, Giovanni da Verrazano, got as far as the mouth of the Hudson River for the same purpose.

Jacques Cartier believed he had found the passage as he sailed up the St. Lawrence and Hernando de Soto died on a fever swamp along the Mississippi believing he was near Anián and Cathay.

Cabrillo and Ferrelo, Spaniards, with two tiny vessels, one without even a deck and manned by conscripted criminals, fought Pacific storms from Mexico to Oregon for six months without finding a passage, but even as Cabrillo lay dying from injury and exposure, he ordered Ferrelo to continue the work.

Francis Drake swaggered around the world looking for Spaniards, gold, and Anián, and when Sir Humphrey Gilbert applied to Elizabeth I for permission to establish a colony in the New World, he intended to use it as a base for the search for the strait. Gilbert went down with his ship, 1583, but his *Discourse,* which argued so eloquently for the existence of Anián, was the prime influence behind the voyages of Martin Frobisher.

It was the golden age of English adventure. Humphrey Gilbert set out to plant a new England in a New World; Francis Drake to "singe the King of Spain's beard" in the far Pacific; Martin Frobisher to find a Northwest Passage and then, with Drake and Howard and Hawkins, to send the Spanish Armada to its defeat.

Martin Frobisher was only less a daredevil than Francis Drake. In the spring of 1576 he headed for Arctic waters with two tiny pinnaces, faulty charts, and little knowledge of where he was going or what to expect. He touched the southern tip of Greenland but because he thought it was one of the islands depicted on the Zeno map he called his landfall "West Friezeland." From there he sailed for the Northwest Passage and glory.

Martin Frobisher found his waterway but time proved his "streight" to be the Frobisher Bay of modern maps, and his "Cathay" to be Baffin Island.

But no matter: Martin Frobisher seized a peaceful Eskimo in his skin kyak, looked at his Mongoloid eyes, plopped him aboard the Frobisher pinnace, collected a handful of Arctic flowers, a lump of black stone, and sailed for home.

Frobisher was convinced he had found the eastern end of a northwest passage and captured an inhabitant of "Cathay." But just then someone noticed that under certain lights the black stone threw off yellow glints.

Gold! The passage must wait.

It was easy to acquire new ships and the Queen's blessing for a second trip. Stopping at "West Friezeland" only long enough to claim it for Elizabeth and rename it "West England" Frobisher hurried on to Baffin Island. From dawn till dark all hands collected the rich black stone, two hundred tons of it. Then home again to the Queen and a hero's welcome.

When an Italian assayer identified the ore as gold all restraints vanished. The Cathay Company, lavishly financed by the Crown and city merchants, sent fifteen ships with miners and settlers, tools, and knockdown houses to far-off Baffin Island—and the Strait of Anián.

But Martin Frobisher forgot the Arctic ice. In one blinding, crashing fury it tore his fleet to shreds. A pitiful remnant of men and ships crawled back to England only to find that Frobisher had previously unloaded two hundred tons of iron pyrites—fool's gold![1]

---

[1] In May of 1860, almost three centuries later, Charles Francis Hall, a poor printer from West Cincinnati, with no exploring experience what-

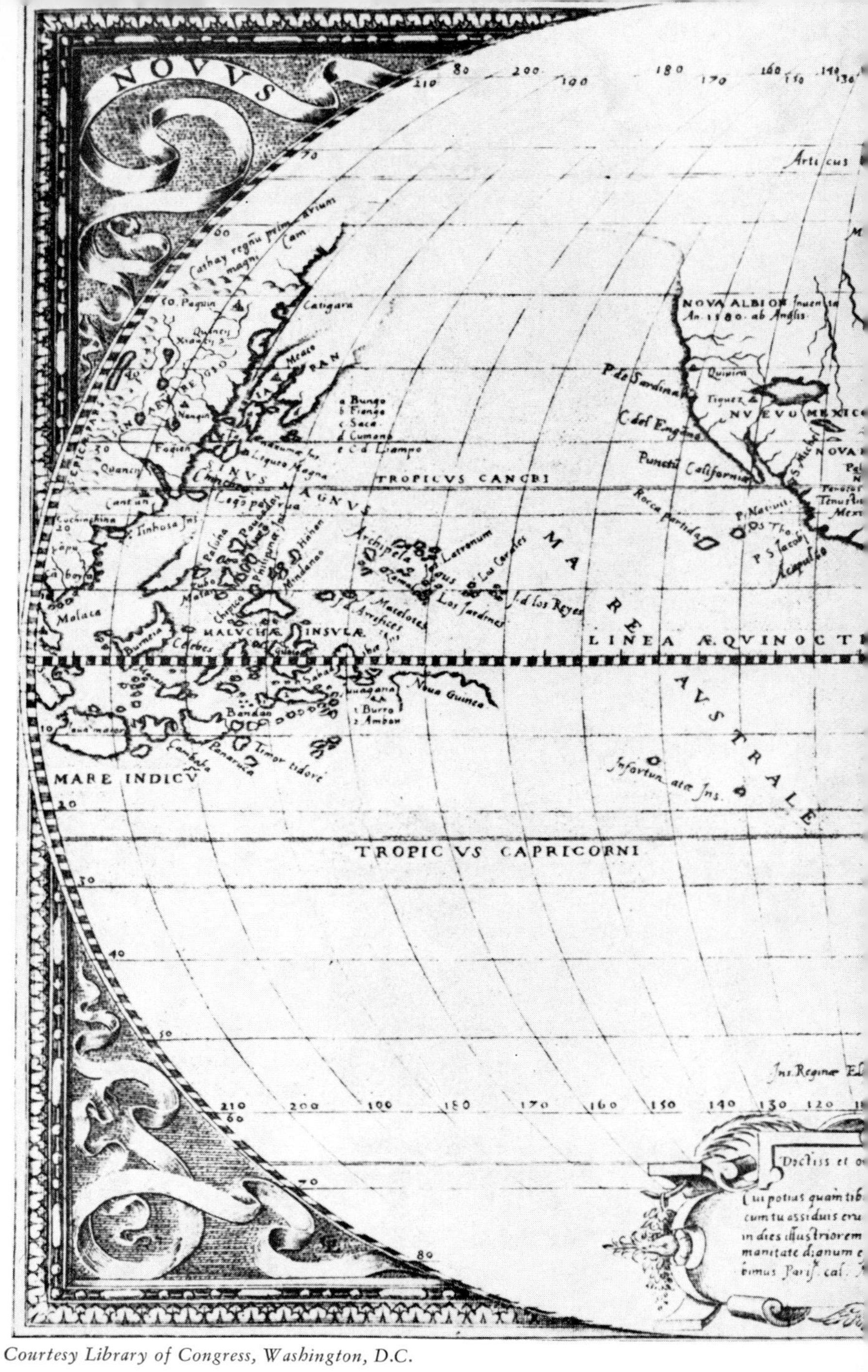

Courtesy Library of Congress, Washington, D.C.

NEW WORLD MAP BY

Not every map of the Ne

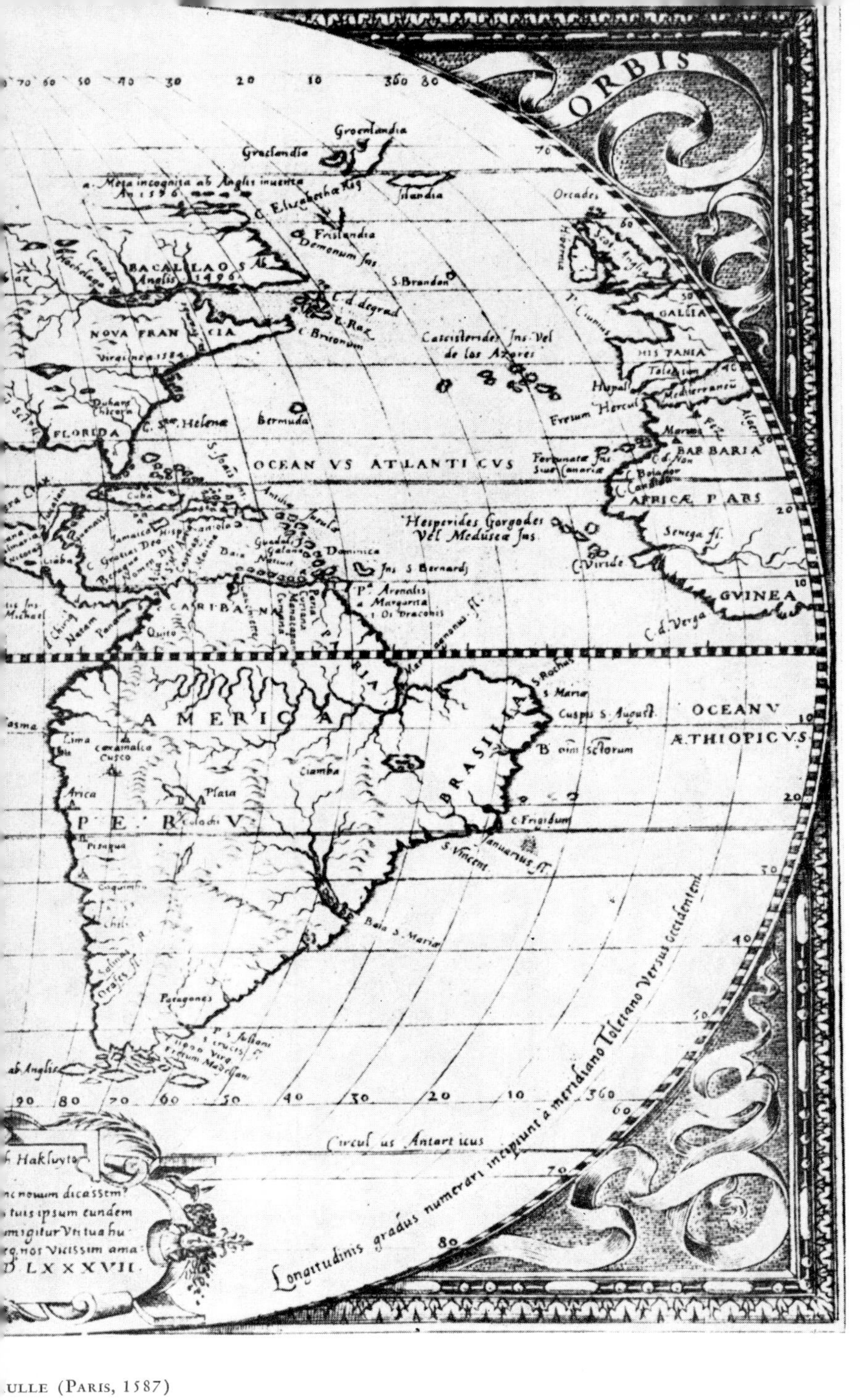

ULLE (PARIS, 1587)
orld considered Anián a reality

Suddenly official England lost interest in the strait.

Nevertheless, there were sturdy Britishers, such as Gilbert, who retained their faith and in 1584 a new North West Company sent John Davis (Davis Strait), perhaps the best navigator of his day,[2] into Arctic waters for a further search. That he failed to achieve victory in no way lessened his belief, "that the north-west passage is a matter of nothing doubtfull, but at any tyme almost to be passed, the sea navigable, voyd of yse, the ayre tolerable, and the waters very depe."[3]

But the Spanish Armada, 1588, gave England other things to do and the search for Anián shifted back to the Spaniards and the Pacific coast.

In 1602-3 Sebastián Vizcaíno, with three ships, sailed from Mexico to Old Oregon and came perilously close to losing his entire command from storm and scurvy. One crew of thirty-four lost twenty-five, and Vizcaíno, himself, once had only two sailors able to mount the mainmasts.

The search for Anián demanded heroes and there was no shortage. If their lives and deaths failed to prove the myth they nevertheless performed a mighty work for they drew the outline of North

---

ever, sailed for the Arctic hoping to find survivors or equipment from the ill-fated Franklin expedition of 1845. He failed in that quest but "he made, however, one astonishing discovery, bringing back to America many relics of Frobisher's unfortunate sixteenth-century expedition, all of which have since and quite unaccountably disappeared." L. P. Kirwan, *A History of Polar Exploration* (New York: W. W. Norton & Co., 1959), p. 182.

[2] *Ibid.*, p. 25.

[3] *Ibid.*, p. 26.

America and, as they sketched a new coastline, found a new river or entered a new harbor, they pushed the possible area for Anián into a narrower and narrower pocket.

With the defeat of the Armada Spain's prestige sagged and the Line of Demarcation meant nothing. Adventurous leaders from every country in Europe entered the scramble for colonies, gold, and the search for Anián. Captain John Smith was looking for the passage when he stumbled into his romance with Pocahontas. The Frenchman Champlain wandered into upstate New York, hoping he had found the way. Father Marquette and the trader, Joliet, were seeking as they drifted down the Mississippi.

Henry Hudson, a professional mariner in the employ of London, had gone farther into Arctic waters, beyond Spitsbergen, than any previous sailor and, on the strength of that voyage, was commissioned to try for a northeast route across the top of Russia. But, faced by ice and two possible routes, he hesitated, listened to a mutinous crew, led by Robert Juet, and returned to England. His failure so discouraged the Muscovy Company it refused to finance another attempt and Hudson contracted with the Dutch East India Company to continue his work. After several changes of plans he was ordered to explore the North American coast in competition with his late employers, the English. His work on the Hudson River convinced the English they had been hasty in relinquishing his services and he was rehired to discover if "any passage might be found to the other ocean called the South Sea."

Without mishap Hudson entered the bay which honors him and in so doing was convinced he had solved the myth of Anián. He explored somewhat at random, then turned south and wintered at the mouth of Rupert River on James Bay. The subarctic days grew short, game disappeared, the sea birds left, ice threatened the *Discovery,* scurvy broke out—and Robert Juet led a new mutiny.

Hudson did nothing effective. When June came the final tragedy was set. Unable either to inspire or control his crew, Hudson was put in the ship's boat just at dawn off Charlton Island. His young son and five loyal seamen drifted with him to their deaths because they had not found Anián.

Juet and the mutineers returned to England and were spared hanging only because they delivered Hudson's charts to the Admiralty and with them a renewed faith that somewhere in that great bay was the eastern end of a strait.

From that day until Samuel Hearne proved there is no Anián there were few years in which some expedition was not plowing northern waters looking for a way either through the continent or around it. To review all these expeditions would defeat the purpose of this volume, nevertheless, certain notable examples may not properly be omitted.

So it was that in 1612 Sir Thomas Button, financed by the "Governor and Company of the Merchants of London, Discoverers of the North-

West Passage," sailed for Hudson Bay to "search and find out a passage by the north-west of America to the Sea-Sur, . . ." With Robert Bylot, another of Hudson's mutineers as chief pilot, Button explored Hudson Bay as far as Southampton Island.

Four years later came the tragic voyage of Jens Munk. A Dane by birth, Munk had led an adventurous life. He had visited Iceland for sulphur; had twice sailed for but failed to reach Novaya Zemlya; had failed to navigate a northeast passage; had joined the Danish Royal Navy and fought the Swedes; had gone to Spain as interpreter-purser for a Crown mission; had escorted a Russian embassador from Copenhagen to his home; had been dispatched to fight pirates in the North Sea; had entered the Arctic whale trade as a personal sideline; and was just now about to be ordered off to India when the plans were suddenly changed and he found himself master of two ships and sixty-four men heading for Hudson Bay in the search for Anián.

Munk was probably the most experienced and resourceful officer of the Danish navy.[4] His natural intelligence and versatility had been richened with years of experience and his appointment to carry the flag of Denmark into the search for a Northwest Passage was entirely logical. He was familiar with Arctic waters as far north as 71°; he was at home in the bleakest camps of northern Nor-

[4] C. C. A. Gosch, *Danish Arctic Expeditions*, 1605-1620 (London: Hakluyt Society, 1897), p. xxviii ff.

way, and he commanded the respect and obedience of his men with ease and efficiency.

Without incident his expedition reached the west coast of Hudson Bay; the men immediately began their work and by the first of December, 1619, had discovered the mouth of the Churchill River on the west side of the bay and elected it as their wintering place. The ships were beached and shored against the ice, already nearly four feet thick. The crews were divided into details for gathering fuel, hunting when it appeared likely to be profitable, melting snow for the cooks (it takes a lot of snow to make a gallon of water), and making such repairs to the ships as conditions permitted.

Salt meat was adequate, fire logs could be felled only a little way up the mouth of the Churchill, and the early December days seemed to promise a winter as sparkling as Munk had so often found along the shores of his North Sea. To be sure, out on the bay where the great north gales had free play and no Gulf Stream tempered the plunging mercury, the ice piled to forty fathoms thick[5] but Jens Munk had seen many an iceberg and gave them no thought.

"The Holy Christmas Day we all celebrated and observed solemnly, as a Christian's duty is. We had a serman and a Mass. . . ."

One week later Jens Munk felt the real hurt from a Hudson Bay winter. "During these days

[5] *Ibid.*, pp. 33, 34n.

. . . we suffered . . . severely from that terrible frost. . . ." This was a cold that defied a blood-stream warmed only with salt meat, Danish woolens, and green wood fires.

And then, the "illness which . . . was very peculiar" came. "All the limbs and joints were . . . drawn together, with great pains in the loins, as if a thousand knives were thrust through them. The body was . . . blue and brown, as when one gets a black eye, and the whole body was quite powerless . . . all the teeth were loose, so that we could not eat any victuals," said Munk.[6]

Scurvy! The dread killer that had so far stalked every Arctic expedition. It was to be a long time before Samuel Hearne tramped to the Arctic fearless of that particular killer because he tossed aside English prejudices of diet and lived on red raw meat and uncooked fish snagged ice cold from the frozen lakes. Had Munk even had smoked meat instead of salt cured it would have helped but he was a scion of a conservative and tradition-bound service and the Danish Royal Navy ate salt meat!

And so every day now a gallant seaman died—every day a shallow grave was chopped from the frozen earth.

On January 25, 1620, as the gunner touched his match to the powder in a final salute to an officer, "the trunnion burst off both falconets

[6] *Ibid.*, p. 47.

[small cannon] . . . so very brittle had the iron become on account of the . . . frost."

Jens Munk was learning that the deadly cold of the American subarctic was not to be confused with the exhilarating winters of his homeland.

A scanty fortnight later, "I again sent to the surgeon, with an urgent request that for God's sake, he would do his utmost, if he knew of any remedy . . . for the crew; to which he answered, as before, that if God would not help, he could not. . . ."

Mid-February. Twenty of the original crew of sixty-four had been carried ashore, each wrapped in his seaman's shroud.

March 1, 1620. ". . . nearly all of the crew lay sick, we had great difficulty in getting the dead buried."

March 30. Munk walked softly "about in the ship to give drink to the sick, to boil drink for them, and get for them what I thought might be good for them, to which I was not accustomed, and of which I had but little knowledge."

April 5. The corpses lay where they died. Ebbing strength and the fearful cold had long ago put an end to burial services of any sort.

On shore, just out of sight, a straggling bit of game huddled against the cold in the shelter of the trees but no one had the strength to kill the game or drag a log to the fires. Even the wine lay untouched in the holds because no man could crawl down the ladders. And so the sick died and the feeble fires were stoked with ship's fittings.

April 14. ". . . only four besides myself, had strength enough to sit up in a berth and listen to the homily of Good Friday."

May 3-4. ". . . not a man left his berth save myself and the under-cook, who could still do a little."

The dead lay untouched. Now and again a corpse was dumped as gently as diseased muscles allowed onto a rough sled, which had been used to haul wood back in the early winter when life was good and hope was high, and dragged off the ship—but it was all really a waste of what little life remained.

May 10. Eleven still alive.

May 12. Nine alive, two dead. "These were the last that we buried in the ground." The rest putrified where they lay.

Munk believed himself near death and scribbled a request that if, on some happier day, a Christian sailor should find him he be given a civilized burial, "Herewith, good-night to all the world; and my soul into the hand of God, etc JENS MUNK."

June, 1620. On the other side of the world a little band of religious fanatics were gathering and sorting their meager earthly possessions preparatory to boarding the *Mayflower* a few weeks hence.

Up on the Churchill sixty-one men lay dead.

June 8. "As I could not now any more stand the bad smell and stench from the dead bodies . . . I managed . . . to get out of the berth . . . considering it would not matter where . . . I died.

Courtesy Library of Congress, Washington, D.C.

The Teixeira Version

ANIAN MYTH, 1630

I spent that night on the deck, using the clothes of the dead," for covering.[7]

Sixty-one dead. Three alive. Jens Munk and two seamen. In a desperate and successful attempt to live Munk literally crawled ashore to eat a few spears of life-giving grass. Broth from a boiled fish gave strength enough to shoot a wild goose, after which life flowed back with miraculous speed.

Six weeks later the three survivors rigged the sloop and sailed for home, July 16, 1620. Once more the search for Anián had failed with ghastly loss of life and once more faith in the myth survived. At home Munk helped plan a second expedition, which for some uncertain reason he did not lead.

In 1623 domestic difficulties arose, he divorced his wife, possibly for adultery, and rejoined the Royal Navy, where he served until his death, 1628.

But if Jens Munk retained his faith in Anián there were skeptics, too. William Baffin believed that the tides and currents of Hudson Bay argued against any great strait leading from it to the west. But his opinions were disregarded and his own notable discoveries, Smith Sound, Lancaster Sound, and Baffin Bay, were discounted.

> William Baffin . . . came nearer to solving the problem of the North-West Passage than any until the nineteenth century. It is one of the misfortunes of polar history that owing to the indolence and parsimony of a popular antholo-

---

[7] The details of the tragedy on the Churchill are from Munk's own *Navigatio Septentrionalis*, Copenhagen, 1624, as translated and published for the Hakluyt Society.

gist, Samuel Purchas, only the bare outlines of Baffin's explorations are known . . . His maps and journals, if Purchas had ever troubled to preserve them, would certainly have shortened many years the search for a North-West Passage.[8]

Time was to prove that some of the foregoing events were to be overshadowed by the chartering of the Hudson's Bay Company, 1670. The "Gentlemen Adventurers Trading into Hudson's Bay" primary purpose then, as now, was commercial profit but even the Great Company (another popular name) could not escape the myth of Anián. Pierre Esprit Radisson and Jean Baptiste Groseilliers, credited with its beginnings, had orders which read in part, "You are to have in your thought the discovery of the passage into the South Sea and to attempt it." And Mere Marie de l'Incarnation, first Mother Superior of the Ursuline nuns at Quebec, wrote a letter in August of 1663, presumably referring to Radisson and Groseilliers, in which she said, "They have discovered a thing that has been sought for a long time, . . . the entrance to the great Sea of the North. . . . It is believed that this sea leads to China and Japan."[9]

Seven years later the charter of the Hudson's Bay Company made it the only legal power in Hudson Bay and if its profits sometimes fluctuated and its policies were less than dynamic, nevertheless, by 1700 it was the established authority on the bay, albeit not an unchallenged one.

---

[8] Kirwan, *op. cit.*, p. 37.

[9] See Grace Lee Nute, *Caesars of the Wilderness* (New York: D. Appleton-Century Company, 1943), p. 93.

In 1697 the pirate, William Dampier, published his *New Voyage Around the World* and, partially because books of travel generally escaped Church censure and partially because the common people sought escape from their daily lives, it soon became a best seller. It is credited with motivating the upsurge of interest in exploration which lasted for seventy-five years, until Cook ushered in a second Age of Discovery[10] to be nurtured by the newly cheap newspapers and paperback books, and paid for by such private foundations as the Linnaean Society, the Royal Society — or Ben Franklin's popular subscription in America.

It was an exciting time with each new voyage or report whetting the appetite for more. With such volumes as Pennant's *Arctic Zoology* spurring the scientists and Cook's *Voyages* firing the adventurers it was easy for furs to be thought of as the staple of world trade and the Northwest Passage as the greatest geographic particular.

And so the Hudson's Bay Company was caught up in the web of world affairs.

Spain had managed to remain great despite the loss of the Armada. Mexican and Peruvian gold, the slave trade, the Manila galleons, papal blessings, advantageous royal marriages—all of them contributed to make her a great imperial power, and she might have continued so had not Louis XIV come to the throne of France and set out to make himself the "Grand Monarch" at the expense of

[10] Kirwan, *op. cit.*, p. 47.

everyone else in Europe. He revoked the Edict of Nantes and attacked the Spanish Netherlands, thereby proscribing his own Protestants and alienating that faith throughout Europe as well as guaranteeing that all Dutch peoples anywhere would rise to defend their position, rivaled only by England, as leaders in world commerce. Louis had laid the basis of his conflict with William of Orange, who, when he became William III of England, induced his new subjects to take up his quarrel and enter the long series of English-French wars which ended only with the defeat of Napoleon many years later.

Louis was not content to expand his power only at the expense of the Protestants and the Dutch. He must rule Spain. To that end he persuaded the weak and childless Charles II to make Philip, grandson of Louis XIV, heir to the Spanish throne. This effectively did three things: made Louis actual ruler of Spain; upset the European balance of power; and insured that England would join with the Dutch to redress that imbalance.[11] A century of war followed, a war which inevitably involved the Hudson's Bay Company and Hudson Bay.

In the New World France held the St. Lawrence and the Great Lakes region while Spain controlled South America, except for Portuguese Brazil, and all the Pacific coast from Central America north-

[11] For a terse statement of these events see Roscoe Lewis Ashley, *Modern European Civilization* (New York: The Macmillan Company, 1919), pp. 64-70.

ward until her realm faded off into the unexplored wilderness.

England and the Dutch owned a narrow slice along the Atlantic coast of North America. It was only natural that Louis XIV and his successors should try to drive them out and that they should resist and even attempt to expand.

All of this took money and England, being the "shopkeeper" which she was, turned to her commerce. Get fish from Labrador, cotton from India, furs from Hudson Bay, and find Anián, the one sure way to deprive Spain of her monopoly of the Pacific-Orient trade and break the backbone of her affluence. A great trading company on Hudson Bay, supported by a powerful fortress, would be a major factor in the struggle for North America.

But here was a conflict of interests. Fur was the cash crop of the north, just as cotton was to be of the south, but pelts could be taken only from a wilderness. No wonder, then, that the Company, British though it was, did not seek too hard for a strait through their fur land—a strait which would certainly bring ships and ports and civilization of a sort and abolish forever the wilderness from which came their wealth.

Nevertheless, their charter imposed upon them the task of seeking Anián, and they must go through the motions, sometimes with sincere zeal, more often with reluctance. And so, when the pressure of public opinion or government power became too strong to ignore, the Hudson's Bay

Company would initiate an explorative venture. The James Knight expedition of 1719 was such.

Knight had just founded Fort Prince of Wales (of which more later), at the mouth of the Churchill River, when he received orders to report to England for a new assignment. In London he was told that he was to command an expedition to "find out the Streight of Anian in order to discover Gold and other valuable Commodities, to the Northwards." Sealed orders, known to Knight but to be opened by his subordinates only in case of his death, explained that the "other valuable Commodities" referred to certain copper mines about which many tales had come to the Company posts.[12]

Knight put to sea the first week in June, 1719, with the *Albany* and *Discovery* and sailed for Hudson Bay. On board was a knockdown house to be used at their most remote base, great chests in which to store precious metals, and a goodly supply of tools and the men to use them.

No word was heard from the expedition the first year but the Company was not alarmed. With the uncertainties of New World travel it often took two seasons to do the work of one. Only when the second season passed with no word did the Company send a relief party.

It was too late.

A half century later, in the summer of 1767,

---

[12] E. E. Rich, ed., *James Isham's Observations on Hudson's Bay, 1743* (Toronto: Champlain Society, 1949), p. xli; J. B. Tyrrell, *Documents Relating to the Early History of Hudson Bay* (Toronto: Champlain Society, 1931), p. 265.

a few months after Samuel Hearne arrived on the Churchill, some broken guns, old bricks, an anvil, two brittle skeletons, and a sunken hulk in a little harbor on Marble Island, far north in Hudson Bay, gave silent testimony.

The tragedy was perhaps unavoidable but fifty years of ignorance regarding it is difficult to excuse. Each summer the Company sent their trading vessels north and by 1767 Marble Island was so well known that it was used as a base for black whale fishing. Yet, beyond the fact that the island was rocky and that the nearest trees were "several hundred miles from the sea-side," as Hearne said later, the Company knew little about it. No effort had ever been made to explore the shoreline and that despite the fact that one of the Company captains, Mr. Garbet, had actually sailed completely around the island on a "fine clear day in the summer of 1766," said Hearne.

Anyway, in the summer of 1767, "they discovered a new harbour near the east end of it, at the head of which they found" the several items listed above. It was the Knight expedition. All that was left were the articles, too heavy for the natives to carry off, or like the ship's figurehead (later sent to the Company in London), of no use to them. On shore were the remnants of the house and in five fathoms just offshore lay the bottom of one of Knight's two ships.

Two years later Samuel Hearne questioned an old Eskimo and received the usual story of a shipwreck on barren or hostile shores. He told Hearne how the Knight party struggled ashore, cold, wet, and frightened; how they established a camp of sorts; how they set up the knockdown house; how the men tried desperately to fashion one new ship from the wreckage of two; how sickness and starvation decimated the crews; how they tried to stave off illness by eating raw whale meat; how the Eskimos gave them what aid their own meager resources allowed; and, finally, how the last, lonely survivor collapsed and died while attempting to bury his immediate predecessor.

In justice to the Company it may be said that it sent, 1721, Captain John Scroggs with orders to search for Knight as far north as 66° 30′.[13] Scroggs arrived on the Churchill River too late in the season and wintered there until June of 1722, when he sailed as far north as Whale Point. He returned with no news except a few signs of accident at Whale Cove which he took to be of a minor nature, not total shipwreck. Marble Island is well north of Whale Cove but far south of 66° 30′, and we must wonder if some of Knight's men might still have been rescued in 1722 had Scroggs fulfilled his instructions.

The failure of the Knight expedition cooled British ardor for the search for Anián and nothing more was done seriously until Arthur Dobbs opened his famous crusade shortly after 1730.

---

[13] Rich, *op. cit.* p. xliii.

CHAPTER FOUR

Samuel Hearne should be interpreted not only in relation to the maps and journeys outlined in the preceding chapters but also in association with the locale and *dramatis personae* of the immediate years before he landed on the Churchill River:

THE CAUSE CELEBRE
THE INHABITANTS OF THE HINTERLAND
FORT PRINCE OF WALES
THE NORTONS, FATHER AND SON

The Cause Celebre

THE most notorious, if not the most noble, British attempt to get action on the myth of Anián was initiated by Arthur Dobbs, prominent Ulsterman, a politician and statesman.

It was no more productive than any of the others but, because it involved the Hudson's Bay Company and reached the rostrums of Parliament where it became a *cause célèbre,* it deserves more detail than some of its predecessors.

Dobbs was a member of the Irish House of Commons, Surveyor-General of Ireland, and, later in life, governor of North Carolina, where he had large land holdings.

Dobbs's initial interest in Anián had grown

into a conviction that the search should not be abandoned and he proposed that the South Sea Company finance a new attempt to find a northwest passage. When they refused he turned to Sir Charles Wager, First Lord of the Admiralty, who in turn presented Dobbs to Samuel Jones, Deputy Governor of the Hudson's Bay Company. Jones was courteous but cited the failure of the James Knight expedition as an excuse for declining to act.

Dobbs, naturally a suspicious man, believed he was being put off and demanded to see the Company charter. His demand was refused but Dobbs forced the issue and of course discovered that the charter specifically charged the Company with prosecuting the search. Sir Bibye Lake, Governor of the Company, readily admitted this but excused the Company again on the grounds that war with France was imminent.

Dobbs then approached a dissatisfied Company captain, Christopher Middleton, from whom he obtained an outline of all previous Company attempts to find the strait.

While these confidences were being exchanged, Sir Bibye Lake sent James Napper, 1736, into the bay as far north as the modern Rankin Inlet to test for ore deposits, contact the Eskimos, and make preliminary preparations for another expedition. Napper died on the return voyage and Sir Bibye then tried to appease Dobbs by voluntarily reporting that the Napper voyage had found no waterway "nor any the least Appearance of a Passage."[1] This report only served to convince both Dobbs and Middleton that the Company was withholding information and falsifying the records. They continued to agitate for action but nothing more was done until 1741 when Middleton was commissioned in the Royal Navy, given command of the *Furnace* and *Discovery*, and ordered into Hudson Bay to explore for the Crown.

The Company frankly resented this invasion of what they considered their territory and sovereign rights and it was only with the greatest reluctance that they ordered James Isham, newly appointed factor at Churchill, that "if Capt. Middleton, who is sent abroad in the Government's Service to discover a Passage to the North West, should be obliged to resort to you, you are to give him the best Assistance in your Power."[2] Such instructions convinced the suspicious Dobbs that Middleton had changed sides and connived with his old employers not to search too diligently lest Anián be found and the Company monopoly in the North be destroyed.

Thus, Middleton left London knowing that Dobbs challenged his integrity but knowing, too, that Isham had orders to cooperate. When he arrived on the Churchill, August 8, 1741, he was met with a volley from the guns of Fort Prince

[1] E. E. Rich, ed., *James Isham's Observations on Hudson's Bay, 1743, and Notes and Observations on a Book entitled "A Voyage to Hudsons Bay in the Dobbs Galley, 1749"* (Toronto: Champlain Society, 1949), p. xlix.

[2] *Ibid.*, p. lii.

of Wales. He ran up the white flag, was escorted to the fort and found that Isham was not present and that Robert Pilgrim, temporarily in command, knew nothing of Middleton's mission.

That Pilgrim dared fire on the Royal Navy was irrefutable evidence of the power of the Great Company.

Both Isham and Middleton were interested in the search for Anián. They were old acquaintances and on friendly terms, and when Isham arrived arrangements were soon made for Middleton to spend the winter at Fort Prince of Wales since it was already too late to explore the northern waters.

The winter passed with the minimum losses from scurvy and some minor friction between the commanders because Middleton tried to replace his manpower losses by hiring Company men away from Isham.

In the meantime Dobbs got a legal opinion to the effect that the Hudson's Bay Company charter was illegal and the first of the long and bitter court battles, Parliamentary investigations, and Committee hearings took place. That the Company always won did not deter Dobbs.

Back at Fort Prince of Wales Middleton was ready to sail for the north, July 1, 1742, with more than one man in his crew so ignorant that he would not know in "what Part of the World he was, without being told."[3]

---

[3] *Ibid.*, p. lxi.

Middleton reached and named Wager River, pushed north up the shores of Roe's Welcome, found Repulse Bay, and named Frozen Strait. He was back at Woolwich, England, in October and reported, "Undoubtedly there is no Hope of a Passage to encourage any further Trial between Churchill and so far as we have gone, ..."[4]

But Dobbs was not satisfied. He openly accused Middleton of double dealing and initiated a Court of Inquiry (which vindicated Middleton) and a Parliamentary investigation; he campaigned for a "public Praemium or Gratuity" for the discovery of the strait; and even James Isham was called home to explain why he had been so helpful to Middleton.

Out of this welter of charges and hearings no one was convinced, but the House of Commons did resolve in March of 1745 (the year of Hearne's birth) "That the Discovery of a North West Passage, . . . would be of great Benefit and Advantage to the Trade of this Kingdom"[5] and offered a £20,000 prize for the discovery of the passage.

Dobbs was indefatigable. He wrote furiously; he sponsored a public subscription and raised £10,000 for a new expedition; he procured the *Dobbs Galley* and the *California;* hired two ex-Company captains, William Moor and Francis Smith, and, escorted by Middleton on *H.M.S. Shark*, sent them to Hudson Bay to find Anián,

[4] *Ibid.*, p. lxii.

[5] *Ibid.*, p. lxxvii.

1746. It was ironical that Middleton must help two ships across the Atlantic for the sole purpose of proving that he had lied.

Moor and Smith accomplished nothing during their first season on Hudson Bay; they stayed too long in northern waters; demanded from Isham the right to winter at Fort Prince of Wales; got into a personal feud and refused to speak to each other, which compelled Isham to act, unwillingly, as envoy of peace and also attempt to restrain drunkenness which "was accepted as a worse enemy than the climate and . . . recognized . . . as capable of upsetting even the defense plans of the posts."[6]

When the ice broke up the following summer Moor and Smith went north again, found nothing, returned to England and permitted two conflicting reports to be circulated: Henry Ellis, agent for the sponsors on board the *Dobbs Galley*, believed that Repulse Bay, if carefully explored, would "shew such a passage,"[7] but Dobbs reluctantly admitted it "would be in vain to push it [the search] any farther that way."[8]

This admission closed the Middleton-Smith-Moor phase of the search for Anián but it did not close Dobbs's fight with the Company. He shifted his attack to the argument that the whole Company structure was illegal and he had the support of thousands of little people and even

[6] *Ibid.*, pp. xiii-xiv.

[7] Henry Ellis, *A Voyage to Hudson's Bay, by the Dobbs Galley and California, in Years 1746 and 1747. For Discovering a North West Passage* (London, 1748), p. 258.

[8] Rich, *op. cit.*, p. xcv.

some big names in England who thought there were grounds for doubting the moral right of any commercial company to hold the power of life and death over human beings as the Great Company did.

But the *Cause Célèbre* did not end in London. Even the redoubtable Ben Franklin became involved in it. Charles Swaine had been with Francis Smith on the *California* and he wrote *An Account of a Voyage for the Discovery of a North West Passage* which came into Franklin's hands. In 1750 Swaine came to America, applied for and received a license from Governor Samuel Ogle of Maryland and then applied to Franklin for financial support. Franklin raised £1,300 sterling toward outfitting the *Argo,* Swaine in command.[9]

On April 12, 1753, Franklin wrote, "Our vessel, named the *Argo,* is gone for the northwest passage."[10]

Thus, for a full twenty years, 1733-1753, Arthur Dobbs made the myth of Anián a *cause célèbre* covering two continents. The news sheets of England and America, Parliament and the Governor's office in Maryland, the streets of London and Philadelphia all buzzed at one time or another over a controversy concerning a northwest passage from the Atlantic to the Pacific.

For the next forty years a considerable part of

---

[9] See B. Solis-Cohen, *An American Search for the North-West Passage,* (Winnipeg: *The Beaver,* September, 1943).

[10] Benjamin Franklin, *Works* (Smyth edition; New York: Macmillan, 1907), III, 123.

the effort to find a sea route from east to west centered in Hudson Bay. Between 1756 and 1764 the Company ordered John Bean, Mr. Christopher, and Magnus Johnston to continue the work and even after Hearne laid the myth of Anián the perversity of history ordained that several others, better known than he, would continue the search even though he had proved its nonexistence.

Captain James Cook did so; the American, Jonathon Carver, placed Anián on his map of 1778 and talked of a string of fur-trading posts along it, "which having been discovered by Sir Francis Drake of course belonged to the English"; Jean Janvier, the Frenchman, still pictured a large "Sea of the West" with a system of inter-ocean waterways; and Jean François Galaup de la Perouse, on his official trip to the New World in 1785, led many to think he had orders to look for the strait. If he had such instructions they would have been disregarded for when he captured Fort Prince of Wales in 1782 he read Hearne's journals and knew they proved the nonexistence of Anián. If La Perouse had any idea of searching for a Northwest Passage in 1785 it must have been one going around the continent, not through it.

As late as 1787, James Colnett, fresh from the British Royal Navy, claimed he had discovered small inlets supposed to connect with Hudson Bay and he thought he had found de Fonte at 53° North.

Myths die hard, if at all, and the military and naval services have almost equally long traditions of independence of thought which sometimes lead into absurd actions. And so the conclusions of Samuel Hearne were not accepted by the British Royal Navy. Hearne was only a commercial employee and his irrefutable proofs were not good enough for the deeply entrenched and conservative Royal officers, and when Captain George Vancouver left Falmouth for the New World, All Fools' Day, 1791, he carried instructions to look for a passage through the continent, twenty years after Hearne. Vancouver was self-confident almost to the point of arrogance but he could write with genuine modesty four years later, "No small portion of mirth passed amongst the seamen, in consequence of our having sailed from old England on the first of April, for the purpose of discovering a north-west passage."

If the English hesitated to accept the demise of the myth of Anián the Spaniards also determined to send out a last expedition in 1792, to prove or disprove, the de Fonte version of the tale. Nothing came of it, as nothing could, but the resolution can serve as a sort of period to the chronology of the search and we can turn to a view of Fort Prince of Wales, the inhabitants of its hinterland, and an interpretation of the man, Samuel Hearne, who humbly proved generations of wise men, geographers, and cartographers were wrong.

C H A P T E R   F I V E

The Inhabitants of the Hinterland

BEFORE we can properly follow Samuel Hearne from Fort Prince of Wales to the Arctic we must meet the Indians who traded at the fort and inhabited the hinterland, including the great Barren Grounds, or the land of "little sticks," as they called it.

No explorer in the New World ever entrusted his life so completely to the natives as did Samuel Hearne. Many men lived with the Indians along the borders of civilization; a few renegades degenerated to savage levels and followed the warpaths; hundreds, at one time or another, married native girls and lived with them honorably; all early travelers called upon Indian guides for varying lengths of time or were compelled to rely on their friendship in specific cases; but only Samuel Hearne took a shaving kit, an extra shirt, and a superb faith in his own destiny and deliberately began a major exploration without any other help than that which he could induce the Indians to give by friendly persuasion.

Two distinct tribes of Indians frequented Fort Prince of Wales and the hinterland: the Northern or Chipewyans, and the Southern, or Home Guards. The name Chipewyan, meaning "pointed skins," was given the Northern Indians by the Home Guards because of the way the former dried their beaver pelts. Deliniation of the tribes is confusing because of family relationships and similarity of names. The Chipewyans called themselves Dinnae, but they are not to be confused with the Chippewas of the Atlantic region, while the Southern, or Home Guards, were actually Crees, a branch of the Algonquins. Little by little Company men came to use one of two names for each: Chipewyan or Northern and Southern or Home Guards. And likewise Chipewyans and Southerns took on very different official and economic status. The Southerns were hired as hunters, for some types of common labor, and for general utility help in and around the posts. They sometimes gave up their native life and became more or less permanent residents at the Hudson Bay factories.

The Chipewyans never quite succumbed to the blandishments of the Company. They were too proud or too lazy to become paid hunters and carriers of water. They came to the factory with their pelts and bartered these for Indian trade goods which they often took to the interior and resold. They furnished guide services and acted as liaisons between the Company and the tribes further inland.

The Home Guards and Chipewyans were not on friendly terms although open war was averted for the most part. The former feared the latter and the Chipewyans considered the Home Guards fair prey for any sharp practices they could put over.

The Southern Indians had unenviable reputations. Hearne said they were "remarkable throughout all their tribe for being the most debauched wretches under the Sun." No man, said he, could keep a Southern woman in chastity. They cohabited with their own mothers, sisters, and daughters, and frequently passed their daughters on to their sons when through with them. How this frigid climate could stir up so much sex amazed the Company men but it was a phenomenon of common knowledge. James Isham, discussing life at Churchill, and presumably referring to the Southern Indians, said, "Maidens are Very rare to be found at 13 or 14 Years, and I believe m'y Safely say none at 15 Years."[1] A plurality of wives was customary and "the Grey mair is the best horse most on End with them as well as other Nations that is more polite."[2] But he hastened to add that the half-breed children were good youngsters, "straight Lim'd active" and "they are pretty Numerous."[3]

Isham recorded a story, which may or may not have referred to the Southern Indians, but one which was going the rounds. According to the tale several Indian women had been forced to live with some French traders and they resented it. Their husbands came with the avowed intent of reclaiming their own. The women offered to co-

---

[1] E. E. Rich, ed., *James Isham's Observations on Hudson's Bay, 1743* (Toronto: Champlain Society, 1949), p. 80.

[2] *Ibid.*, p. 95.

[3] *Ibid.*, p. 79.

operate and at a prearranged time, "the women took an oppertunity to wett all the french fuzes with their 'urin'e, and then gave the Signal." The husbands slipped into camp; the guns were useless; and all the French were killed, "being 8 in Number."[4]

Hearne thought the Southern Indians inferior even in the matter of drying meat. They prepared theirs over a hot fire, dried the life out of it, left it half burned, bitter, hard, and sooty. Chipewyan game was prepared over a slow fire or in the sun, thus retaining the juices and flavors. Although many Europeans preferred the Southern variety Hearne favored the Chipewyan, on which he "could travel longer without victuals than after any other kind of food."

The Chipewyans were full of contradictions, from childlike beliefs to sophisticated and even cynical philosophies and customs. Perhaps that is why they liked Samuel Hearne, for he, too, was essentially contradictory. They refused to stretch two nets across the same stream because one would be jealous of the other and neither catch fish. They amused themselves imitating the groans of their dying neighbors and left their own aged to die alone and unburied. They plead poverty with a cynicism worthy of a better cause and when they found a Company governor who would not be taken in by the wailings of the women and the flattery of the men they shrugged their shoulders

[4] *Ibid.*, p. 95.

and said, "he is no child and not to be deceived."

They held no code of honesty as we know the term and would defraud their neighbors, enemies, and the Company with equal aplomb and equal efficiency. When apprehended in deceit they would resort to aliases, change of costumes and even masks to cheat or avoid debt to the Company.

Withal this they were a mild and peaceful people except for their everlasting hatred of the Eskimos whom they blamed for conjuring whenever an important Chipewyan died.

David Thompson was impressed with the "steady frugality they strictly observe" as this "never allows distress to come on their families."[5] This opinion was flatly disputed by Hearne who repeatedly gave evidence of their lack of foresight in providing for their dependents. We must accept Hearne's judgment. He lived longer with them and was more sympathetic to the people of the North than was Thompson.

The Chipewyans drank less than other tribes and most of their violence was vented in loud and profane talk.

Physically, the Chipewyans were medium size with typical North American Indian features. Both men and women were almost devoid of body hair and when it did appear in middle life they sometimes pulled it out.[6] The women were not

---

[5] J. B. Tyrrell, ed., *David Thompson's Narrative of His Explorations in Western America, 1784-1812* (Toronto: Champlain Society, 1916), p. 129.

[6] The 1795 edition of Hearne's journal has this version: "Neither sex have any hair under their armpits, and very little on any other part of

beautiful according to our standards but they had clear, soft brown skins and "When they are dressed in clean clothing they are as free from offensive smell as any of the human race."

As a mark of decoration the Chipewyans carried three or four black streaks on their cheeks acquired by the simple but painful device of pushing an awl through the skin, withdrawing it and rubbing in charcoal before the skin healed. Neither men or women possessed combs but used their fingers instead. This was unusual since certain primitive artifacts tend to be common to all people and some appliance for dressing the hair is one of them.

Chipewyan women were held in about the same low esteem as in most Indian tribes. Girls from the age of eight or nine until they entered the tent of a man were not allowed to play with boys although true to their contradictory nature, both boys and girls were subjected from birth to witnessing the most intimate discussions and acts of family life.

The first matches of the young girls were made by the parents or next of kin and always to men many years older. That man was most eligible who had the most monetary standing, a standard not peculiar to the Chipewyans. There was really no marriage ceremony and divorce, which was common, consisted in giving the offending wife a good drubbing and tossing her out of the family

the body, particularly the women; but on the place where Nature plants the hair, I never knew them attempt to arradicate it."

tent. Chipewyan men were jealous of their females and "thinking [was] the greatest privilege they [the women] enjoy," said Hearne. Chipewyan men would spend a night now and then with a friend's wife as the highest tribute he could pay to that friendship. After such tribute the death of either man obligated the survivor to assume responsibility for both families. Hearne, tongue in cheek, said this was more than European godfathers were wont to do!

The first marriages had the flavor of custom more than marriage for although the Northern women were "more backward" than the Home Guards, "neither . . . lost any time." However, children from these early relations were rare and Hearne thought pregnancy among the Chipewyans was less common than among civilized peoples. He could have been wrong on this score because other travelers in the north reported the native women used herbs to produce abortions at will and thus the actual ratio of pregnancy to population may have been comparable to any other people. Nevertheless, Chipewyan mothers seldom had more than five or six children and usually two or three years apart.

Births were generally easy; if traveling, the mother dropped behind, gave birth, tied a bit of moss between the newborn's legs, strapped him to her back, and resumed her trek. If the birth took place while the tribe was encamped the mother was shunted into a camp set far enough away that her cries would not annoy the rest of the family and if labor lasted longer than usual she was visited regularly by other women of the tribe.

These tents were also used periodically while the women were "thun-nardy." At this time they were not allowed to use the regular tent flaps but were required to crawl out under the edge of the tent. But they had the last word! Whenever they became angry at their men or weary of being half slave-half woman they crawled out under the tent and took a few days off, "thun-nardy." And the men, following a custom as old as time, pretended not to know the truth. One wife once became so infuriated she lived alone for several weeks in a stretch and her husband said not a word, just kept a sharp lookout to make sure she *was* alone. All in all it was a most satisfactory solution to several marital problems.

Social life among the Chipewyans was very simple. The men participated in target shooting as might be expected. They played "Holl," a game faintly like quoits, and they danced at night. But neither their dances nor their music were their own. They borrowed both from neighboring tribes. And they borrowed only the most primitive. The dance was little more than a shuffle. The men, three or four at a time, stripped naked except for a loin cloth (which was often discarded as the evening wore on) and performed their simple steps to the "Hee, hee, hee, ho, ho, ho" of their companions, who in turn were accompanied by a crude buffalo-hide drum and rattle.

The women danced by themselves, fully clothed, but for some unknown reason with their music always inside a tent while they performed outside the same tent.

In addition to the above the men (women not allowed) played a sort of who-has-the-button game which ended when one man acquired all the tokens. His prize was a single load of powder or shot.

It was only natural that in that rugged country the most popular and rewarding social events were the feasts. These came whenever the kill warranted them and were prepared with great care and skill. But of them, more later.

When two parties of Chipewyans met on the trail they advanced to within a short stone's throw of each other, then sat or lay on the ground in complete silence for several minutes. One of the elders then rose and recited the lists of deaths and misfortunes visited upon the group since they last met. When he finished an elder from the opposite side did the same. Each side pleaded deep poverty and they became so mutually sorry for themselves they broke into a great "crying match." After the last shred of enjoyment was extracted from this activity pipes were passed and presents were exchanged. Some of these latter were to be kept as real gifts, some only as decoys for larger return gifts.

In the realm of religion, too, the Chipewyans pursued their contradictions. Matonabbee, their greatest leader, said they had "nothing to do but consult their own interest, inclinations, and passions; and to pass through this world with as much ease and contentment as possible, without any hope of reward, or painful fear of punishment in the next." James Isham said, "I observe in these Norther'n parts the natives have but obscure notions of a Diety &c.: however they believe there is a good spirit which concerns itself not with them, therefore pay him no adoration,—an Evill spirit they Believe in & worship him from fear, ..."[7] David Thompson said, "I never saw any act of a religious tendency; they make no feasts, have no dances, nor thanksgivings."[8] However, they had the idea that a manito took care of the migrations of the animals and "they believe in a future state, and that it is much the same as in this life; they appear to have no high ideas of it, but somewhat better than the present; they dread death as a great evil, but meet it with calmness and fortitude; . . ."[9] And despite these contradictions, and true to the pattern of all peoples, ancient or modern, savage or civilized, they had their own version of the Creation, and one not without a rough beauty. The "Mother of the world" was a lone woman living entirely on berries. One day she found a doglike animal and took him to her cave. At night he became a handsome young man, but at daybreak turned into a dog again. "Mother of the world" thought

[7] Rich, *op. cit.*, p. 65.

[8] Tyrrell, *op. cit.*, p. 130.

[9] *Ibid.*

her memories of the night's passions and pleasures were dreams and delusions and scarcely understood her own pregnancy. Then, a man, so tall his head was in the clouds, came with a huge walking stick to level the jumble which was the earth. He marked out the lakes and rivers and filled them with water; he took the dog, tore him to bits and threw the entrails into the water to become fish; the flesh over the land to become animals; the skin to become birds; and told "Mother of the world" and her child to kill for their sustenance. The tall man returned to his own abode and the Chipewyans never saw him again.

This story plus their belief that the aurora borealis was "Ed-thin," the deer, having his fur stroked "up there"; that certain fairies were responsible for the good and evil events in their lives; and that there are both good and evil spirits would seem to contradict the statement that the Chipewyans had no religion; for it would be difficult, indeed, to separate a code of good and evil and a story of Creation from religion. Doubtless the Chipewyans had no formally organized religion, as recognized by the theologians, but one dares to believe the Power "up there" neither did, nor will, make any such distinctions.

When old age and death came the Chipewyan knew he would lose the respect and care of his family and would be left to die alone and unburied. Where, indeed, could he be buried in those frozen wastes where nine months of the year the frost is never out of the ground; where three or four feet down one finds ice in midsummer; where even the sea freezes to a depth of ten feet or more?

It was a hard, cold, ruthless life and that any love, loyalty, fidelity, and joy crept in at all was something of a miracle.

A smallpox scourge in 1781 carried off nine tenths of the Chipewyans, and civilization and time have almost completed their elimination as a cultural entity.

C H A P T E R S I X

Fort Prince of Wales

HUDSON'S BAY COMPANY factories[1] were both commercial and military in nature and were the centers for every facet of life in the northern American wilderness.

And that wilderness was in itself unique. Millions of human beings have moved to new lands but they normally departed from a thoroughly organized society and penetrated, peacefully or by war, another organized society. When the Romans invaded England they found an established society; when the Goths swarmed into Rome they encountered a civilization; when the hordes of Jenghis Khan moved across Asia they met other millions with a fixed way of life. There were roads and judges in England; aqueducts and theaters in Rome; temples and tea houses in old Asia.

It remained for those who invaded this continent to experience the peculiar drama that was the American frontier and one encompassing an entire continent.

When the European came to North America he was trying for the first time in history to in-

[1] "Factory" derives from the Portuguese, *feitoria,* office or administration of a factory, estate, colony, or business. A "factor," from *feitor,* was the manager or agent for such a factory.

vade, conquer, and live in an unorganized frontier void. Here were no roads, no courts, no husbandry, no temples to desecrate, no consecrated grounds of the dead; no man-made supplies of food or water; no dispenser of pills; no priesthood to marry or mumble a ritual at one's passing. Thousands of square miles had no inhabitants to enslave or rape; no domestic animals to carry burdens (if we except the half-wild dog) ; no place to buy, or even steal, the necessities of life; no organized amusement to alleviate boredom—in truth, nothing the invader had a right to expect to find.

And no place in North America more graphically illustrates this unorganized, empty, frontier than the hinterland of the Hudson's Bay Company posts on the western shore of Hudson Bay.

Little wonder, then, that the well-run, highly self-contained factories of the Company became more than buildings and military outposts and took on some of the attributes of human beings. Inside their walls was the only planned food and clothing supply within months of time; the only medicine and knowledge of how to use it; the only sure supply of fuel against death by exposure.

Wandering sluggishly across this vast wilderness west of Hudson Bay are many rivers, among them the Churchill, known to the Indians as the Missinipi and sometimes as the Tzan-dézé, or metal river, probably because of the iron they got from the ship of Jens Munk who wintered there, 1619-20, when his entire crew, save two, died of scurvy.

The Churchill begins in La Roche Lake near

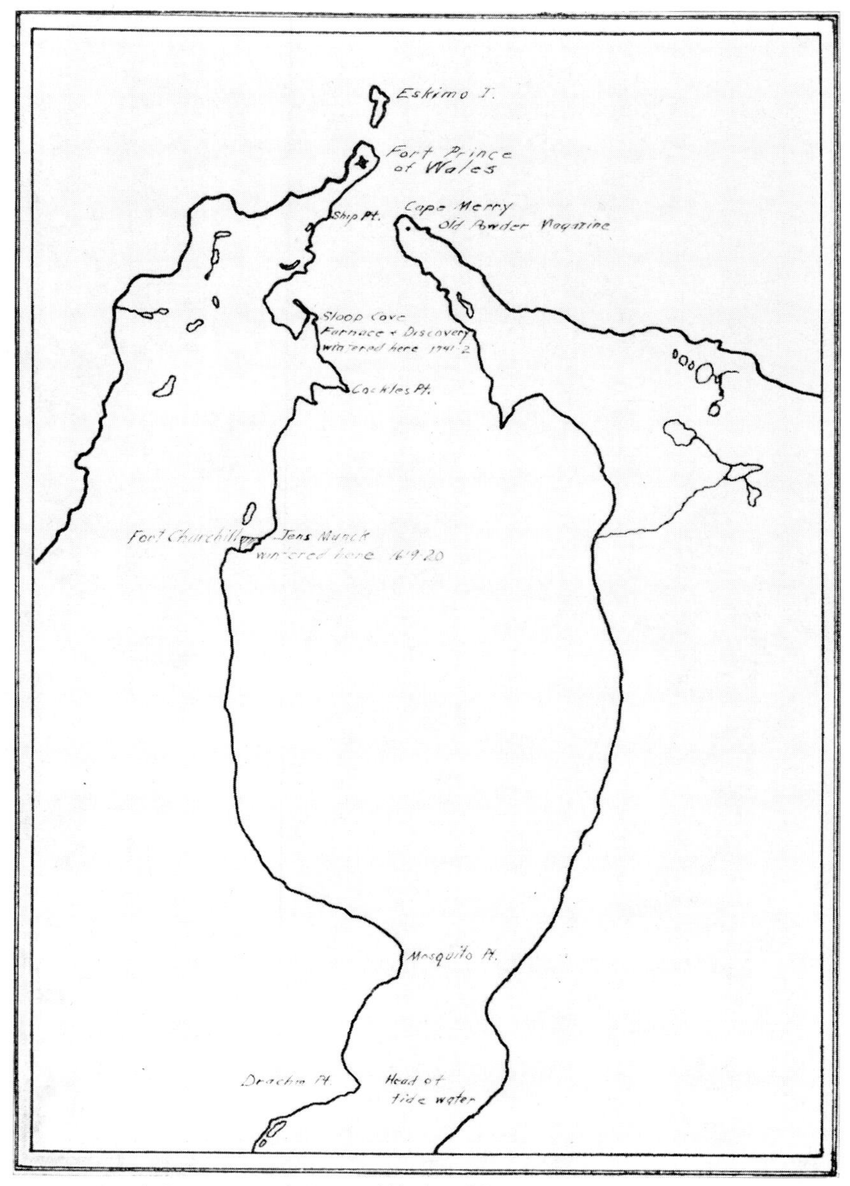

Courtesy Canada Department of Mines and Technical Surveys, Ottawa

INSTALLATIONS AND SITES AT THE MOUTH OF THE CHURCHILL RIVER

the border of Alberta and Saskatachewan and flows for a thousand miles northeast across Saskatchewan and Manitoba until it debouches into Hudson Bay at the modern port Churchill.

Although discovered in 1619 by Jens Munk while he was searching for the Northwest Passage, its headwaters were unknown until the Frobisher brothers, Peter Pond, and Alexander Henry, North West Company men, explored them at the time of the American Revolution a century and a half after Munk.

The mouth of the Churchill is almost a mile and a half wide and helps form the only natural harbor on the west coast of Hudson Bay. The north and south shores of the river are low points of rock and sand, and on Eskimo Point at the end of the narrow isthmus, just west of the mouth, are the remains of Fort Prince of Wales, designed by the English military to be one of the mightiest fortresses ever built in colonial America. Even now it is an imposing and formidable pile. It was begun in 1733 and completed in 1771, and it replaced the earlier post established by James Knight.

James Knight was almost eighty years old when he built the first temporary buildings of Fort Prince of Wales. He was currently master at York Factory but had held an enviable list of important positions with the Company, both in London and on the bay. He had been servant and executive, and at one time he was creditor to the Company for a considerable sum.

Knight was widely traveled, an astute Indian

trader, a good commander, and by virtue of his advanced age and wide experience was listened to with respect by Company officials.

Despite his years of contact with the northern frontier, however, he never quite got used to it. The sharp contrast between British tea with scones and Indian raw meat washed down with warm blood left him slightly disturbed. Had he been obliged to live for any length of time in the interior behind the bay he would have found that both customs had great merit.

James Isham, in his *Observations on Hudson's Bay, 1743*, says Governor Knight was the moving force in building the post, Fort Prince of Wales; that the site was chosen in July, 1717 (Hearne has it 1715); that Knight went to England, convinced the Company of the value of the Churchill location, then came back to the bay in 1719 and chose the name, Fort Prince of Wales.

Knight's own description of the founding of the fort is as follows:

Tuesday 16 July (1717 In the morning wee did gett up our anchor and went in. When wee gott in I went a shore, but I never see such miserable place in all my life and there was but one little place where the Danes[2] had wintered wch is upon a point as hardly contains so much compass of ground as the Royall Exchange stands upon and when I saw it I was not at all surprised to think of so many of the Danes as lost their lives in comeing so late to this place and here is no other place to build at this river but the outer point where the Iskemays tents is wch is impossible for any European to

[2] Jens Munk.

live at. Wee pitched our tents and I gott my bedding ashore but was wellcom'd by such a quantity of musketos that as soon as they light or whereever they fix their sting like great wasps that wee are nothings in the worls but knotts and bumps our flesh is. I find here is no fresh water to be gott nigher than a quarter of a mile wch is in the clifts of the rocks like a great cistern. Our people as I sent here in the boat have been 2 or 3 times up the river as farr as they could go for rocks and stones but could not find a fitting place to build a house upon but at one place wch was worse than this is where formerly the English had built one wch they found so badd that after they had built it I believe they were so disscouraged that they sett it a fire to run away by the light of it. Here is the sign of the Danes building here formerly by the stumps of trees they left cut down but all as rotten as dirt. We found a peice of a brass gun hear near 7 foot long. It was a 12 pounder for I have one of the shott as wee took out of her by me. There was 2 of them but the Indians have broke one all to peices and carryd it clear away and this is a great peice of the mussell is broke of and wee have found several peices of cast barr iron 3 or 4 foot long 4 inches thick as the Danes used for a stove as the Indians have found by digging abt.

Saty 20 July. I burnt and cleared a place where I design the ffactory for to stand wch I believe to be the very place where Capt. Monk built upon when he wintered here by the brass gun and square peices of cast iron as wee have found there and by the Northern Indians digging up the moss and stones abt the rocks for above ½ mile round. The place is the best in this river both for landing of goods and the house standing but here is no good place at all.

Sunday 28 July. One of our men covered in the mudd a great gun lying a good way of on the flatts but cannot tell yett whether it is brass or iron and sevll barrs of cast iron wch I will seek after shortly. The gun is 12 pounder without doubt it was a very great ship, as was lost here by its having such great guns.

Monday 29 July. It proves to be a brass gun.

Tuesday 30 July. Wee are forced to back all the timber at a great distance and hardly can find one peice to bring out to carry upon the mens backs but what is as farr as it is from the Hudsons Bay Company's house as it is to Ludgate.

Wed 14 Aug. 1717. [The ship] came to an anchor in ye channel opposite to where wee are building. Capt. Ward and Mr. Stanton came a shoar before the ship came to an anchor which I found to be the *Hudsons Bay* ffriggot. They brought the Companys packett a shoar by which I found they were all well and told me as the *Port Nelson* was gon to York Fort and ye *Albany* with a small vessell to ye bottom of the bay.[3]

When the new post was finished the Company ordered Knight to leave it in charge of his second in command, Richard Staunton, and report to England for another assignment—the search for the strait and the copper mines, from which he never returned.

In the meantime England and France continued their fight for world control. On the Continent Louis XIV, who had set out to create a new empire at the expense of England, Spain, and the Dutch, was close to the end of his reign. A reign which had seen him toasted as the embodiment of divine right but one, too, now that he was old and worn with the dissipations and defeats of seventy-two years, which had seen him accept the Treaty of Utrecht, 1713. It was a bitter potion for a Crown that had once dominated all of North

[3] Canadian Archives, *Hudson Bay Company Journal at York Fort, 1716-1717*. Quoted in J. B. Tyrrell, *Documents Relating to the Early History of Hudson Bay*, pp. 33-34.

America that seemed to it worth while. To be sure, his flag still masted from New Orleans to the St. Lawrence and on down to the sea, but Louis had been obliged to give up Acadia and Newfoundland, which guarded the door to Canada, and to recognize British and Hudson's Bay Company claims to the empire of fur draining into Hudson Bay.

France now had the enemy officially before her and behind her.

Time after time, though, Louis had played the double cross: Years ago, before the Company was formed, he had ordered Radisson to give up all the pelts held by the French on Hayes River while at the same time he sent his military to seize the area, capture Radisson, and any ship daring to leave the bay with furs.

This particular episode became something of a comic opera when the Englishmen captured their supposed captors, sent one French commander, Jean Péré, to London, and dumped two of his brother officers on a deserted island to make their way back to Montreal as best they could.

Nevertheless, their report, when they arrived, sent Pierre Le Moyne d'Iberville on the first of his five famous raids into Hudson Bay. With thirty-three Frenchmen and sixty-six Indians, all on snowshoes and in the dead of winter, he moved from Montreal to the bay and caught the Company flat-footed. Moose Factory, Fort Rupert, and a Company ship were soon French prizes. Fort Albany got wind of the attack but officials were

Courtesy The Champlain Society, Toronto, Canada

HEARNE'S DRAWING OF FORT PRINCE OF WALES. NORTHWEST VIEW, 1777

unable to convince the Company servants it was worth dying for an organization which paid such low wages and Albany, too, fell to the French, who posted a garrison, booted thirty Company men into the winter wilderness and then headed back for Montreal, one thousand miles away.

Thirty Englishmen died of starvation.

Louis now suggested that violence might be avoided if joint occupancy were practiced and when this idea seemed acceptable to the English he ordered d'Iberville back into the north to grab all the territory he could hold by force.

In the light of such dealings it is little wonder that, despite the gloom which the Treaty of Urecht cast on the French Court, the Company had no faith in Louis's good behavior and little more in the provisions of peace included in the treaty.

And their doubts were justified.

Louis died two years later and the new reign was soon embarked on another thrust for empire. France repudiated the Treaty of Utrecht when she fortified Cape Breton Island with the fortress of Louisburg and deliberately inflamed the Indians against England all the way from Louisiana to the lower St. Lawrence. Years of savage attacks and counterattacks followed. It became increasingly obvious that either France or England must be driven from the continent.

A well-organized trading company holding every important river mouth on Hudson Bay and backed by a powerful fortress would be no mean weapon with which to defend British interests

Courtesy The Champlain Society, Toronto, Canada

INTERIOR OF FORT PRINCE OF WALES SHOWING WALLS OF OLD DWELLING HOUSE

and attack France. With that end in view the plans were drawn and work commenced on a new Fort Prince of Wales, 1733.

The new fortress, the remains of which have become a tourist attraction, is more than three hundred feet square. Walls thirty to forty feet thick taper to twenty at the parapets and are faced with hammer-dressed stone. Four bastions guard the corners. Forty cannon could be mounted atop the walls and these supported from across the river by the lesser Cape Merry Battery with six twenty-four-pounders.

Inside the massive walls were a powder house, shops, warehouses, water-storage facilities, and the quarters for the staff and troops.

The personnel consisted of a council made up of the chief factor, second factor, surgeon, sloop and brig masters, and the captain of the Company ship when it was in port. In addition there were soldiers, clerks, artisans, *coureurs, voyageurs,* and hunters to a total of sixty.

The chief factor lived in the "big house," over one hundred feet long and thirty feet wide. Tradition says that it was roofed with lead. At each end of the large mess hall and common room were enormous fireplaces facing each other across flagstone floors. These furnished the only heat permitted, either winter or summer, for Fort Prince of Wales is very near the timberline and fuel was scarce and difficult to get.

The common room bore little resemblance to the rustic lodge of our time. It was a Spartan

Courtesy The Champlain Society, Toronto, Canada

Gateway of Fort Prince of Wales

room. A Company flag: the English ensign with H.B.C. in white on a red ground, or in reverse colors; benches and tables, a few clothes pegs, a candle holder, a whale-oil lamp and some items too worthless to invite native cupidity were all that could be allowed.

Outside the walls were the tents of the Indians and sometimes a tiny garden of peas and turnips planted with the generally vain hope of giving some variety to a preponderantly meat diet.

All employees swore fidelity to and secrecy about all matters pertaining to the Company and a portion of their wages was withheld to enforce compliance. Only Company officials were allowed to trade with the Indians and the enlisted men were subjected to personal search on leaving or entering the post lest they smuggle for their own gain.

The annual ship from London docked late in August or early September and signaled a semi-festive relief from an otherwise restricted life. The docking was the beginning of the factory season and was, therefore, a sort of Company New Year.

However, there was much work to do. All hands must help unload, for everything had to be tugged, lifted, and carried by human labor and it was a major task and took from ten days to two weeks to complete. It must be done with the greatest possible dispatch because a good ship's captain got his ship cleared and sailed to warmer waters before it was too late. More than one captain spent a lonesome winter away from home because he failed to outrun the inexorable ice.

After the ship departed for the Thames the posts settled down to the winter's work. Ten or a dozen of the best marksmen, accompanied by Indian aides, were sent to shoot the fall flight of geese. Each man carried two guns and with luck could bag as high as seventy-five birds per shoot.

Twenty-five or thirty axmen sharpened their steel and trudged upriver to cut the following year's supply of fuel. The green spruce, which they insisted on calling "pine," was felled, cut into the longest lengths possible to carry, taken to the river and stacked in piles to dry until the river would be free of ice the following summer when it would be floated downstream to the fort.

As the cold and Arctic darkness closed in the work took on a slower tempo. The geese and caribou were gone and the hunting parties were broken into smaller groups and sent after the staple winter diet, ptarmigan and Arctic hare. Each of these smaller detachments was equipped with a rude sled, guns, fishline, traps, a tent, and the necessary supplies to last several days (or weeks), as the situation might demand. And always there was at least one Indian girl to do the cooking and furnish a domestic note.

As the game was killed it was frozen, packaged, and sent back to the factory to feed those engaged in repairing fort equipment and small boats and invoicing the goods. This latter was a never-ending task for the natives considered trade a social as well as a business proposition and when they came to buy and sell they stayed for many weeks and did business a little at a time.

Since Fort Prince of Wales and the other Company posts were in northern latitudes the winter temperatures were major factors in all activities. Early in the fall about three feet of dust-dry, hard-frozen snow came, blew into long drifts, and settled down to await the spring thaw nine months away. The mercury dropped lower and lower: zero, $-10°$, $-15°$, then a plunge to $-25°$ or $-30°$, or even $-50°$, when the ice in the rivers and along the shore "froze," contracted, and exploded into great cracks with a noise like heavy artillery.

Gloves were useless; only heavy mittens offered any protection. It was dangerous to load the frozen steel Company guns; one's hands might become useless before the charge could be placed, or, the gun, itself, might burst into deadly pieces when fired. Axes became brittle and splintered with the tinkle of broken glass unless handled with skill; each day the sun rose a little later and went to bed a little earlier, and the evening fires warmed ever smaller circles before the stone hearths.

By December it took a gayer song, a bawdier joke, a larger portion of rum to bring a smile. "This dull month of long nights we wish to pass away, ... Christmas when it comes finds us glad to see it and pass; we have nothing to welcome it with."[4]

---

[4] J. B. Tyrrell, ed., *David Thompson's Narrative of His Explorations in*

In the safe retrospect of two centuries and civilized comfort, life at Fort Prince of Wales carries a certain frontier magic, but to those who fought through its mosquito-cursed summers and its lonely winters it was a serious and treacherous life. Death by exposure and starvation came to both natives and whites, and those who made mistakes seldom had a second chance.

Western America, 1784-1812 (Toronto: Champlain Society, 1916), p. 122.

C H A P T E R   S E V E N

The Masters of Fort Prince of Wales

JAMES KNIGHT, Richard Norton, Moses Norton, Samuel Hearne—these four may be said to have given Fort Prince of Wales the characteristics which made it different from all other Hudson's Bay Company posts. Within a period of seventy years these men picked the site, built the post, developed the business, administered the fortifications, saw the fortress fall to the French and eventually be regained and rebuilt—all without a shot from its parapets, except for those fired as salutes.

There were other governors at Fort Prince of Wales between and after these four, but they left no imprints worthy of the term. They had no dreams of greatness, no drives beyond a Company retirement—not even a sin to lend color to their regime.

James Knight, eighty years old and long past the accepted age of adventure, reconnoitered the site of Fort Prince of Wales, went to England to persuade the Company, returned to the bay, raised the first buildings, and then, with an assurance worthy of his life, sailed north to die with his crew in one more futile search for the Strait of Anián.

Overshadowing Knight as central figures at Fort Prince of Wales were father and son, governors Richard and Moses Norton.

Richard, apparently with Knight when he established Fort Prince of Wales, had entered the service of the Company while very young. When Knight left the new post in charge of Richard Staunton and went to seek Anián, he sent the "boy Richard Norton" to live with the Indians with instructions to "divert'em from going to warre and to desire'em to go to trade at York Fort"—a mission so successful that he arranged a truce among the natives which "has not been broke since (1750)."[1]

Young Norton had an affinity for Indian trade and politics. He understood native customs; he could be aloof without snobbery; he did not sneer at their simple beliefs or rail at their irresponsibility; he neither sank to their barbarism nor expected them to be civilized. Without apology or condescension, he took an Indian mate who bore him their half-breed son, Moses Norton.

Gradually the Company moved Richard Norton up its hierarchical ladder until he became master at Fort Prince of Wales. He had a sound business sense and he and the fort matured together.

In the meantime the Company was sampling new sources of wealth and responsibility. It had never limited its interest to furs. It had bought

---

[1] E. E. Rich, ed., *James Isham's Observations on Hudson's Bay, 1743* (Toronto: Champlain Society, 1949), pp. xxvii, xlii.

and sold anything—goose quills or ermine. It mattered only that it be remunerative.

The Strait of Anián might bring the wealth of the Orient to the Thames without the frightening voyage around the Horn or Good Hope; England's power in North America must be supported; the French free traders from the St. Lawrence must be watched lest they invade Company domains and by offering better goods at lower prices defeat the Company on its own preserve; a whaling industry must be established; more Indians must be coaxed to Fort Prince of Wales to trade more pelts for fewer goods; and, cognizance must be taken of the constantly recurring tales of large copper deposits somewhere to the north and west—probably on Anián.

These mines were a major factor in the history of Fort Prince of Wales and the career of Samuel Hearne, the fourth member of the quartet of great governors on the Churchill.

The pressure to look for the deposits had been building for a long time. The Company charter provided that the Hudson Bay posts be used as bases for further exploration of the interior of North America, but as long as profits were reasonable Company officials had, quite naturally, subordinated exploration to trade. The Company, because of its somewhat high-handed rule and its extreme secrecy concerning its business, was not overly popular in either England or America. When dividends began to fluctuate angry criticism flared up

Courtesy The Champlain Society, Toronto, Canada

A SOUTHWEST VIEW OF FORT PRINCE OF WALES
Published by J. Sewell, Cornhill, March 1, 1797

with demands that the terms of the charter be honored.

The Company must find Anián before Spain or France could do so; it must ransack every Indian band for more pelts; and, it must ferret out the truth about the copper mines, which, after all, might pour more millions into London than all the furs in the New World.

Only thirty years after the Company was chartered the natives brought to the bay several artifacts pounded out of pure copper which they said they got far to the north. There was no question about the genuineness of the artifacts—only the whereabouts of the source of the raw material.

When Knight sailed on his last voyage, 1719, he knew that the term "valuable Commodities," contained in his orders, referred to these copper mines. He had talked with the Indians and believed he knew the way to the deposits as "well as to my own bed," he said. And he doubtless thought he did for his ships, the *Albany* and *Discovery,* carried iron-bound boxes in which to store the copper.

It was cruel irony that when he did not return when expected, many people insisted that he had found Anián and gone, *via* it and California, to the South Sea—testimony that two centuries after Columbus the world was almost as confused about California and the South Sea as it had ever been.

Almost without exception Company officials believed in the value of the copper deposits, and there were numerous tales with as many variations.

Richard Staunton, Knight's immediate successor at Fort Prince of Wales, believed that "if we can find a Communication by Navigation nothing can hinder us from so rich a purchass"; the "boy Richard Norton" was supposed to have found both Anián and the mines while living with the Indians; someone said that Company ships could easily load at mine side; Captain Carruthers, commanding a Company vessel, claimed he had sent a canoe inland to induce the Indians to bring out ore; Alexander Brown and Edward Thompson, Company surgeons, believed in the mines; and when Captain Scroggs and Richard Norton went to search for Knight the captain is said to have had the proverbial birch bark and charcoal map, drawn by an Indian, on which the copper mines were located.

And thus the search for Anián became entangled in the search for copper; and the search for copper somehow became the Coppermine River; and the Coppermine River became Anián for some but mutually exclusive for others, and it was left for time and Samuel Hearne to set it all straight.

But before either could be effective, Richard Norton passed away and his half-breed son Moses became governor of Fort Prince of Wales.

The frontier always produces excesses: saints and sinners, heroes and cowards, mental dwarfs and physical giants, and Moses Norton encompassed both extremes. One is inclined to compare him with the great Russian, Baranof of Alaska, but there is no need to do so. Moses Norton was big enough to cast his own shadow.

His father sent him to England for nine years to be educated and acquire a veneer of civilization, but the frontier has a way of scrubbing off veneers and when the blood of his Indian mother ran hot in his veins Moses shucked off his English training and became a primitive.

He was hated as bitterly by the Indians as by the whites and for the same reasons. He was exceedingly fond of women and kept, in addition to his wives, several young Indian girls for his personal enjoyment.

Moses Norton was brutal when drunk; he poisoned his enemies and two of his wives died in like manner. At the same time his shy, gentle daughter, Mary, was pampered and allowed to loiter about the officers' mess because she did not like to associate with the full-blooded Indian women.

Moses Norton used the whipping post for both natives and whites; he flogged soldiers for no offense more serious than speaking to one of his wives; he preached sobriety and reverence to his men while he drank to excess and made no effort to curb his own blasphemy. His staff was indignant with this "hypocritical cant of [the] selfish debauche."

He locked all doors at night and put the key under his pillow, "so that in the morning his dining room was generally, for want of necessary conveniences, worse than a hog stye."

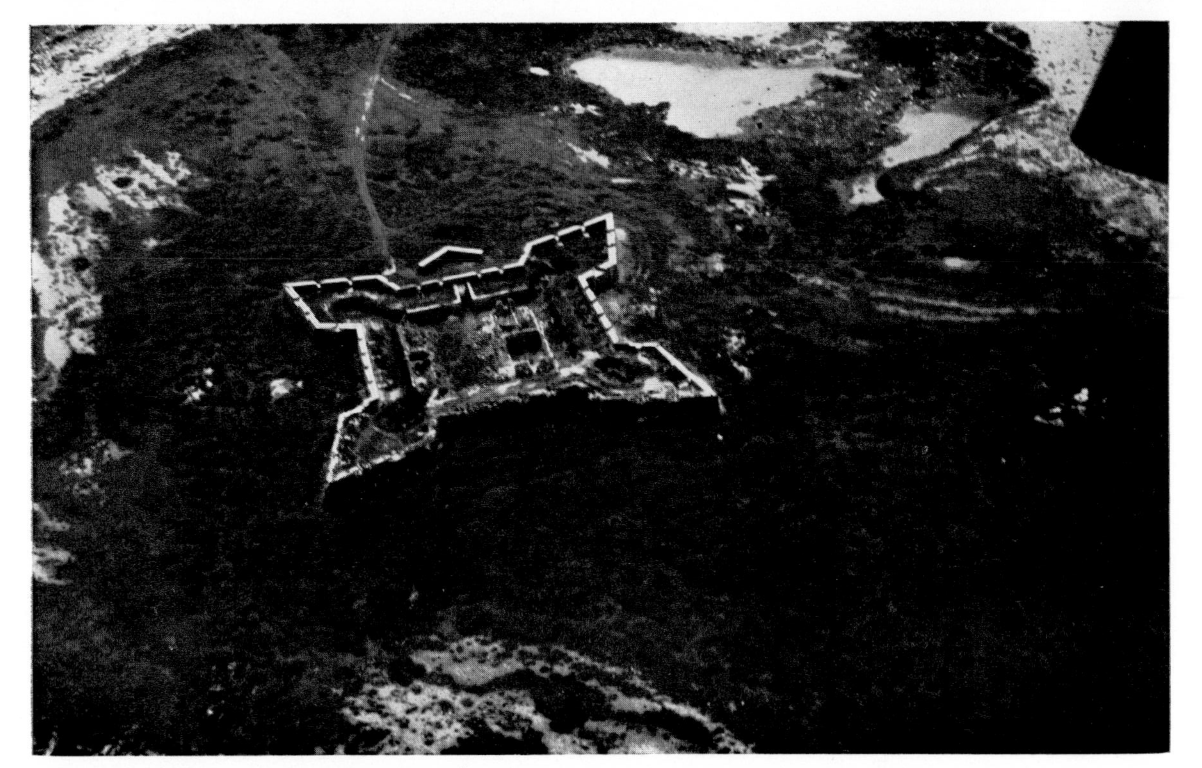

Courtesy Royal Canadian Air Force, Ottawa, Canada

OLD FORT PRINCE OF WALES FROM ALMOST DIRECTLY OVERHEAD
Note the remains of the "Great House" inside the walls

He smuggled constantly but turned all profits to the Company.

Despite all this there was another side to Moses Norton. If he was a moral dwarf he was not a mental one and his worst enemies credited him with governing Fort Prince of Wales at least as well as his father, and when the time came he was to prove that his interest in exploration and the advancement of Company interests was greater than his predecessors'.

"Inflamation in his bowels" caused his demise four days before Christmas, 1773. His death was as violent as his life. As he neared the end the pain was great and his wives and officers gathered by his side. One officer, forgetting for the moment, Norton's insane jealousy, took the hand of one of his wives upon which Norton raised up and screamed, "God d-n you for a b-h, if I live I'll knock out your brains." "This I declare to be the real character and manner of life of . . . Mr. Moses Norton," said Hearne.[2]

Moses Norton was a brutal and evil man but he was also one with courage and vision and we shall see how he used both to promote the career of Samuel Hearne and benefit the Great Company.

---

[2] E. E. Rich, *The Hudson's Bay Company, 1670-1870* [Hudson's Bay Record Society Publications, Vols. 21-23] (London, 1959), Vol. II, p. 45, takes issue with Hearne's interpretation of Norton.

CHAPTER EIGHT

The First Expedition Is Planned

THE Treaty of Paris, 1763, ended the Seven Years' War and seated England firmly as the first power in Europe. From the sophistication of London to the savagery of the South Seas and the ancient rites along the Ganges, the British flag flew almost unchallenged, certainly undefeated.

Spain had been eclipsed, France driven from North America, and Clive of England was taking India away from the Frenchman, Dupleix.

But England was more than the first military power in the world. Dr. Samuel Johnson ruled her *belles lettres;* Jeremiah Horrox capped her astronomers; Dr. James Lind had found a cure for scurvy; Alexander Dalrymple, choleric and egotistical, was, nevertheless, a world authority on hydrography; Dr. Daniel Solander, Englishman by adoption, was a renowned botanist; Thomas Pennant had an enviable reputation as a zoologist; and dominating them all was the young, newly elected Fellow of the Royal Society, Joseph Banks, who used his neighbor, the corrupt but powerful Earl of Sandwich, a fabulous personal fortune of £6,000 per annum, and his own reputation as a botanist to go to Labrador aboard the *H.M.S. Niger* as botanical scientist and to accompany James Cook to the South Pacific on the *Endeavor,* and then, through the remainder of his life, drive the Royal Society in a relentless search for knowledge. "Among the men of science the rule of Sir Joseph Banks was as absolute and undisputed as was that of his friend, Dr. Johnson, among the men of letters."[1]

Indeed, England was more than a great naval power. She was the leader of world culture.

It was, therefore, no coincidence that following the Treaty of Paris, 1763, the Royal Society headed up the scientific studies undertaken to maintain England's position of world leadership.

Among the many problems facing the scientists and the military were two geographic questions and one tactical situation which demanded immediate attention.

There was an almost universal belief in the Strait of Anián and there was also a well-accepted hypothesis that there must be a *Terra Australis Incognito* somewhere in the South Seas to maintain the land balance between the northern and southern hemispheres.

Anián and *Terra Australis Incognito* could be resolved only by further exploration.

Only months after the Seven Years' War, the Crown financed two round-the-world expeditions devoted to science and the search for a southern continent but both had ended in disaster. The Admiralty, which worked in close harmony with

[1] Hector Charles Cameron, *Sir Joseph Banks* (London: The Batchworth Press, 1952), p. xix.

the Royal Society, might have hesitated to do more but pressure from the scientists, plus the growing tactical fear that Spain was about to revive her attempt to make the Pacific a Spanish lake and thus thwart England's expansion in the Orient, compelled action.

To block Spain was the duty of the Royal Navy but it could best be done by discovering Anián (which Spain very much wanted *not* discovered) and by locating and seizing strategic lands in the South Sea. These projects would be immeasurably furthered if the navigators knew a great deal more astronomy than they did.

Thus, the Royal Society sent a memorial to the king, November 12, 1767, reminding him that exploration was necessary to maintain England's leadership; that efficient exploration was impossible without astronomy; that the transit of Venus across the sun, June 3, 1769, offered an opportunity for further study; that the Russians, Swedes, Spaniards, French, and Danes had already made arrangements for such observations; that the South Sea, Spitsbergen and Fort Prince of Wales were advantageous locations to observe the transit, and, would the Crown furnish £4,000 to finance such a study?

The Crown would.

The stage was being set for the conclusive attack on the myth of Anián.

The Royal Society ordered William Wales, F.R.S., and Joseph Dymond to Fort Prince of

Wales to make the observation and there they found Samuel Hearne.

Hearne had arrived on the bay two years earlier, had been assigned to a coastal trading vessel, and was doing little more than "keeping shop," the very task he had joined the Royal Navy to escape.

He was, frankly, bored. He had scant interest in trade as such; he did not like his ship's captain; he detested Moses Norton, and there seemed little likelihood of any improvement as long as he remained on board his present ship.

He appealed to London for a new assignment, "where there is greater probability of my making some returns, and giving satisfaction to my Employers."[2]

It was just then that three seemingly disconnected events favored Hearne's fortune: Wales and Dymond arrived at Fort Prince of Wales; the discovery of the remains of the James Knight expedition on Marble Island in the north bay proved only that Knight had failed to find Anián, not that it did not exist; and, at the very time of the arrival of the Wales' staff, the Chipewyan Indians brought in another specimen of copper from their "copper-mine river."

These events combined to give Hearne his chance. Moses Norton permitted him to study with Wales, who set up his equipment on the parapets of the fort; there was new hope for discovering Anián; and, Norton suddenly took such an

---

[2] J. B. Tyrrell, ed., *Journals of Samuel Hearne and Philip Turnor* (Toronto: Champlain Society, 1934), p. 27.

intense interest in copper that he decided to go to England himself and present a new plan, namely, that the Company finance an expedition by land to locate the copper mines. This was an entirely new approach to the problem for no serious attempt had ever been made to penetrate the interior of the continent north and west of Hudson Bay.[3]

The home office agreed to finance a very small expedition, preferably one man, who was to live and travel with the Indians, or by their sufferance, and make what progress he could.

Norton's return from London was quickly followed by this letter to Hearne, dated May 25, 1769:

From the good opinion we entertain of you, and Mr. Norton's recommendation, we have agreed to raise your wages to .... per annum for two years, and have placed you in our Council at Prince of Wales's Fort; we should have been ready to advance you to the command of the *Charlotte*, according to your request if a matter of more immediate consequence had not intervened.

Mr. Norton has proposed an inland Journey, far to the north of Churchill, to promote an extension of our trade, as well as for the discovery of a North West Passage, Copper Mines, &c.; and as an undertaking of this nature requires the attention of a person capable of taking an observation for determining the longitude and latitude, and also distances, and the course of rivers and their depths, we have fixed upon

[3] Five years before Norton had informed London that he was "Certain and Shure that there is no Passage into the Western Ocean in this Hudson's Bay." E. E. Rich, *Hudson's Bay Company, 1670-1870* [Hudson's Bay Record Society Publications, Vols. 21-23] (London, 1959), II, 46.

you (especially as it is represented to us to be your own inclination) to conduct this Journey, with proper assistants.

We therefore hope you will second our expectations in readily performing this service, and upon your return we shall willingly make you any acknowledgement suitable to your trouble therein.

We highly approve of your going in the *Speedwell,* to assist in the whale fishery last year, and heartily wish your health and success in the present expedition.

We remain your loving Friends,

Bibye Lake, *Dep. Gov.*
John Anthony Merle.
Robert Merry.
Samuel Wegg.
James Winter Lake.
Herman Berens.
Joseph Spurrel.
James Fitz Gerald.

What manner of man had the Company hired to make the last significant search for the Strait of Anián? What had a fatherless boyhood meant in terms of adulthood? What had war and blood and death meant in terms of character? What had three years of frozen frontier meant in terms of a philosophy of life?

The evidence is conclusive: Samuel Hearne was always molded by his environment but that did not infer that he invariably approved of it; he could accept good or evil with understanding patience; he had a stoicism worthy of any frontiersman, but he had, also, a warmhearted sympathy for the sufferings of his fellowmen.

He had learned that to survive, especially in the North, one must know when to compromise and when to fight, and his "fighting" became a quiet, dogged determination to do a given task regardless of obstacles or previous failures.

Courtesy Royal Canadian Air Force, Ottawa, Canada

Aerial Photograph Showing Fort Prince of Wales on the Long Tongue of Land at the Mouth of the Churchill River.

Button Bay is to the right, the Churchill River on the left

His personal courage was unlimited but of such a gentle and retiring sort that it might appear as cowardice to those who did not know him; he rarely boasted but he could back his words with deeds.

Samuel Hearne was not a glittering leader but he was diligent and thorough. He was a contradictory mixture of indecision and persistency, and his weaknesses seemed always on the verge of overwhelming his strengths, but, unlike the tragic Bering whom he most resembles, he had a habit of coming out on top.

He was not a trained explorer but he was a natural and keen observer and it might be demonstrable that a large percentage of the greatest explorers were not professionals. Neither Lewis nor Clark was so trained; Stanley, of Africa, was a newspaperman; Balboa was a soldier of fortune; La Salle was a Jesuit novice and nobleman; George Vancouver was a naval officer; Robert Gray was a Yankee trader; Vitus Bering belonged to the military. Certainly Samuel Hearne was as well fitted for his task as they.

But he was pitting his youth and gentle perseverence against gigantic odds. From Columbus to 1769 men had been exploring America and the losses had been staggering. Magellan left Europe with more than 200 men—a remnant of eighteen reached home; John Smith of Virginia lost 80 of his 120 within twelve months; the Humphrey Gilbert and John Cabot expeditions perished without trace; Jens Munk, trying desperately to live one winter on the mouth of the Churchill a few hundreds yards from Fort Prince of Wales, lost every man but two; Pánfilo de Narváez sailed with five ships and 600 men—and nine years later Cabeza de Vaca, the Negro Estivanico, and two companions reeled into Mexico.

There had been no end to the appalling losses.

And the Company proposed that Samuel Hearne leave the Churchill alone in midwinter and head into the Arctic night without any human help or supplies except what he might get by sufferance from a frozen land and a savage people!

It was the first week in November, 1769. Fifteen hundred miles to the southeast Patrick Henry and Sam Adams were stirring their fellow citizens into revolt against their king.

But on the Churchill it was a different world. There was little real warmth in the bright sun. By midafternoon the shadows were long, by teatime it was dark, cold, and still, with a stillness peculiar to those latitudes. The usual human sounds were all there—talk, a snatch of ribald song, a grumbled curse, the crackle of the evening fire, and the short, sharp report of expanding metal and stone. But it was, nevertheless, so very still. The booming ice as it froze too hard and exploded only accentuated the quiet. There were no bird calls now; no small animals running about with their tiny noises added to the sum total; the giant flies were still; there were no traffic sounds; no bells striking the hour; no rush of water over rocks; no rumble of wheels; no distant whistles.

In this quiet Samuel Hearne sorted out a handful of trade goods — "ammunition, useful iron work, some tobacco, a few knives." He had an outline map covering twelve degrees of latitude north and thirty degrees of longitude west of Churchill on which he "sketched West coast of Bay on it, but left the interior blank, to be filled up during my Journey"; there were small maps of one degree on which to put each day's travel and to be transposed later to his master sheet; he would use, with something less than professional skill, his "very portable" quadrant; and he would write his daily log, not for the "critical geographer, but for the interested public," the public which still remembered the *Cause Célèbre*.

No serious preparations at all were made for food or clothing "as the nature of travelling long journies in those countries will never admit of carrying the most common articles of clothing: so that the traveller is obliged to depend on the country he passes through, for that article, as well as for provisions.

"I took only the shirt and clothes I then had on, one spare coat, a pair of drawers, and as much cloth as would make me two or three pairs of Indian stockings, which, together with a blanket for bedding, composed the whole of my stock of clothing."

The paucity of his equipment is testimony enough to Samuel Hearne's bravery and the incredible risk he was taking. Few explorers ever gambled their lives on less.

When the final determination of personnel was made Moses Norton, using his authority as Chief Factor at the fort, overrode the Company's suggestion of an expedition of one man and assigned two white companions, William Isbester and Thomas Merriman, to go with Hearne.

These three were to be guided by a "Captain Chawchinahaw" and accompanied by a small detachment of Chipewyans and a few Home Guards who would presumably supply the labor force. However, these initial numbers really meant nothing because desertions and new attachments took place almost daily.

Whenever an expedition is undertaken those who pay the bills invariably issue instructions and the manner in which the commander obeys these orders presents a not unsatisfactory key to his character. If he lacks perspective and tries to fulfill impossible orders and thereby wastes lives or defeats the major purposes for which he was chosen he forfeits the right to be classed among the top few, though he may, indeed, achieve fame just below them. But if, given orders impossible or impracticable to obey, he ignores them and proceeds on his own judgment, thereby accepting the risks, he assumes the stature of a great explorer, whether he is permitted to achieve his goal or not.

It is pertinent, therefore, to study Hearne's orders.

ORDERS and INSTRUCTIONS for Mr. Samuel Hearne, going on an Expedition by Land towards the Latitude 70° North in order to gain a Knowledge of the Northern Indians Country, &c. on Behalf of the Honourable Hudson's Bay Company, in the Year 1769.

MR. SAMUEL HEARNE,

SIR,

Whereas the Honourable Hudson's Bay Company have been informed by the report from Indians, that there is a great probability of considerable advantages to be expected from a better knowledge of their country by us, than what hitherto has been obtained; and as it is the Company's earnest desire to embrace every circumstance that may tend to the benefit of the said Company, or the Nation at large, they have requested you to conduct this expedition; and as you have readily consented to undertake the present Journey, you are hereby desired to proceed as soon as possible, with William Isbester sailor, and Thomas Merriman landsman, as companions, they both being willing to accompany you; also two of the Home-guard Southern Indians, who are to attend and assist you during the Journey; and Captain Chawchinahaw, his Lieutenant Nabyah, and six or eight of the best Northern Indians we can procure, with a small part of their families, are to conduct you, provide for you, and assist you and your companions in everything that lays in their power, having particular orders to do so.

2dly, Whereas you and your companions are well fitted out with everything we think necessary, as also a sample of light trading goods, these you are to dispose of by way of presents (and not by way of trade) to such far-off Indians as you may meet with, and to smoke your Calimut of Peace with their leaders, in order to establish a friendship with them. You are also to persuade them as much as possible from going to war with each other, to encourage to exert themselves in procuring furrs and other articles of trade, and to assure them of good payment for them at the Company's Factory.

It is sincerely recommended to you and your companions to treat the natives with civility, so as not to give them any room for complaint or disgust, as they have strict orders not to give you the least offense, but are to aid and assist you in any matter you may request of them for the benefit of the undertaking.

If any Indians you may meet, that are coming to the Fort, should be willing to trust you with either food or clothing, make your agreement for those commodities, and by them send me a letter, specifying the quantity of each article, and they shall be paid according to your agreement. And, according to the Company's orders, you are to correspond with me, or the Chief at Prince of Wales's Fort for the time being, at all opportunities: And as you have mathematical instruments with you, you are to send to me, or the Chief for the time being, an account of what latitude and longitude you may be in at such and such periods, together with the heads of your proceedings; which accounts are to be remitted to the Company by the return of their ships.

3dly, The Indians who are now appointed your guides, are to conduct you to the borders of the Athapuscow Indians country, where Captain Matonabbee is to meet you in the Spring of one thousand seven hundred and seventy, in order to conduct you to a river represented by the Indians to abound with copper ore, animals of the furr kind, &c., and which is said to be so far to the Northward, that in the middle of the Summer the Sun does not set, and is supposed by the Indians to empty itself into some ocean. This river, which is called by the Northern Indians Neetha-san-san-dazey, or the Far Off Metal River, you are, if possible, to trace to the mouth, and there determine the latitude and longitude as near as you can; but more particularly so if you find it navigable, and that a settlement can be made there with any degree of safety, or benefit to the Company.

Be careful to observe what mines are near the river, what water there is at the river's mouth, how far the woods are from the seaside, the course of the river, the nature of the soil, and the productions of it; and make any other remarks that you think may be either necessary or satisfactory. And if the said river is likely to be of any utility, take possession of it on behalf of the Hudson's Bay Company, by cutting your name on some of the rocks, as also the date of the year, month, &c.

When you attempt to trace this or any other river, be careful that the Indians are furnished with a sufficient number of canoes for trying the depth of water, the strength of the current &c. If by any unforseen accident or distaster you should not be able to reach the before-mentioned river, it is earnestly recommended to you, if possible, to know the event of Wager Strait; for it is represented by the last discoverers to terminate in small rivers and lakes. See how far the woods are from the navigable parts of it; and whether a settlement could with any propriety be made there. If this should prove unworthy of notice, you are to take the same method with Baker's Lake, which is the head of Bowden's or Chesterfield's Inlet; as also with any other rivers you may meet with; and if likely to be of any utility, you are to take possession of them, as before mentioned, on behalf of the Honourable Hudson's Bay Company. The draft of Bowden's Inlet and Wager Strait I send with you, that you may have a better idea of those places, in case of your visiting them.

4thly, Another material point which is recommended to you, is to find out, if you can, either by your own travels, or by information from the Indians, whether there is a passage through this continent. It will be very useful to clear up this point, if possible, in order to prevent further doubts from arising hereafter respecting a passage out of Hudson's Bay into the Western Ocean, as hath lately been represented by the American Traveller. The particulars of those remarks you are to insert in your Journal, to be remitted home to the Company.

If you should want any supplies of ammunition, or other necessaries, dispatch some trusty Indians to the Fort with a letter, specifying the quantity of each article, and appoint a place for the said Indians to meet you again.

When on your return, if at a proper time of the year, and you should be near any of the harbours that are frequented by the brigantine *Charlotte*, or the sloop *Churchill*, during their voyage to the Northward, and you should chuse to return in one of them, you are desired to make frequent smokes as you approach those harbours, and they will endeavor to receive you by making smokes in answer to yours; and as one thousand seven hundred and seventy-one will probably be the year in which you will return, the Masters of those vessels at that period shall have particular orders on that head.

It will be pleasing to hear by the first opportunity, in what latitude and longitude you meet the Leader Matonabbee, and how far he thinks it is to the Coppermine River, as also the probable time it may take before you can return. But in case anything should prevent the said Leader from joining you, according to expectation, you are then to procure the best Indians you can for your guides, and either add to, or diminish, your number, as you may from time to time think most necessary for the good of the expedition.

So I conclude, wishing you and your companions a continuance of health, together with a prosperous Journey, and a happy return in safety. Amen.

MOSES NORTON, *Governor*.

Dated at Prince of Wales's Fort, Churchill River, Hudson's Bay, North America, November 16th, 1769.

There was nothing unusual about most of these orders but certain items bring into focus the state of the Company ignorance regarding the northern frontier.

". . . you are to correspond with me . . . at all opportunities," just as if there were a post system! And Moses Norton knew better! Hearne said later that in all his travels he had only one opportunity to send a report and that by means of a very casual encounter and with no assurance at all that it would be delivered.

"Be careful to observe . . . the nature of the soil," and it was November and already thousands of square miles lay white and silent and frozen!

". . . know the event of Wager Strait"—hundreds of miles from the area Hearne was to explore. He said he would pay no attention to this order as the Company already had that information and had formally taken possession. Its inclusion, however, indicated how tenaciously the Company held to the idea that Wager Strait or Chesterfield Inlet, might, after all, be Anián.

". . . whether there is a passage through this continent. It will be very useful to clear up this point, . . ." Here, indeed, was a notable item. Not only did it point up the search for Anián as a major purpose of Hearne's voyage but offers refutation to the sometimes expressed opinion that Hearne and Norton were unaware of the worldwide importance of the expedition. To Norton, educated in England and at least as well informed as most on northern affairs, the search for the strait was a familiar theme and Hearne was no less acquainted with the story. Hood had most assuredly talked in Hearne's presence of the many expeditions in which the Royal Navy had participated and it is inconceivable that Hearne was not aware of the millions spent on the search. And aware, too, that the man who proved or disproved its existence across the continent would either usher in a golden age of New World commerce or release an enormous amount of wealth and energy to be expended elsewhere.

And, "If you should want any supplies . . . [You are to] dispatch some . . . Indians to the Fort . . . and appoint a place for the said Indians to meet you again." But, as Hearne remarked, the Indians did not inhabit North America, they roamed over it and one met them only by chance or by their choice, not by making appointments.

And so, Samuel Hearne proposed to obey such of his orders as were practicable and ignore the remainder and thus made the first essential decision of all great explorers.

CHAPTER NINE

The First Coppermine Expedition, 1769

IT WAS not yet daylight when Samuel Hearne told Moses Norton that the first Coppermine expedition was ready, November 6, 1769.

In a few weeks it would be the shortest day of the year and even now, north of Fort Prince of Wales, the sun barely rose above a red horizon before it sank back into an Arctic night.

Hearne knew that most of his work would be done regardless of day or dark. The Indians ate when they had food, slept when they were sleepy, and traveled when they chose.

November 6 broke too warm for the time of year and the snow was soft and heavy and would make hard going for the Indian sleds on which the goods were packed. But Hearne had dallied long enough. From the day he sailed with Hood to avoid a shopkeeper's life he had been building for today. He was ready to "make a name for himself." He wanted to get started.

The Indians with whom he was to travel had finished their business at the fort; they had exchanged their furs for another year's supply of the things they coveted most: guns which might explode at the first shot, diluted whiskey, bright ribbons and yardage, small pieces of iron, and fancy garters for their women. They were unwell from too much drinking, from "civilization," and anxious to return to their normal life.

Captain Chawchinahaw, the Cree guide, was ready, and Isbester and Merriman had completed their simple preparations.

As the straggling company left the stone fort shortly after daybreak they were given a seven-gun salute. It was more than they expected and, in truth, more than they yet deserved. The time was to come when Samuel Hearne well deserved that salute and did not get it but he accepted both the salute and its later omission with equal calm.

Naturally, Hearne was unaware of the total magnitude of the task he had undertaken. No one knew the expanse of North America or where the Arctic was. Only a generation ago Vitus Bering had at last found the Alaska coast. A whole continent lay between his landfall and Samuel Hearne. No one had ever crossed it; no one had ever tried.

The Indians did not pretend a knowledge of the Pacific and their information concerning the Arctic was fragmentary.

Hearne knew the forest would soon disappear; that he must cross the great Barren Grounds; and that somewhere out there in that vast expanse of white were surely the copper mines, and perhaps Anián. But that was all. All that Hearne knew, all that anyone knew.

Thus, aware of the risks but without looking

back, Hearne followed Chawchinahaw west and north, crossed the Knife River twenty miles away and awoke the third morning to find one of his Chipewyans already gone. Hearne slipped the thongs of the deserter's sled, with its sixty-pound load, across his own shoulders. He would rather drag the goods himself than compel someone else to pull a double load.

These native sleds, pulled with a trace across the chest, were crude but efficient under normal conditions. They were made of thin boards, or light poles, of any convenient length laid parallel and turned up and back at the forward ends into rough semicircles fifteen or twenty inches in diameter. Across these were lashed crosspieces which in turn supported the load. Their very crudity contributed to their efficiency for any scraggly brush would serve for repairs. However, they were easily damaged by the twists and stresses of boulders and frozen drifts and demanded frequent mending.

When the expedition left the Knife River and moved toward the Barren Grounds, Hearne asked Chawchinahaw how far it was to the next timberline and the Indian replied that it was only four or five days' travel. Ten days later there was no sign of woods in the direction in which they were going although Hearne could see them "looming . . . to the southwest." And finding trees was fast becoming a necessity. Exceedingly rough terrain had made the sleds almost useless; the cold was now intense; the minute supply of European food which they had stuffed in their pockets as they walked out of Fort Prince of Wales was gone many days ago and there had been no replacement. Once they had seen a deer track,[1] once a partridge had been killed. Less than two weeks away from the Churchill Hearne faced starvation and death by exposure. Out on the Barren Grounds there was rarely any fuel for fire and they could do no more than turn the sleds sidewise, wrap their single blankets about them, then lie down beside their equipment and hope that the drifting snow would offer enough protection to prevent death.

They had already reached their first "point of no return." Food and fire and life might be ahead; most assuredly they were not close enough behind.

On November 20 Chawchinahaw found a small stand of trees and water. The squaws cut holes in the ice, squatted on their heels and fished; the men found three deer but the "Indians have such enormous stomachs" there was very little left after two or three meals, said Hearne.

They wandered on, north and west, living on one-half partridge per person per day. Chawchinahaw suggested they return to Fort Prince of Wales.

Hearne refused.

During the night of November 29 more Chipe-

---

[1] The "deer" so often referred to in Hearne's journals were, in fact, North American caribou, closely related to the European reindeer. *Since Hearne always spoke of the caribou as deer we shall follow his usage.* For a further description of the caribou see the Appendix.

wyans deserted, taking ammunition, iron goods, and other miscellaneous items. Hearne tasked Chawchinahaw with encouraging the desertions but the Indian denied any involvement and again suggested they return to the Churchill.

Again Hearne refused.

Now Chawchinahaw dropped all pretense. He arrogantly tossed Hearne a few remaining supplies, told him in what direction he might find the Seal River, a stream just north of the Knife, and, in company with his friends, set off towards the southwest, "making [the] woods ring with their laughter and left us to consider our unhappy situation," two hundred miles from home.

Where was the first Coppermine expedition when this desertion took place? Except that it was approximately two hundred miles north and west of Churchill, no one knows. Hearne's quadrant was a poor one and he was not expert in its use.

Faced with his first defeat Hearne stoically lightened the loads of his remaining companions and tramped southeast.

One can argue that Samuel Hearne deserved his present fate since he had broken a cardinal rule of a good commander: assume the risks, issue orders and see them obeyed. But Hearne was very young and dealing with older and wiser rascals. He had not yet learned that gentleness seldom swayed the savage mind.

The return to the Churchill was marked by a general disintegration of command. Others beside

Chawchinahaw laughed, and while the three white men went hungry on half a partridge the few remaining Indians walked ahead, flushed the game, and ate in moderate plenty.

December 1, Hearne, Isbester, and Merriman reached the Seal River where they accepted an invitation from a chance-met Chipewyan band to join in "taking a beaver house," fifteen miles away. The thought of food was welcome and they hurried over the miles; arrived near midnight; were welcomed to a feast, and then, early next morning, raided the beaver dam. In the division of the spoils Hearne came out on the short end but he made no very serious objection and resumed his journey.

One of the Chipewyans announced his intentions of going along. ". . . at first I could not see his motive," said Hearne. But when they finally arrived at the fort, December 11, 1769, the Indian demanded payment for the food Hearne had eaten, and helped catch, back at the beaver pond.

Governor Norton, who had expected the expedition to be gone "twenty months or two years" and had had great confidence in Chawchinahaw, probably even greater than in Hearne, accepted the guide's desertion, the fake food bill, and Hearne's defeat without recriminations.

Hearne's journal of his first Coppermine expedition ends on a mundane note: a long entry detailing facts and fables about beaver; an expression "of my own great mortification," and, without Anián.

CHAPTER TEN

The Second Coppermine Expedition

DISDAINING alibis, Hearne proposed an immediate second expedition and Norton agreed. The only important problem to be resolved was personnel and the Indian complement was easily settled. A band of Chipewyans had recently arrived at Fort Prince of Wales in "great distress" and among them was Conne-e-quese who said that he had been very near the copper mines. On that statement Norton hired him to guide the second Coppermine expedition.

Hearne argued it was necessary to include women in the command to do the camp work but for some unknown reason Norton refused and Hearne gave in.

There remained only the question of white companions. Ibester volunteered again but Merriman pleaded a "cold" and asked to be relieved. Hearne refused to have either, saying they were both useless. He preferred to go without European comrades.

Modern explorers do not plan to challenge the Arctic in midwinter. Months are spent collecting and testing supplies and machines; weather reports are mapped for weeks; and the command moves only when it can make use of every daylight hour, every degree of warmth, every shred of natural protection.

But Samuel Hearne, accompanied by three Chipewyans and two Home Guard Indians walked out of the gates of the fort on the Churchill, February 23, 1770, with a single leather tent, homemade sleds, a Hadley quadrant, a cheap gun each, a few trade trinkets, and a stubborn determination to find the Coppermine and Anián if they existed.

There were no salutes this time as "I readily relinquished everything of the kind," although Norton "insisted on giving me three cheers," said Hearne.

Hearne, now properly impressed with the risks he had assumed, believed that his best chance of survival was to follow the rivers when possible and he made a fifty-mile swing around Button Bay northward to Seal River, thence up it for approximately ninety miles. The weather was bad. For days at a time storms lashed the land with a fury even the Indians would not challenge and the six men huddled in their tent and waited.

Two weeks after leaving Fort Prince of Wales they were without food. Early in the morning of March 8 they retreated to a small lake on which Conne-e-quese selected a location for net fishing through the ice.

Trout and pike proved plentiful and the Indian suggested they stay there until the geese came, about May 15. There was no shelter farther north and if they wished to keep to the trees they must make a long, out-of-the-way swing to the west-southwest. If they waited until good weather they could cut almost due north over the Barren Grounds. Hearne agreed and a semipermanent camp was made, probably on the rapids at the western end of Shethanei Lake just below 59° north and 98° west.

The snow was cleared away down to the moss which was then hacked out lest it become a fire hazard as it thawed and dried. The tent, the familiar wrap-around tepee of moose hide, was placed over this cleared area. At the bottom around the outside brush and snow were tightly packed. One could live without fire for a very considerable length of time in such a shelter.

Except for the monotony of an all-fish diet Hearne rather liked it. He trapped marten with a morsel of fish attached to a center pole around which were arranged other poles in such fashion that when the bait was disturbed the logs fell on the marten either killing it or holding it prisoner until it froze to death; he brought his journal up to date; and, most important, he drew maps, not very complete, perhaps, but the first ones ever made of the interior of northern Canada.

March passed with no apparent progress toward the Coppermine or Anián. On April 1, 1770, "Early in the morning we arose" with only food enough for two men and on the eighth, ninth and tenth there was less, "a pipe of tobacco and a draught of water." The fish were gone. The expedition resumed the trail.

Anyway, with the advent of spring the partridges would arrive: the wood partridge, the willow partridge or ptarmigan, and the rock partridge.

In season the ptarmigan was a staple. Hearne said they were often killed in such numbers they were fed to the hogs at Fort Prince of Wales. Sir Thomas Button, who wintered at Port Nelson in 1612 while on an abortive search for the Northwest Passage, said his crew killed 1,800 dozen that winter. Mr. Jeremie (Governor at York Factory on the Nelson River when the French held it and called it Fort Bourbon) claimed the eighty men stationed under him ate 90,000 ptarmigan and 25,000 rabbits in one winter!

Because of the long months of snow the ptarmigan were forever short of gravel for their crops and the Indians took advantage of this fact to catch them easily. They set up a pole, tied a net to it and baited the net with a heap of gravel. The grit-starved ptarmigan rushed for the net, the cord was yanked and the Indians piled on the flapping partridges and killed them by "biting them at the back of the head." With luck, three men could "bite" three hundred birds in a forenoon.

By June 1, Hearne had moved beyond Shethanei Lake, turned north, and was at Shoal Lake, the modern Beralzone, between Shethanei and the timberline to the north. There was almost constant daylight with soft snow and patches of bare ground. Snowshoes and sleds were thrown away and the goods arranged into packs. Hearne, contrary to the custom of English commanders, carried his share: the quadrant, the compass, his small trunk, extra clothes, some books and paper. Sixty pounds. No paths, insecure footing, the "most laborious task I ever encountered," said Hearne.

There was no sign of copper and even less of a transcontinental waterway. And again there was no food. On June 20, 21, and 22 they carried their sixty-pound loads on tobacco and water although Hearne found it not so unpleasant as when they had traveled for seven days on cranberries, water, scraps of leather and burned bones from old fires. Then their stomachs shrank, their strength ebbed, and when food was taken again they dared eat only "2 or 3 ounces."

The Indians and Hearne were never far from starvation. "I have frequently seen the Indians examine their wardrobe, . . . and consider what part could best be spared." In the last extremities the subarctic Indians sometimes resorted to cannibalism but it was never from choice or was it ever a religious ceremony. The guilty were shunned and despised. Hearne said he once saw such a wretch almost killed when he could not explain how he had traveled two hundred miles without weapons yet had fragments of meat in his pack, fragments which the women said were human flesh.

The second Coppermine expedition was now crossing the Barren Grounds almost due north along the ninety-third meridian, a hundred miles away from the nearest trees. There were no fires; it rained incessantly; and the loose leather shirt, long stockings, and soft, wet moccasins were cold and slippery comfort.

Stung by the rain, and plagued by a growing suspicion that the Coppermine and Anián might be much more illusive than Conne-e-quese had pretended, Hearne moved farther and farther north, battling a mounting hunger until its satisfaction became the only aim in life.

Three old musk-oxen with shaggy heads hunched down into huge shoulders and bleary eyes staring vacantly stood at the shore of a small lake. The Indians killed all three. They were old and tough and reeked but while the rain came down in great wind-driven sheets the second Coppermine expedition ate raw most of "one buffalo."

After seventy-two hours the downpour ended, the men dried their clothes in the sun, jerked a few strips of musk-ox, and headed for the Kazan River the last of June.

The Kazan is typical of northern rivers. It winds and slithers over four hundred and fifty miles, widening at dozens of places into small lakes then drifting on to a narrower, deeper channel before it stops again to form a new lake. It rises in the southwest corner of Mackenzie District and empties into Baker Lake, which in turn reaches Hudson Bay via Chesterfield Inlet. The Kazan was a favorite Chipewyan hunting ground because the caribou crossed it on their annual migration.

On one of these crossings, near "White Snow

Lake," the Yathkyed of modern maps, Hearne came upon another Chipewyan leader, Keelshies, traveling to Fort Prince of Wales. The Indian offered to carry dispatches and meet Hearne at a later rendezvous with tobacco, ammunition, and knives, which were always in short supply.

We shall meet Keelshies again much later.

With the discovery of Yathkyed Samuel Hearne had penetrated deeper into the American subarctic than any other white man. His suspicion that the land draining into Hudson Bay was only a small part of the Canadian north had been verified. The upper Seal River, Shethanei, the Kazan, Yathkyed—new worlds to the white man, old trails to the Chipewyans. And yet the miles lay beyond. Where were the copper mines? Was there an Anián?

Late in July, after moving northward from Yathkyed, Hearne met a small band of Chipewyans with whom Conne-e-quese fraternized in a most suspicious manner. When questioned he replied that since it was already too late to get to the Coppermine this season the expedition should spend the winter with this band.

Hearne was unprepared for this turn of events but he was in no position to force the issue and reluctantly agreed to accompany the Indians while they wandered northwestward toward the south shore of Aberdeen Lake, approximately 125 air-line miles from Yathkyed. It is not likely, however, that Hearne ever saw Aberdeen Lake, for just before actually arriving there the Indians turned at right angles and headed southwest seventy-five miles to the Dubawnt River where it leaves Dubawnt Lake, 63° north.[1]

Now, even a casual study of his journals will demonstrate that it is almost impossible to keep the man, Samuel Hearne, in focus. He is forever slipping out of sight behind the scenes he remembers. Thus, since he reached the Dubawnt River just where it leaves the lake he could hardly have avoided being the discoverer of Dubawnt Lake, sixteenth largest in all North America, but he takes no credit for it and his journal passes lightly over the day: "In our way to the Westward we came to several rivers, which, though small and of no note, were so deep as not to be fordable, particularly Doobaunt River."

Almost daily other bands joined the expedition and by the end of the month Hearne was surrounded with six hundred persons, ". . . and in the morning, when we began to move, the whole ground, . . . seemed alive, with men, women, children, and dogs."

One day early in August, Hearne, wishing to get away from the racket of six hundred Indians, entrusted his quadrant and a supply of powder to one of them and went hunting. On Hearne's return the Indian had decamped. It was too late that night to go after him and Hearne indulged in a bit of self pity: the Chipewyans were a dis-

---

[1] Dubawnt, more properly "To bon," is Chipewyan for "water-along-the-shore," referring to the fact that the lake seldom has more than a narrow ice-free channel along the shore.

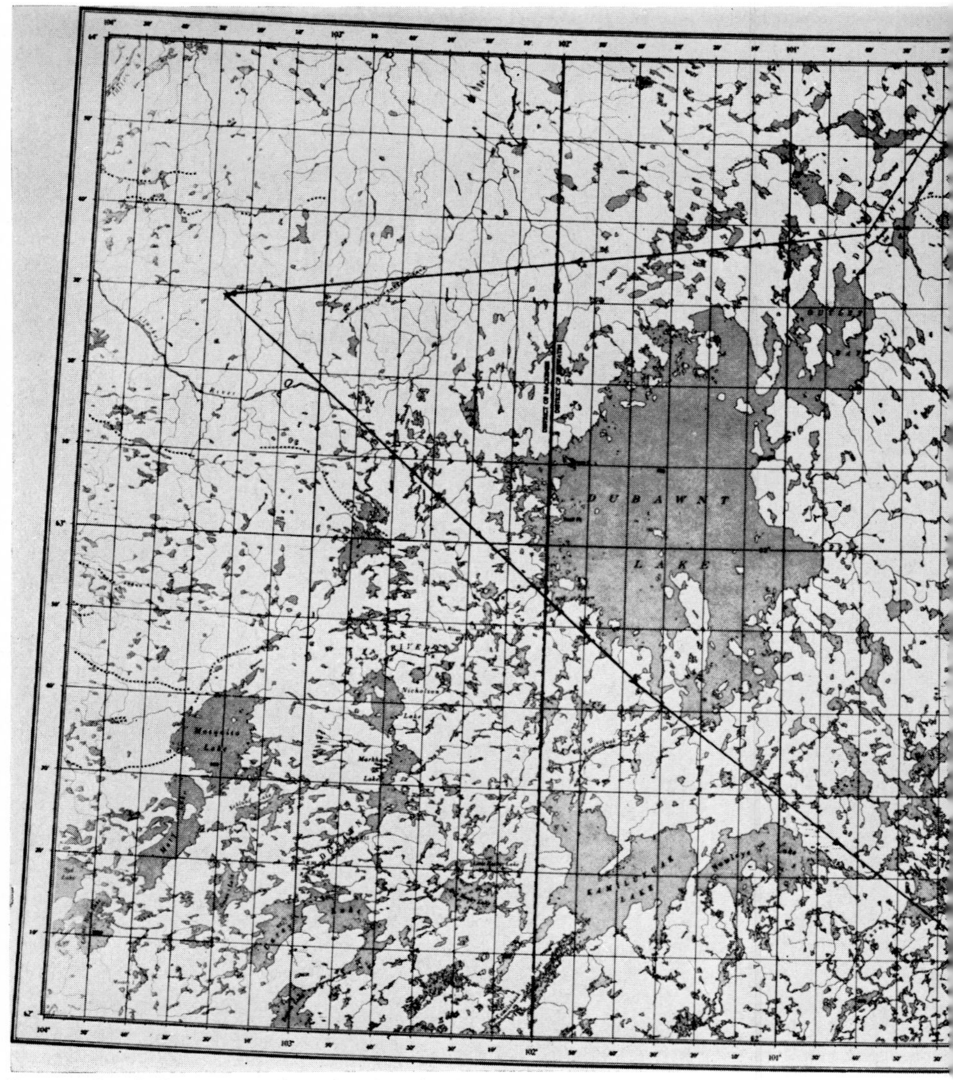

Courtesy Canada Department of Mines and Technical Surveys, Ottawa

THE DUBAWNT LAKE SEGME

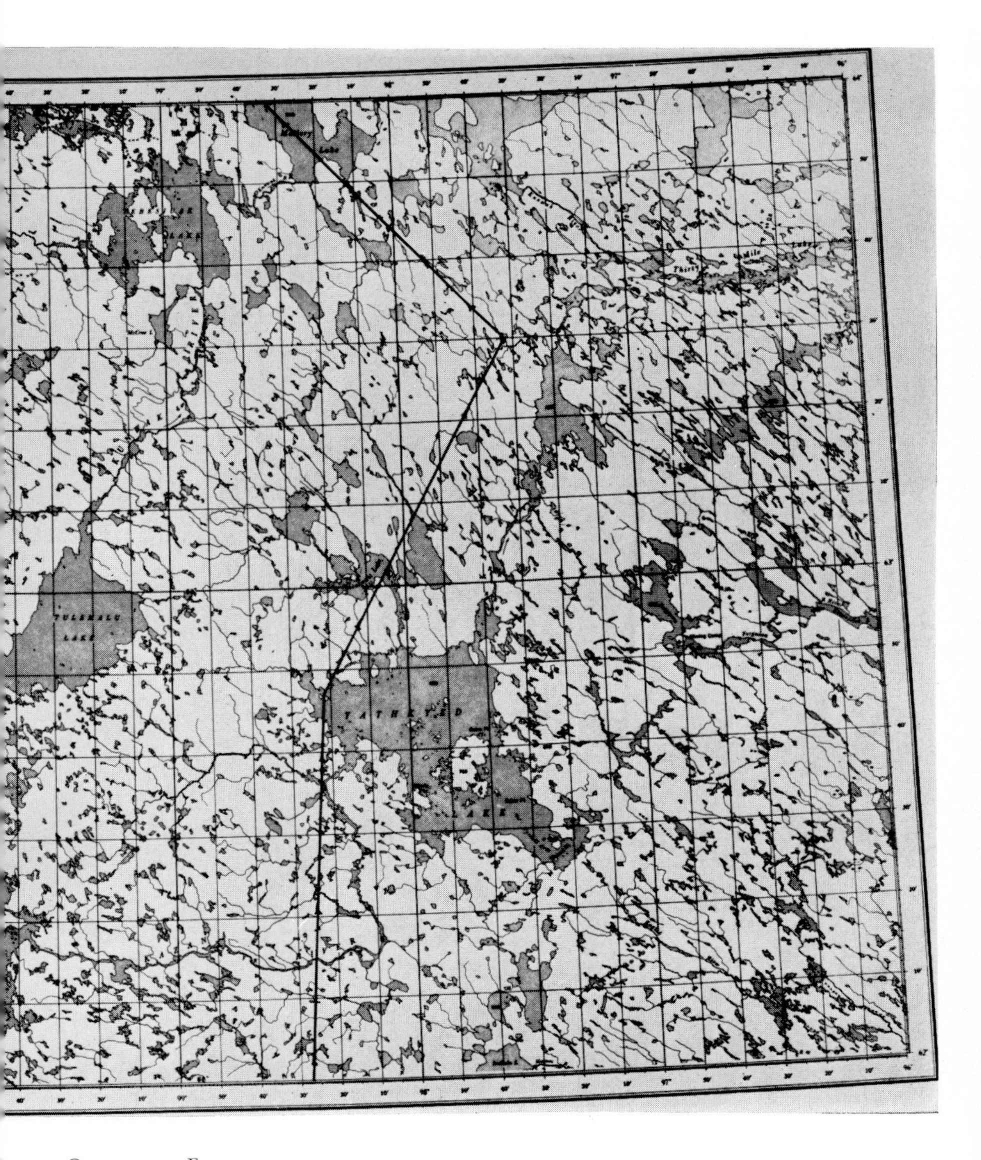

ECOND COPPERMINE EXPEDITION

courteous lot; they seemed to think he had brought the whole Fort Prince of Wales with him; and because he had only "knick-knacks and gew-gaws" they denounced him as a "poor servant, noways like the Governor at the Factory, who . . . they never saw, but [who] gave them something useful."

It had turned out an unpleasant, discouraging day.

Gradually the moss fires died down; children stopped bickering; the women left off their gossip and petty quarrels, and Samuel Hearne soothed himself to sleep reciting:

> Tir'd Nature's sweet restorer, balmy sleep!
> He, like the world, his ready visit pays
> Where fortune smiles; the wretched he forsakes;
> Swift on his downy pinion flies from woe,
> And lights on lids unsullied with a tear.

Next morning, very early, Hearne and two Southern Indians went after the deserter. Without result they returned at evening to the place where Hearne had last seen the porter and there found tracks leading toward a river. Following these he found the quadrant and part of the powder laid out on a stone. Hearne then returned to his previous night's camp but found that all six hundred Indians had moved on. They had, however, left him a direction marker. He tightened his belt, grumbled, and set off after them. It was 10:00 P.M. when he caught up, ate a big supper, and went to bed. He needed no poetry to put him to sleep that night. He had walked, probably, thirty or forty miles since sunup.

August 12 was a fine summer day and the Indians were resting and catching up on various chores. Hearne mounted the quadrant and recorded "63° 10′ No and 10° 40′ w from Churchill." Because of a slight cloudiness he left the quadrant in position intending to take another reading after lunch. He never got his second shot at the sun. A gust of high wind slashed across the camp and before he could reach his instrument it was useless—glass, sight vane, and vernier broken.

A sudden windstorm had put an end to the second Coppermine expedition. With no means of verifying positions and distances the goals of the venture would be impossible to attain: find the copper deposits and be able to return to them; and prove or disprove the existence of Anián.

Hearne was now on the vast plain west of Dubawnt Lake and northwest of Dubawnt River, probably a thousand miles of meandering trail from Fort Prince of Wales. While he thought of this and Governor Norton's displeasure at a second failure several Indians came to him and asked for his "skipertogan," a small bag, richly ornamented with quills, beads, and moose hair, in which he kept his flint, steel, pipe, tobacco and other personal effects. Before he could answer their request they seized his other baggage, helped themselves, handed him the empty sack, and robbed the five men who had come with him from Fort Prince of Wales.

Hearne was now in a precarious position: a lone white man, far from home, surrounded by six hundred Indians who accepted theft as a way of life and without any possibility of regaining his property by force. He gambled on Chipewyan psychology. Knowing their unpredictability he requested they return a knife, an awl, needle, his razors and soap in order that he might travel in safety. They readily agreed, except that they restored only one of his razors. "Luckily they chose [to keep] the worst," he said.

Hearne submitted to these attacks with what grace he could and after another week with the Indians started home, accompanied by some of the very men who had robbed him.[2]

The five Indians Norton had assigned Hearne had no personal interest in copper mines and much less in Anián. At the moment their sole concern was recouping their personal fortunes and acquiring and preparing the eight or ten caribou hides necessary for each suit of winter clothes and it was a laborious task. They must mix the brains and soft fat of the newly killed animals into a lather, soak and wash the hides, hang them in the smoke of a slow fire for several days, soak and wash again in warm water, dry and rub and

[2] Professor Rich criticizes Hearne for failing to prevent these thefts by exerting his authority! Just how a single white man was to compel six hundred Indians to do his will is not made clear. See E. E. Rich, *Hudson's Bay Company, 1670-1870* [Hudson's Bay Record Society Publications, Vols. 21-23] (London, 1959), II, 50-51.

stretch until all moisture was exhausted, after which they were carefully scraped.

All this was women's work.

But Norton had refused to assign women to the expedition and it had now been robbed of the means of paying for women's services and they would do nothing without pay. "I never saw a set of people that possessed so little humanity, or that could view the distress of their fellow creatures with so little feeling and unconcern; for though they seem to have great affection for their wives and children, yet they will laugh at and ridicule the distress of every other person who is not immediately related to them."

And certainly Hearne was in distress for he had neither clothes nor a proper tent. During the summer a blanket tossed around a chance-found pole would serve, but now it was September and the beginning of winter. Almost any morning might break lead gray with little puffs of snow and before one was aware he would be enveloped in a swirling desolation of white in which life was perilous and travel almost impossible.

On September 17 Hearne awoke to such a world, and once again faced a very-present death. The Chipewyan camp was far behind and his supposed companions were racing ahead and "we could not keep up with them for want of snow shoes."

Hearne seldom mentioned personal dangers and the entry, "we could not keep up. . . ." was his way of saying he had been abandoned. If he was to live this day he must plow through miles of soft snow, desperately trying to "keep up" and knowing that if he failed there could be but one result.

Perhaps it is such crises which have led historians generally to think of the second Coppermine expedition as a bootless errand instead of what it was: a feat of exploration the like of which has awarded lesser men world renown.[3]

Hearne had penetrated the American subarctic farther than any white man had ever done—300 miles inland from Hudson Bay, 400 miles north of the Churchill. He had explored the upper Seal; he had discovered Yathkyed, larger than Lake Champlain; he had touched the borders of the great Thelon game preserve south and west of Aberdeen Lake; and he had discovered Dubawnt Lake, larger than Great Salt Lake. He had, in effect, traveled a giant, crude X across 120,000 square miles of northland, drawing maps and recording the natural history as he went. And if his maps were less than perfect his natural history was a product of almost faultless observation.

But on the mornings of September 18, 19, and 20, 1770, Samuel Hearne was not thinking of his place in history. He was concerned with survival. For three days the deadly struggle without snowshoes had gone on. Only a superb physique and his quiet, stubborn will had kept him on his feet. Each night he stumbled to sleep a little later and with a little less hope, but he would not admit

[3] "Hearne's second journey . . . was . . . as disappointing as his first." *Ibid.*, II, 50.

defeat. Then, sometime during the day of September 20, 1770, Samuel Hearne crossed the path of the Chipewyan chief, Matonabbee, longtime favorite at Fort Prince of Wales, whom Norton had mentioned as a messenger in the official orders for the first expedition.

CHAPTER ELEVEN

Matonabbee

IT HAS BEEN said that some men deserve to be known only by a single name, one which identifies them and their work without more ado.

Matonabbee was such a man.

Matonabbee's parentage was extremely humble. His mother was a slave purchased from the Southern Indians when they came to trade at Fort Prince of Wales. His father was a Chipewyan. Governor Richard Norton is reputed to have arranged the match.

Probably not even his own mother knew the date of Matonabbee's birth. The year 1736 was generally accepted around the fort and, if that is correct, he was about ten years older than Samuel Hearne.

While Matonabbee was a boy his father died and Governor Norton adopted him, probably according to tribal customs rather than English law. The little Indian was a likable youngster and popular at the "Big House," and because of his adoption by the Chief Factor he had certain privileges not extended to other Indian boys.

But when Richard Norton went to England and an interim governor assumed the duties on the Churchill Matonabbee's relatives came and carried the boy away with them. He stayed with the Chipewyans until Ferdinand Jacobs took charge at Fort Prince of Wales in 1752 and hired him as a hunter. Samuel Hearne said, years later, that Jacobs engaged Matonabbee out of respect for the elder Norton who had passed away in the meantime.

In the intervening years Matonabbee had grown from a gangling adolescent into a six-foot giant: powerful and proud but friendly and tolerant according to his wonts.

He became a master of the Southern Indian language and acquired a working knowledge of English along with a smattering of the Christian religion.

Christianity was too complicated for him to understand but he maintained a tolerant respect for it as he did for the simpler faiths of his own people. At the same time he insisted that he, personally, would go out of the world as he came into it, without religion. As is so often the case he belied his own words and "notwithstanding his aversion for religion, I have met with few Christians who possessed more good moral qualities, or fewer bad ones," said Hearne. "Matonabbee . . . could tell a better story of our Saviour's birth and life, than one half of those who call themselves Christians; yet he always declared to me, that neither he, nor any of his countrymen, had an idea of a future state. . . . I have seen him several times assist at some of the sacred rites performed by the Southern Indians, apparently with as much zeal, as if he had given as much credit to them as they did: and . . . I am persuaded [he would] have assisted at the alter of a Christian church, or Jewish synagogue; not . . . to reap any advantage to himself, but . . . to assist others who believed in such ceremonies."[1]

For an Indian, Matonabbee's table manners were impeccable. Hearne mentioned how Matonabbee would often put five or six of his "strapping wives to work to louse their hairy deerskin shifts, the produce of which being always very considerable, he eagerly received with both hands, and licked them in as fast and with as good a grace as any European epicure would the mites in a cheese." Hearne here referred to the *Arachnidae*, or cheese mite, common in all cheese in those days. The ripest cheese, and concomitantly with the most mites, was the greatest delicacy.

Matonabbee loved Spanish wine but never used hard liquor and seldom drank anything to excess. This was the more remarkable since drunkenness was taken for granted on the American frontier.

Matonabbee was not faultless, of course. In fits of wild jealousy he could step beyond the "bounds of humanity" and commit brutal and savage acts. But altogether he was a worthy and lovable man, who, if the most important part of his life were

[1] Samuel Hearne, *A Journey from Prince of Wales's Fort in Hudson's Bay to the Northern Ocean, Undertaken by Order of the Hudson's Bay Company, for the Discovery of Copper Mines, a Northern Passage, etc., in the Years 1769, 1770, 1771 & 1772.* (Dublin: P. Byrne and J. Rice, 1796), pp. 344-45.

not tied inextricably to that of Samuel Hearne's, would deserve his own biographer.

A summary is in order even here.

Some time after the elder Norton died but before Moses Norton became governor on the Churchill, Matonabbee served on a Company sloop under Magnus Johnston.

Later Governor Jacobs sent him to make peace between the Chipewyans and their neighbors. Matonabbee entered enemy territory, was seized and prepared for death by torture. As the savages worked themselves into a frenzy Matonabbee taunted them either to commit their murder or be quiet. This effrontry so astounded his captors they released him.

The next year he again entered their territory and was captured a second time. Once more he dared them to do him bodily harm, overawed them, was released and then became a lifelong friend of the enemies he had just bluffed.

Matonabbee went to the Coppermine River with another Indian leader, I-dat-le-aza, and reported his trip to Moses Norton in 1769; went with Hearne on the third Coppermine expedition; was made head of all Chipewyans in the north; spent several years in the fur trade; saw Fort Prince of Wales captured by the French as part of their campaign to aid the American colonies during the American Revolution, and, disillusioned about the impregnability of the fort and the infallibility of his English friends, threw a rope around his neck and hanged himself, leaving his six wives and four children to starve to death during the winter of 1783.

Matonabbee was the only Indian ever known to commit suicide in all the years Samuel Hearne was on Hudson Bay, but Matonabbee demanded life on his own terms and if it could not meet those terms he had no use for it.

This, then, was the man who rescued Hearne, September 20, 1770, as he was fighting a losing battle against early winter without proper clothes, snowshoes, or sleds.

Matonabbee immediately gave Hearne a suit of "otter and other skins"; ordered his own women to prepare additional clothes; directed Hearne to a nearby supply of material for snowshoes and sleds; gave a feast in Hearne's honor, thus raising his sagging prestige; and, asked Hearne if he intended to try again to find the copper mines and Anián.

Samuel Hearne was sometimes hesitant and overgentle but Matonabbee found him positive and stubborn now. He would find the copper mines and prove or disprove Anián if he forfeited his life in the attempt, he said. And he would go again with, or without, Norton's permission.

Matonabbee understood those rules. They were of the pattern of his own life and the two men became fast friends. Matonabbee sometimes laughed at Hearne's civilized qualms and English manners and Hearne often berated the Chipewyan for his jealous temper and disregard of life, but these things never seriously interfered with their deeper esteem.

It was soon agreed that Matonabbee would act as guide for the third attempt to reach the Arctic if Norton would agree to pay the proper wages.

Matonabbee then listened to Hearne's recital of his two failures and immediately analyzed their cause, not as broken quadrants or treacherous guides, but the lack of women. For, said he, "when all the men are heavy laden, they can neither hunt nor travel to any considerable distance; and in case they meet with success in hunting, who is to carry the produce of their labour? Women . . . were made for labour; one of them can carry, or haul, as much as two men can do." All this was an exaggeration, of course, but it suited Matonabbee's argument of the moment. He continued, "They also pitch our tents, make and mend our clothing, keep us warm at night; and, in fact, there is no such thing as travelling any considerable distance, or for any length of time, in this country, without their assistance. Women, though they do everything, are maintained at a trifling expense; for as they always stand cook, the very licking of their fingers in scarce times, is sufficient for their subsistance."

Hearne slyly confided to his journal that he suspected that women had to eat as well as men and dipped their fingers in the pot when the men were not looking. Hearne was indeed right. The comic-tragic code of female behavior provided that the men ate first but the women were expected to taste the dish before serving. If they did this furtively there was no objection, but if observed the penalty was a beating and the culprit's value as a wife declined.

From October 23 to November 6 Hearne detoured after snowshoes and sleds, then returned to the Indians' camp and was given such a warm welcome by Matonabbee that Hearne said he was the "most sociable, kind, and sensible Indian I have ever met with." Since the Chipewyan had just saved his life these feelings were logical.

By the third week in November the weather was much worsened and Matonabbee told Hearne to hurry ahead before his meager equipment caused him serious trouble.

Next morning Hearne, accompanied by one Home Guard Indian and three Chipewyans, headed for the Egg River, spent that night south of it, then moved toward the Seal River next day. But in late afternoon a gale came roaring in from the northwest and piled the snow in huge drifts. There was no wood or fire. To lay huddled together for twelve or fourteen hours waiting for daybreak, or death by freezing, whichever came first, did not seem a fitting way to prove to Matonabbee that he was worthy of a third chance at Anián so Hearne ordered the men to keep walking, using the stars and moon as guides when they could be dimly seen, now and again, through the swirling snow.

During the night and the next day the men passed clumps of trees but the snow was too thick to see the woods and they went on without shelter or fire. Hearne's dog, presumably acquired from Matonabbee, froze to death and Hearne hauled the sled himself, "a very heavy one," he said. Sometime before midnight the second night the party stumbled over a tuft of willows and two or three old tent poles. This was enough. They dug into a drift; put up a deerskin against the wind, and fought green wood until a tiny blaze gave them some psychological warmth if very little real heat.

They had hardly built their fire when the storm died as suddenly as it came; the moon threw a brilliant glare against the drifted snow and the aurora borealis "shone out with great splendor."

As Hearne squatted on his heels beside his fire and deerskin and watched the lights play up and down the sky he remembered how the Chipewyans called the aurora borealis the "Ed-thin" and their belief that "up there" was a celestial deer having his fur rubbed and throwing off sparks just as his earthly counterpart would do if properly stroked.

Next morning was "excessively sharp" and Hearne moved quickly. He crossed the Seal River, circled around Button Bay, and on November 25, 1770, reentered the gates of Fort Prince of Wales.

After reporting to Norton that Matonabbee would be along shortly Hearne's journal ends and we are left to assume that he resumed work in the post just as if he had never gone away.

Samuel Hearne left the Churchill February 23, 1770, and returned November 25. Where had he been in those nine months? For part of the time he did not know exactly where he was and so neither do we, but we can trace his route in its essentials: He got as far toward the Arctic and the copper mines as the southern edge of Aberdeen Lake; he broke the quadrant on the plain west of Dubawnt Lake and northwest of the Dubawnt River; and, his journey home, not counting side trips or meandering, was substantially as follows: he crossed the Dubawnt at 63° north, near where it flows into Dubawnt Lake, turned southeast and skirted the south end of the lake; then went overland to the Kazan River just above Angikuni (Titmeg) Lake; kept to the south of Angikuni; then continued east and south to the Thlewiaza River; then pushed on to the Egg and Seal rivers; crossed them and moved around the south end of Button Bay to Fort Prince of Wales.

More significantly, we may ask what the second Coppermine expedition had accomplished? Certainly Hearne had found neither the ore deposits nor the Strait of Anián but he had crisscrossed a hitherto unexplored 120,000 square miles of North America in which he had proved there was no Northwest Passage. If Anián existed it must be still farther north.

And with that knowledge in mind Samuel Hearne laid his plans for the third Coppermine expedition—without recriminations, dramatics, or regrets.

CHAPTER TWELVE

The Third Coppermine Expedition Begins

THERE have been hints and statements that after the second Coppermine expedition Hearne was considered a hopeless incompetent. "Not even the distrust of Norton, who wrote home to the Company that Hearne was unfit for the task in hand, could discourage him (Hearne) from making a third attempt," said Beckles Willson.[1]

But all such criticisms do not ring quite true. Norton was governor at Fort Prince of Wales and as such was the depository of enormous power. Quite enough to have scotched any third excursion by Samuel Hearne had he so desired.

Hearne, himself, states flatly that Norton recognized his "abilities and approved courage," and the Company increased his wages to £130 per year (his beginning wage had been £25), a most peculiar proceeding if his superiors were dissatisfied with his work.

And there is the item regarding personnel. Hearne refused to include several of Norton's relatives in his third company and the governor, although very angry, accepted the decision. If

[1] Beckles Willson, *The Great Company* (New York: Dodd, Mead and Co., 1906), p. 305.

Hearne was held in low repute what was the lever which permitted him to defy his superior? Company governors, especially Moses Norton, were not accustomed to having their orders questioned. We must either resolve these discrepancies or accept Hearne's own statement that the governor recognized his "abilities and approved courage."

In any event Moses Norton gave full official support to the third Coppermine expedition; appointed Matonabbee as guide; authorized such supplies as could be taken; and issued the required formal instructions, which merely referred Hearne to his previous orders and reminded him to look for the "North West Passage, Coppermines or any other thing which might be serviceable . . . etc."

Anián was again given a top billing!

Hearne, although young and sometimes inefficient, had learned that a really great commander delegates authority to those better prepared for a given task than himself, and Matonabbee was at once assigned the duty of organizing their scanty equipment.

And this time, too, there was to be no nonsense about leaving the women at home. Matonabbee saw to it that there were sufficient females to do the domestic work and maintain some semblance of family relations. As for himself, Matonabbee seldom had less than three wives to do his bidding.

Hearne was again the only white man in the company.

In our day of elaborate preparations for such expeditions it is difficult to realize the magnitude of Hearne's faith in himself, and, to a lesser degree, Matonabbee. About the only parallel in this century being Richard Byrd's winter alone in the Antarctic and that is not really analagous for while Byrd gambled his life without human companions he had every known scientific aid. Hearne went without a vestige of prearranged civilized supplies beyond the first few miles.

On the third Coppermine expedition it is sometimes difficult to determine just who made the plans or issued the orders at a given moment. Hearne almost invariably said "we" and there are those who insist that Hearne was, therefore, only a figurehead and that Matonabbee was the real leader. Such an interpretation disregards one of Hearne's greatest attributes—his willingness to accept a subordinate with superior knowledge in a given field. It is as specious to argue that Matonabbee was the leader of the third Coppermine expedition as to say that Sacajawea commanded the Lewis and Clark expedition because her advice was accepted.

Thus, Hearne delegated to Matonabbee the day-by-day details and seldom interfered with the Indian's orders, but that did not mean that Hearne relinquished the search for the Northwest Passage, or map making, or the study of the natural history of the lands they crossed. Those projects were quite beyond the ken of the Indian and Hearne reserved them for himself. He and Matonabbee could share in the search for the mines.

On December 7, 1770, the final valid expedition for the search for Anián was ready to start. When its work was done there would no longer be any legitimate excuse to spend fortunes and risk lives looking for the myth of Anián. If certain governments and certain individuals refused to accept the finality of Samuel Hearne's work they but illustrated a senseless intransigence for he settled without justifiable quibble the question of a Northwest Passage through North America.

There was no fanfare when Hearne departed Fort Prince of Wales on the third Coppermine expedition. Nor did he expect otherwise. Twice before he had been dispatched with salutes and huzzahs which he had been unable to justify as far as Anián and the mines were concerned and he was willing to wait for an earned salute.

And so, on an unseasonably warm day, December 7, 1770, Samuel Hearne, Matonabbee, and an unknown number of Indians drifted out of the gates of the fort and headed for the Arctic.

One of Matonabbee's wives was ill and he had her hauled on a sled, an unusual practice, but woe to him who hinted that the chief was soft with his women! The sick wife and the soft snow slowed travel and Hearne did not reach the Seal River until the end of the first week.

On December 16 they arrived at the Egg River. Food was almost gone; caches from a previous trip by the Indians had been robbed but it was useless to talk of revenge; plod on; sixteen or eighteen miles per day and hope for food tomorrow; two days more and the discovery of an old camp with enough frozen leftovers for one good meal; then out on the great Barren Grounds where man and beast travel at their own risk; a treeless waste where only a little "wish-a-ca-pucca" grows and sometimes a "thin sod of moss . . . so palatable, that all who taste it generally grow fond of it"; where a bit of scrubby willow and a few spears of stunted grass form the only visible life. "The land . . . is scarcely anything but one solid mass of rocks and stones and in most parts very hilly, particularly to the Westwards among the woods."

The great Barren Grounds!

Four hundred thousand square miles of permafrost—earth frozen forever to a depth of hundreds of feet; but a place where the greatest extremes of temperature on earth take place; where 100° F. has been recorded in summer and –82° F. in winter;[2] a land where even the scorching summer sun thaws only the top few inches of soil and half of every square mile is a shallow lake or a sluggish river; a realm where there is no darkness from May to July but where the still dry air, scant rainfall, and short growing season creates the anomoly of Arid Zone life surrounded by eternal water. Water which cannot sink into the frozen earth or run off to the sea before another winter sets in and each lake and pond in its turn becomes another layer of the everlasting ice; a domain where freezing and thawing and expanding and contracting raise geometric patterns of tiny pebbles as if

[2] See *Life* magazine, June 7, 1954.

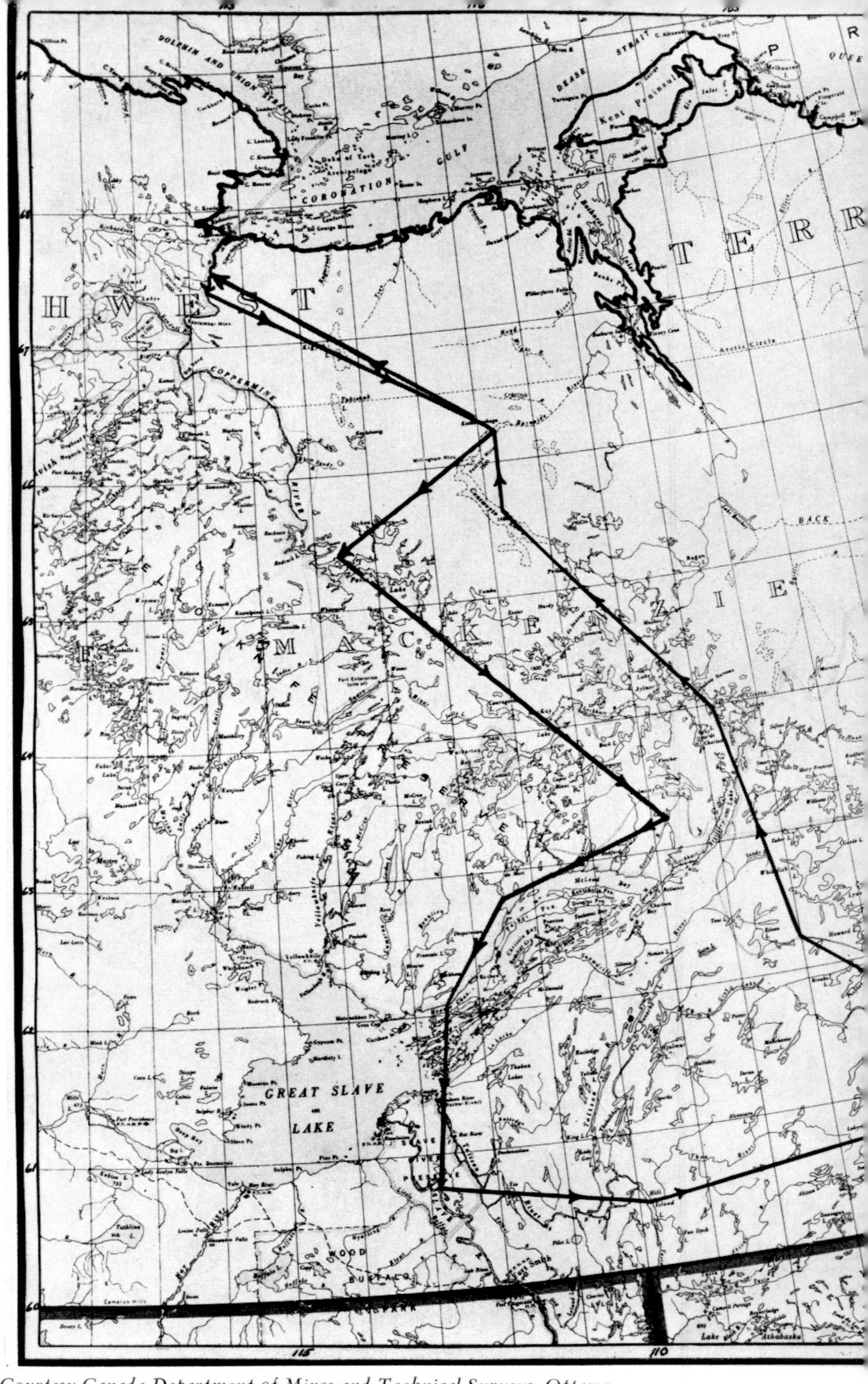

Courtesy Canada Department of Mines and Technical Surveys, Ottawa

A STRAIGHT-LINE PROJECTION OF THE SECOND AND T

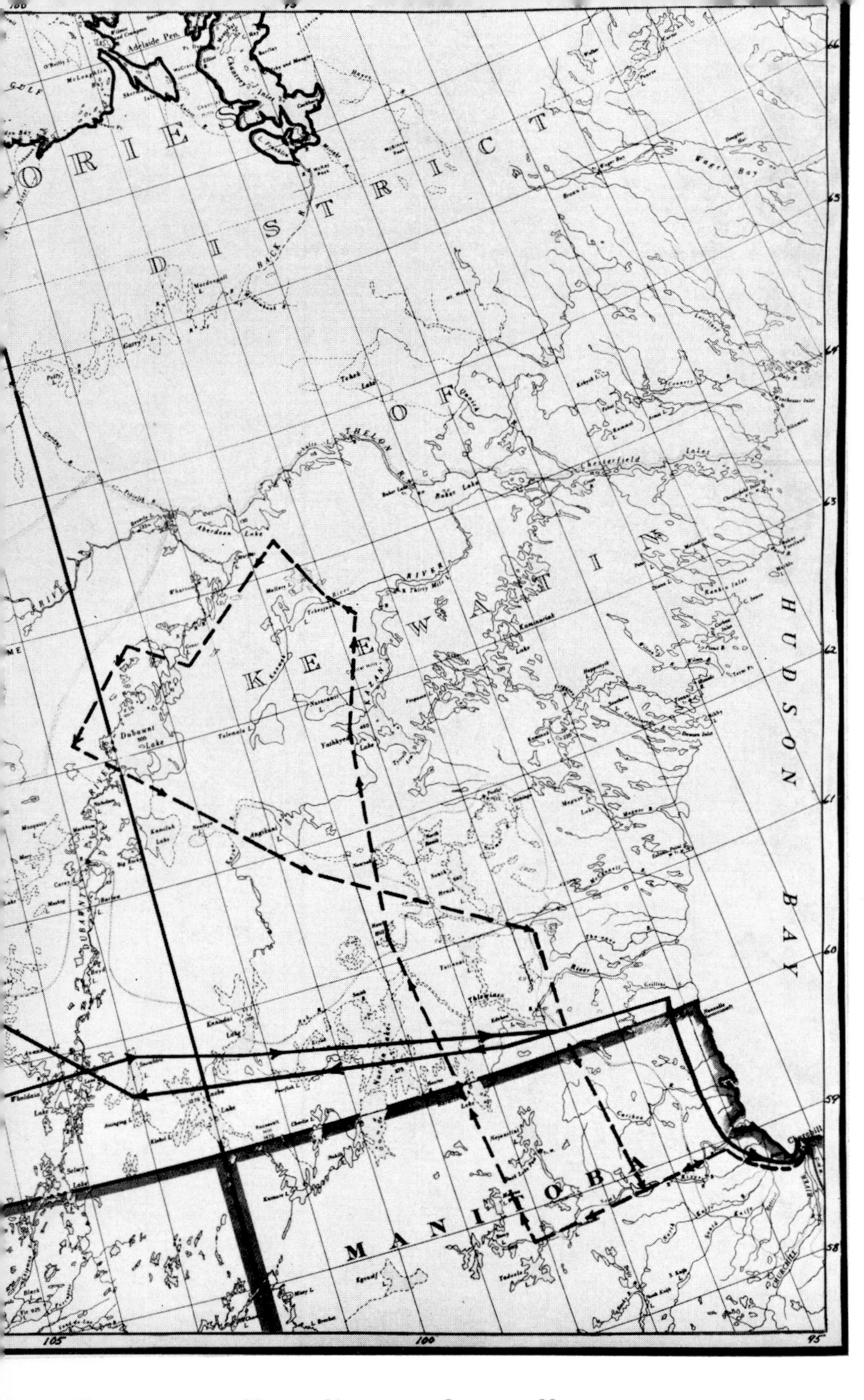

ermine Expeditions on a Modern Map of the Canadian North

some giant mathematician had practiced his art with a world for a slate; a waste where volcano-shaped pingos of unfrozen material are squeezed between the surface ice and the permafrost until they bubble to the surface as pockmarked scars.

But for all that, here is a world with its own fascination and charm. A land where the ptarmigan swarmed by the thousands in the nesting season; where the white Arctic fox trotted hour after hour hunting his lesser prey; where the rare north wolf left her cubs to be found and have their little fuzzy faces painted red by the Chipewyans as a joke on their canine mothers; where tradition said the she-wolves knew how to make fire and cook; where "I have frequently seen [the northern frogs] dug up with the moss, frozen as hard as ice; in which state the legs are as easily broken off as a pipe stem, without giving the least sensation to the animal; but by wrapping them up in warm skins, and exposing them to a slow fire, they soon recover life, and the mutilated animal regains its usual activity."

The great Barren Grounds—where the white-headed and golden eagles snatched a meal but were never known to nest; where the snowy owl pounced on a young ptarmigan or a lone mouse; where the rare whooping cranes sometimes passed overhead; where myriad geese hatched their young and gossiped among their kind; but, nevertheless, a place unfit for human habitation with thousands of square miles of frozen white nine months of the year; a place to be shunned, if possible, or endured heroically if it could not be avoided.[3]

Samuel Hearne was the first white man ever to cross the great Barren Grounds and it is a mark of his greatness as an explorer that his description of the Grounds is authority even today.

It was less than two weeks from Fort Prince of Wales but already starvation walked silently beside every man and woman under Hearne's command. Already he must accept the terrible responsibility of following Matonabbee deeper into the Barren Grounds or order a retreat and fail a third time.

Perhaps there would be food tomorrow! December twentieth; the twenty-first; surely Matonabbee could find a deer; the twenty-third; walk slower, talk less, save what strength remains; another day; a bit of leather wardrobe will push death aside a few more hours; tomorrow and tomorrow. Why can't Matonabbee find a deer?

For eight days they "traversed nothing but entire barren ground, with empty bellies, till the twenty seventh." Then the timberline and four deer!

The Indians stopped under the pretense of repairing equipment but "I was led to think that the want of food was the chief thing that de-

---

[3] Ernest Thompson Seton visited the Barren Grounds early in the present century and compared them to New England meadows or Indiana prairies. His own findings contradict such a comparison for he described, "Another dwarf [spruce] but 8 feet high, was twelve inches through. It had 205 rings plus a 5 inch hollow. . . . This tree was at least three hundred years old." Indiana prairies could do far better than that in three centuries! See Ernest Thompson Seton, "The Arctic Prairies," *Scribner's Magazine,* XLIX, 61-65.

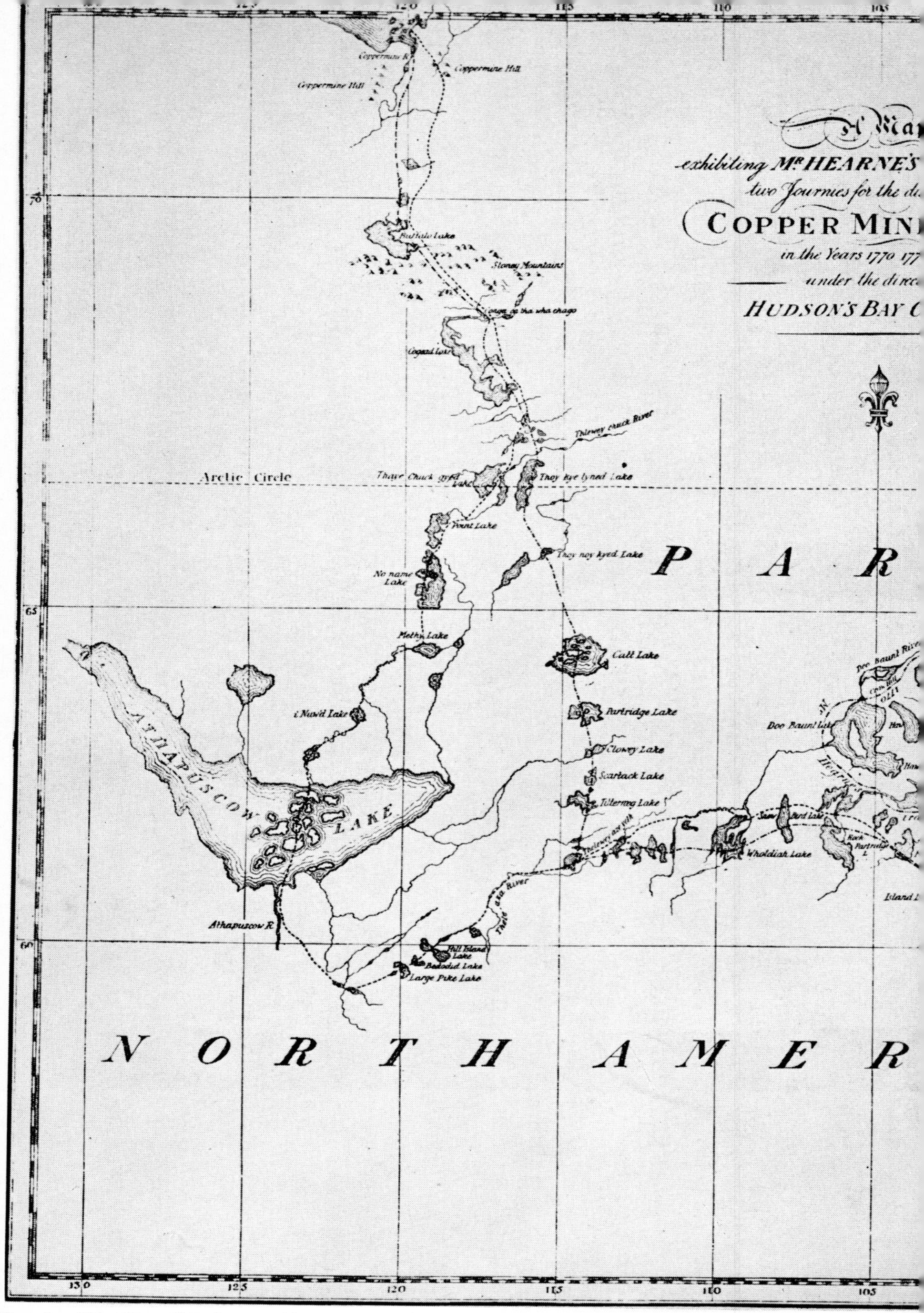

Courtesy The Champlain Society, Toronto, Canada

HEARNE'S MAP OF HIS SECOND

o Coppermine Expeditions

tained them, as they never ceased eating the whole day."

Was that so strange? They had been in "great want, and for the last three days had not tasted a morsel of anything."

It was the holiday season. "I must confess I never spent so dull a Christmas." The fires roared high across the great common room at Fort Prince of Wales; the boards were heaped; the cups were filled. And Samuel Hearne dropped his defenses for a moment and wished he were back in England and away from the Chipewyans and the cold and the silence. Today he was willing to leave Anián and glory to other men.

New Year's Eve, 1770, Hearne and Matonabbee reached the ice of Nueltin Lake, a narrow, indefinite mass of water a hundred miles long, straddling a nine-hundred-foot elevation of earth between 99° west and 100° west. Hearne had possibly touched the northern end of the lake as he returned from the second expedition, and lesser Company men may have crossed Nueltin ice but Hearne's New Year's Eve contact marked the effective discovery of the lake. Hearne Bay, an arm on the east shore, honors the event.

Matonabbee luxuriated, riding across the lake on a sled, too ill to walk, or so he said. Hearne chided him that he was only paying the penalty for his recent gorging but the big chief pooh-poohed the idea, saying he knew when he had eaten enough, the same as all animals did. Hearne countered that this was a childish argument and said that even the bears had sense enough to regurgitate when they ate too many berries.

There was really no fire in the argument. Hearne and Matonabbee were only showing their affection in the inverse manner of men who thoroughly understand one another.

Next day Matonabbee resumed walking, thus relieving an already overworked wife, who, of course, had had to act as draft animal.

On New Year's Day, 1771, the expedition logged sixteen miles across the ice and, once across Nueltin, they found more than twenty wives and children belonging to two of Hearne's men.

Matonabbee, too, had extra wives scattered here and there all over the North, and soon after moving west from Nueltin they met a band of "strangers" with whom Matonabbee found one of his spare mates.

The term "strangers" appears to be used by Hearne to denote nonrelatives more than anything else, but this is inconclusive, for like all primitive peoples the Chipewyans' sense of relationship was ill-defined.

Throughout January Hearne moved west and a little north at a leisurely eight or nine miles per day. Food was relatively adequate but they always faced potential starvation. "It is a truth well known to the natives . . . that there are many extensive tracts of land in those parts, which are incapable of affording support to any number of the human race even during the short time they are passing through them." The rivers generally had fish but catching them was uncertain and this uncertainty was the "means of many hundreds being starved to death."

The Chipewyans often went three or four days without food and considered it mildly amusing, the men asking each other, "Any inclination for an intrigue with a strange woman?"

Nevertheless, January was no time to again challenge the great Barren Grounds, and when they reappeared February 3, 1771, a few miles ahead and to the north, Matonabbee suggested keeping closer to the straggling trees and bushes, which in turn offered the best chance for game.

In so doing they came upon a second band of "strangers," some of whom unceremoniously attached themselves to the expedition while the remainder wandered on, forever seeking the feast which, when found, was sure to be followed by dreary days of hunger. But it was their nomadic way and they neither knew nor perhaps desired any other.

CHAPTER THIRTEEN

Hearne Learns to Hunt and Feast

THE third Coppermine expedition was moving generally westward, keeping well inside the tree line. Northward lay the modern Windy Lake; directly in their line of march was Poorfish Lake; and still farther ahead, some ninety miles air line from Nueltin and four hundred feet higher in elevation, was Kasba, a sprawling, crablike lake sitting solidly across 102° west and just above 60° north.

Easily half of this white world was frozen lakes interspersed with a shrinking forest and scarred beneath the snow with esker, narrow ridges of rocks and sand left from a subglacial stream. When gales whipped the snow from these ridges they became travel hazards of no mean proportions. Samuel Hearne risked broken bones many a dark day as he stumbled over them while following Chipewyan trails laid down by an instinct unknown to civilized man.

The weather was bitterly cold. "Several of the Indians were much frozen, but none of them more disagreeably so than one of Matonabbee's wives, whose thighs and buttocks were in a manner incrusted with frost; and when thawed, several blisters arose, nearly as large as sheep's bladders.

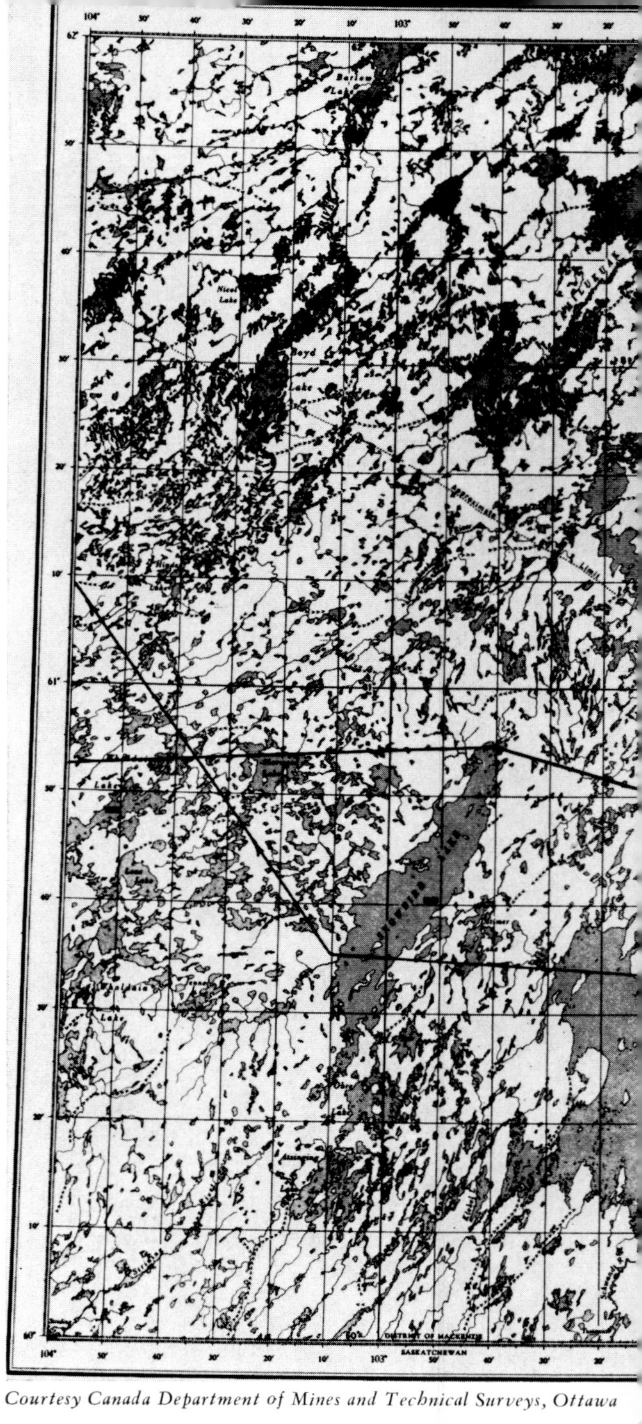

Courtesy Canada Department of Mines and Technical Surveys, Ottawa

A Portion of Hearne's T

The Kasba Lake area richly demonstra

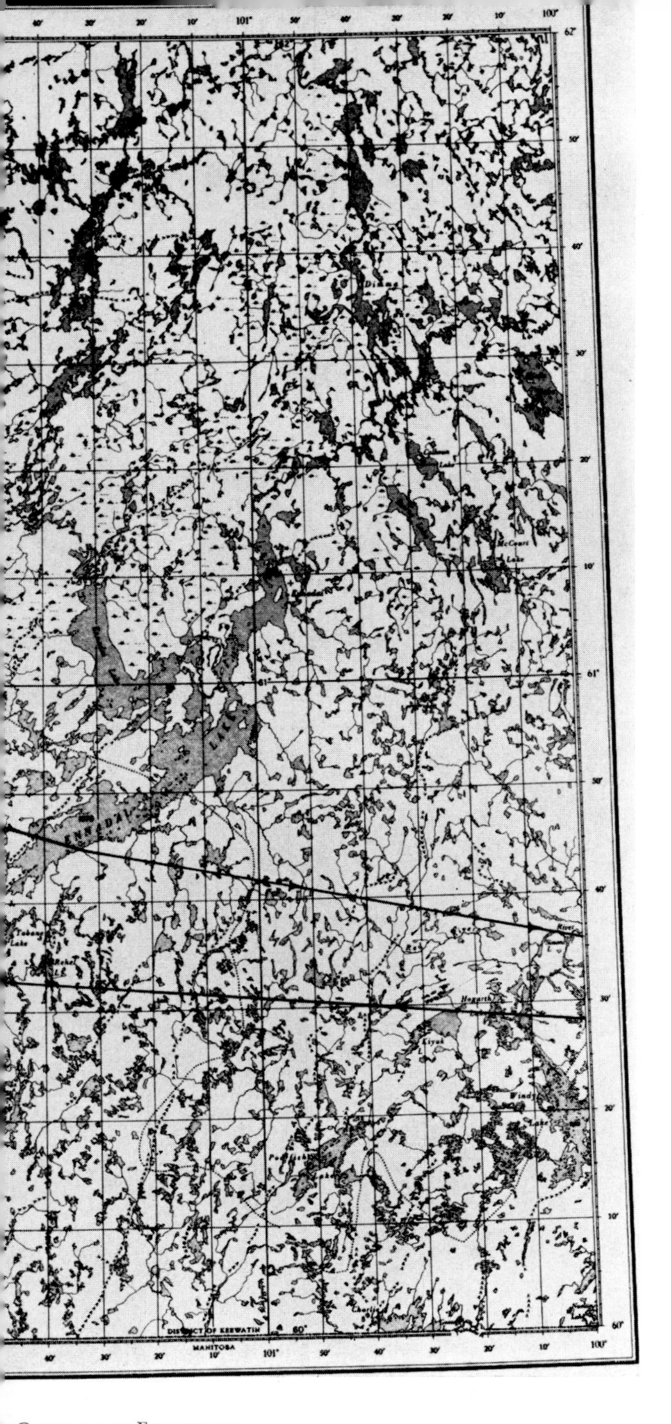

Coppermine Expedition

lty of travel through the northern lake region

The pain the poor woman suffered on this occasion was greatly aggravated by the laughter and jeering of her companions, who said that she was rightly served for belting her clothes so high. I must acknowledge that I was not in the number of those who pitied her, as I thought she took too much pains to shew a clean heel and a good leg; her garters being always in sight, which, though by no means considered here as bordering on indecency, is by far too airy to withstand the rigorous cold of a severe winter in a high Northern latitude."

At Kasba Lake Matonabbee told Hearne it was impossible to get to the Coppermine this time of year and Hearne wisely made no objection. Instead, he drifted on from Kasba to a nearby lake, not now identifiable, and joined an encampment of Indians who were having great fun catching deer in a pound.

These pounds were enclosures of trees, saplings and the like, in a rough circle, perhaps a mile in circumference. Inside the single opening were mazes and snares designed to confuse and trap the animals.

Outside the opening a "fence" of sticks or stones was erected in such a manner as to create a long, acute triangle, the base of which opened on a small river or plain. This "fence" was often two or three miles long with a deer trail in the center.

A lookout was posted and when the deer arrived the women and children closed in behind them and the animals, thinking the "fence" was more

Courtesy Canadian Wildlife Service, Ottawa, Canada

TRANSPORTING MEAT BY DOGSLED IN SUMMER

Except for the addition of strap-iron runners, the sled is constructed essentially as it was in Hearne's day

humans, rushed madly to the apex of the triangle and through the opening into the enclosure to become entangled in the mazes, traps, and snares.

Precious powder was never wasted now. Game caught in the snares were speared, others were brought down by bow and arrow, although this latter routine was not performed with much finesse. Hudson's Bay Company guns had already dulled the co-ordination of arm and eye and the Chipewyans were anything but expert with the ancient weapon.

Samuel Hearne was not normally given to introspection but on occasion he lapsed into a dour mood and for some reason the sight of the Indians driving deer into the pounds brought on one of these turns. Such a simple way to make one's livelihood! Too easy, by far! No incentive! No wonder the young men would not work the trap lines and bring pelts to the Company! No wonder they were forever without the means of purchasing yardage and beads at Fort Prince of Wales!

But even as he wrote the last of these complaints Hearne was confiding a different viewpoint to his journal. After all, their life was not so bad! Why work if one did not have to? Those who do work end a life having had only food and clothes enough to last that life—the same as those who drove deer into a pound and prepared a feast of smoked stomach!

Good Company man that he was, Hearne encouraged the Indians to hunt and trap but, "I

Courtesy Canadian Wildlife Service, Ottawa, Canada

STONE AND SOD DRIFT FENCE TO GUIDE THE "DEER" TOWARD THE HUNTING POUNDS

must confess, that such conduct is by no means for the real benefit of the poor Indians . . . it being well known that those who have the least intercourse with the Factories are by far the happiest."

With these bits of philosophy recorded, Hearne again turned his attention to food.

"I have frequently made one of the party who sat around a fresh killed deer, and assisted in picking the bones quite clean, when I thought that the raw brains and many other parts were exceedingly good . . . even to this day I give preference to trout, salmon, and the brown tittemeg, when they are not warm at the bone."

But such casual eating was not feasting. To feast, one must have the desire to feast, the components needed, and time. Time to prepare the food and to enjoy it. The Chipewyans knew these things and their feasts were prepared with great care.

When all the factors coincided the Chipewyans laid aside their work and travel, started fires to give the exact heat needed, and set about preparing their favorite dish:

Fat from the freshly killed animal was first cut into mouth-sized pieces and given to selected men and boys to chew. The recipients of this favor must be particularly clean and with no imperfect teeth which might impart an unwanted flavor. After the fat was properly chewed it was mixed with pieces of meat of approximately the same size and stirred into the blood and half digested contents of the animal's stomach with enough water added so the whole would boil into a porridge. This was then returned to the stomach and hung up for several days in the smoke from the fires. Natural fermentation gave it "such an agreeable acid taste, that were it not for prejudice, it might be eaten by those who have the nicest palates . . . I no longer made any scruple, but always thought it exceedingly good."

If time did not permit the several days needed for such a feast, unborn calves, fawns, and tiny beaver were good. "I am not the only European who heartily joins in pronouncing them the greatest dainties that can be eaten."

This was also true of geese and ducks still in the shell. In fact, "Whoever wishes to know what is good must live with the Indians."

There were other food favorites, of course. Chipewyan men and boys always ate the genital organs unless overtough, in which case they were burned lest the dogs consume them and bring bad luck to the hunters.

Smoked womb was highly esteemed although Hearne objected to eating his share of this Indian delicacy. With an obvious, but unimportant discrepancy, Hearne said in another place that the only Indian food he could not eat were lice and grubs from the hairy garments, a day by day tidbit of the Chipewyans. He avoided this experience by saying that since it was unlikely that he could obtain them when he returned to Fort Prince of Wales it was not worth while learning to like them.

And so Samuel Hearne learned that it was possible to live without tea and scones, and that, under certain circumstances, smoked stomach was preferable.

CHAPTER FOURTEEN

Hearne Seeks Anian to 64° North

FEW explorer journals are more devoid of references to the task in hand than those of Samuel Hearne. He had been ordered to seek Anián, find the copper deposits, and investigate Company business opportunities. His journals refer to these orders at the outset of each expedition and they are seldom mentioned again.

In consequence it would be easy to conclude that Hearne himself had lost sight of the reasons for his weary travel and was floundering in the trivia of the day. Nothing could be less true. The Northwest Passage never lost its initial position, the copper mines were never subordinated to a study of Chipewyan life.

But Samuel Hearne could keep items in their proper focus without harping. Since Anián obviously was not caught in a Chipewyan deer snare why not enjoy the hunt for what it was: an adjunct of today's feast. And search for Anián tomorrow!

Nevertheless, when Matonabbee observed at Snowbird Lake, some twenty miles west of Kasba, that the feasting was over because the deer were leaving for the Barrens, Hearne was ready to go. Consequently, the third Coppermine expedition, now augmented to seventy souls, slanted north-westward from Snowbird Lake. Other crews joined them; they ran head on into a wild storm and must wait it out; and they met a band planning to visit Fort Prince of Wales and Hearne sent a letter to Norton giving his location as 61° north and more than 19° west of Churchill, which latter was in error, being much too far west.

Spring was on the way but it was "never so warm as to occassion any thaw, unless in such places as lay exposed to the mid-day sun, and were sheltered from all the cold winds."

Early in April the expedition camped for ten days, making inch-square tent poles for use on the Barren Grounds and knockdown canoes so carefully cut they could be put together without further shaping any time the ice broke on the lakes.

It was a busy time. Not since leaving the Churchill had Hearne had an opportunity to actually see the surface of the earth over which he had traveled so many hundreds of miles. He spent the lengthening days describing the land, its flora and fauna, and recording the many changes in Chipewyan life which accompanied the new season.

It was mid-April and Matonabbee had spring fever. Every new woman in sight caused a roving eye and a few days later he purchased his seventh wife, a big, hulking female, to be added to his other half dozen, "most of whom would for size have made good grenadiers," said Hearne. Matonabbee "prided himself on the height and strength of his wives, and would frequently say few women would carry or haul heavier loads; and though they had, in general, a very masculine appearance, yet he preferred them to those of a more delicate form and moderate stature."

Ability to carry up to 140 pounds in summer and drag much more than that in winter were the first consideration in Chipewyan wives.

In general, Chipewyan women were not likely to be thought beautiful by European standards. "Take them in a body, the women are as destitute of real beauty as any nation I ever saw, though there are some few of them, when young, who are tolerable." They were "old" at thirty and the more "ordinary ones at that age are perfect antidotes to love and gallantry. . . . Ask a northern Indian, what is beauty? he will answer, a broad flat face, small eyes, high cheek bones, a low forehead, a large broad chin, a clumsy hook nose, a tawny hide and breasts hanging down to the belt."

By late April the lakes were deicing and Matonabbee sent his brother with a small party ahead to Clowey Lake[1] to set up the precut canoes while Hearne attempted to aid a Chipewyan wife who was overlong in labor. He thought a midwife as used in England might help. The Chipewyans sarcastically replied that the "many hump-backs, bandy legs, and other deformities, so frequent among the English, were undoubtedly owing to

[1] Clowey Lake is not now identifiable states Secretary G. M. Munroe, Canadian Board on Geographical Names, Ottawa, 1958. A map published in 1818 and illustrating the voyages of Hearne and Mackenzie has a Clowey River flowing off the southwest corner of Slave Lake. See R. A. Skelton, *Explorers' Maps* (New York: Frederick A. Praeger, 1958), p. 132.

the great skill of the persons who assisted in bringing them into the world, and to the extraordinary care of their nurses afterwards."

Hearne had nothing to say.

Presently, the Chipewyans, completely contrary to the usual practice, held up all travel for fifty-two hours until the baby arrived, after which they moved at once, the woman nursing her new child and carrying her regular load although another woman did relieve her of pulling a sled for one day only.

Hearne was much saddened over the incident but "it was not in my power to relieve her."

On May 3, 1771, the expedition arrived at Clowey Lake and remained there several days awaiting completion of the canoes. Two hundred more Indians congregated with Hearne for a like purpose and this undisciplined and irresponsible influx could have been as disastrous for the third Coppermine expedition as much smaller bands had been to the first and second excursions. But Hearne had learned much and Matonabbee was a different Indian than Chawchinahaw or Conne-e-quese. He told the newcomers of Hearne's position and the extent of his supplies and that closed the matter except that "on some occasions it was scarcely possible to get off without presenting a few inches [of tobacco] to them."

Meanwhile, Matonabbee had acquired an eighth helpmeet, whom he promptly renamed "Marten" as he had each of the other seven. He took no chances on domestic jealousy over names, and besides, one shout might bring the services of half a dozen wives!

Toward the end of May Hearne received the agreeable news that Keelshies, the man with whom he had sent a letter to Norton asking for supplies when they had met on the Kazan River on the second expedition, was only one day's walk to the south. Carriers were immediately dispatched for the goods Hearne had ordered. They returned, however, saying that Keelshies, himself, would deliver the freight within a few days. With anticipatory pleasure the third Coppermine expedition moved beyond the timberline where a few old stumps from a dim past when the ice was farther north gave the only relief from the cold of the subarctic spring.

But this warmth was short-lived. On May 26 a vicious storm again stopped all travel and forced Hearne, his Chipewyans, and their wild dogs to huddle together in their wet leather tents outwaiting the elements.

The expedition was moving slowly. Hearne had been gone from Fort Prince of Wales for six months; he had taken enormous risks, suffered great hunger and cold, and it is safe to say that for every air-line mile covered he and his companions had walked two miles by trail. They had, therefore, tramped not less than 1,200 to 1,500 miles.

Inasmuch as lakes are the outstanding topographical features of this bleak domain Hearne's route is best followed in relation to them. He had

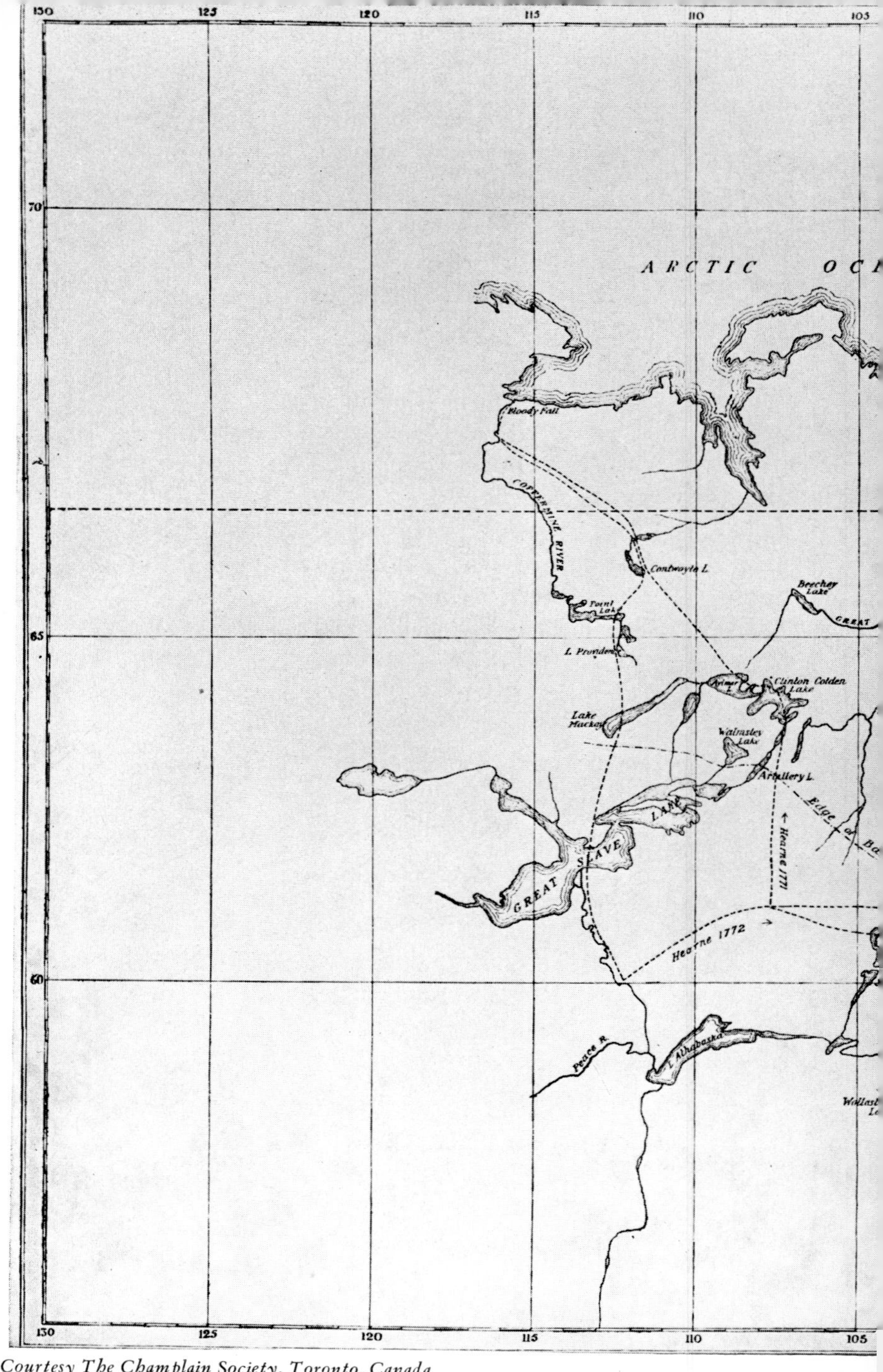

Courtesy The Champlain Society, Toronto, Canada

A MAP EXHIBITING HEARNE'S TRACKS ON HIS

The journeys were made in the years 1770, 1771, and 1772. Adjusted,

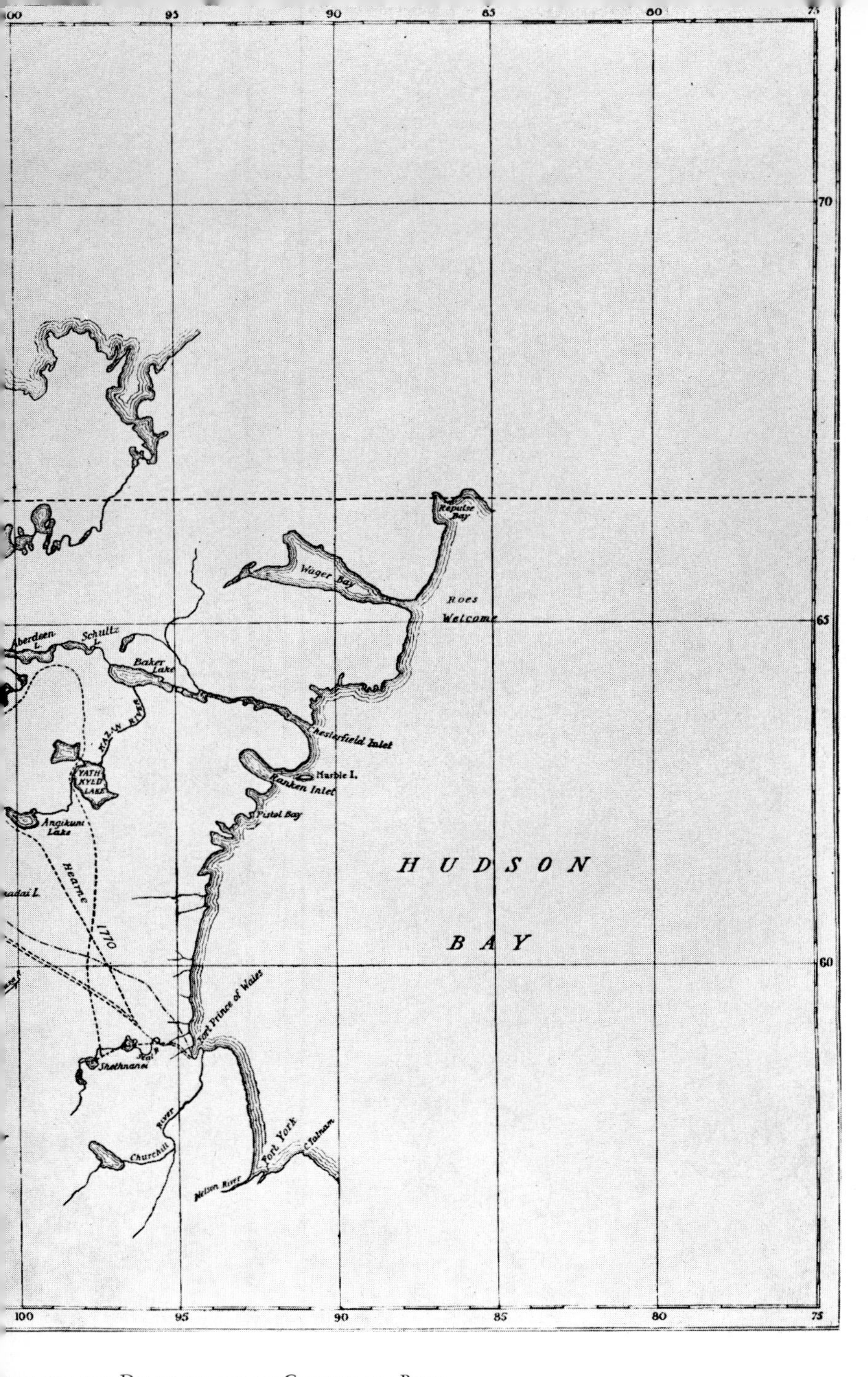

EYS FOR THE DISCOVERY OF THE COPPERMINE RIVER
possible, in accordance with the latest maps by J. B. Tyrrell (1909)

discovered Nueltin, Kasba, and Snowbird lakes and crossed or skirted literally hundreds of others, unnamed even today. Tomorrow, May 27, 1771, he would discover Clinton-Colden Lake, 64° north and 107° 30′ west of Greenwich. To date it was the white man's "farthest north" in the interior of North America.

Nueltin is almost twice the size of Lake Champlain, Kasba is three and a half times the size of Yellowstone, and Clinton-Colden equals Lake Pontchartrain at New Orleans. Even Snowbird outranks Tahoe in size if not in tourists.

The ice on Clinton-Colden had not yet softened from the late May sun and Hearne and Matonabbee crossed twenty-two miles to an island and pitched camp to await the arrival of Keelshies.

That night, or rather early next morning, there was great excitement in camp. Matonabbee's newest, youngest and most attractive wife, whom he had but recently taken by force from a younger husband, had decamped with another woman.

Matonabbee had taken the girl under the Chipewyan wrestling code which allowed any able-bodied male to challenge another for his wife, provided there were no children involved. Wrestling was so popular that it was difficult to tell whether the woman or the game was the main attraction.

Sometimes all the men would wrestle for a given woman, one after the other, and she would change hands a dozen times in an evening. Sometimes a little man would slip into his tent, cut off his hair and grease his ears, then rush out and throw a larger opponent before the latter was properly aware of the attack.

The girls were not always happy over the outcomes but even when they were secretly glad to be thus won "custom, or delicacy if you please, has taught them to think it necessary to whimper a little, let the change be ever so much to their inclination."

Unfortunately, brutality was sometimes used. "On those occassions their grief and reluctance to follow their new lord has been so great, that the business has often ended in the greatest brutality; for, in the struggle, I have seen the poor girls stripped quite naked, and carried by main force to their new lodgings."

Matonabbee's latest wife represented one of these unwilling exchanges. She said she would rather be the single wife of a poor man than "have the seventh or eighth share of the affection of the greatest man in the country."

After Matonabbee had taken her by force, her previous husband had unwisely made a critical remark about the big chief. Matonabbee's mad jealousy immediately flared out of control. He walked stiff-legged and blind with fury into his tent, "opened one of his wives's bundles, and, with great composure, took out a new long box-handled knife, and, without any preface whatever, took him [the ex-husband] by the collar and began to execute his horrible design."

His intention was murder.

Matonabbee seemed to sense his guilt for when his jealous frenzy was spent he washed his hands, turned to Hearne and demanded if he had not "done right."

Despite the savage knifing the young man recovered and Matonabbee was spared the two penalties automatically assessed perpetrators of the capital sin: ostracism and the cry, "There goes the murderer."

By the time the excitement of Matonabbee's attack had died down Keelshies had arrived with a packet of letters, two quarts of brandy and a mass of excuses for having none of Hearne's supplies. One of his relatives had died, and, following Indian custom, he had stripped naked and given away all his possessions as a sign of his grief. His family reclothed him but it was not part of their duty to return his extra goods and he had used Hearne's freight to pay his way in his Chipewyan world.

How much of this tale was true and how much alibi for embezzlement Hearne had no way of knowing but he accepted the *fait accompli* with what grace he could muster.

Keelshies, in turn, saved his face by shedding the proper tears and presenting Hearne with four partially cured moose hides not worth 5 per cent of the goods he had used but more acceptable at the moment because Hearne was short on moccasins while powder and shot were relatively plentiful.

Hearne had barely completed this bit of native diplomacy with Keelshies when Matonabbee got into trouble again and bid fair to wreck the whole third Coppermine expedition. The chief was a very powerful man but he could be bested by even more powerful Chipewyans and one of those chose the day of Keelshies arrival to demand Matonabbee's favorite wife. The chief had one of three choices: refuse to wrestle and lose both wife and "face"; wrestle and lose the wife anyway; or, still according to code, buy his wife back from the prospective new husband even before she had left the old tent. Matonabbee knew when he was beaten and paid up: a quantity of ammunition, some iron, and a kettle! A young fortune!

To make the day even more unpalatable he had lost another wife and much prestige through attempting a bit of chicanery which had recoiled.

Matonabbee was much disgusted and announced he was quitting the expedition to join the "Athapuscows" who would treat him with proper respect, choosing to forget, of course, that only a few days before he had attempted murder while taking a woman from her more favored husband.

In this crisis Hearne's real leadership came into play. As long as everything was going well he was willing to let Matonabbee pretend to the most important position but two previous failures had taught Hearne his lessons and he did not intend to have the third Coppermine expedition blow up in his face—and over a woman at that!

Knowing Matonabbee's vanity, Hearne appealed to it: he was a great man; his grandchildren would boast of his leading Hearne to the Coppermine; his exploit would be talked about from the bay to the Arctic; and so on until Matonabbee became so fired with his own importance that he ordered an immediate advance although it was already late in the afternoon.

This was more than Hearne had bargained for but he was too wise to crowd his luck and he acquiesced with apparent enthusiasm. They walked seven miles more across Clinton-Colden before putting up for the night, a term of little importance at the moment since it was almost June and the sun's drop below the horizon was "so short and its depression even at midnight so small" that it did not interfere with any normal daytime activity.

Next day Matonabbee called a halt on the north side of Clinton-Colden and began preparations for a final northward push. Women and children were sorted out and given into the command of a rear guard who were to protect and provide for them until the return of the advance party.

These separations brought such a flood of tears, wails, and general confusion that the Chipewyan chief had to exert all his authority to restore order.

Plans for a rendezvous were made and at 9:30 P.M., May 31, 1771, the smaller command headed toward the Arctic, Matonabbee taking two of his young wives with him and allowing the other men similar rights.

As far as known Hearne had no personal feminine attachment and relied entirely on the services of women belonging to others.

For some weeks now Samuel Hearne had been intermittently concerned with certain behaviors of the Indians which did not seem to fit into the pattern of exploration. There had been an unusual influx of small bands which attached themselves to the larger group without any obvious reason; as far back as Clowey Lake, the first week in May, the Indians had begun making shields, nearly an inch thick, two feet wide and three feet long, and decorated with rude symbols designed to bring aid and protection to the bearer, shields which manifestly had nothing to do with hunting. There had been long, quiet discussions about Eskimos—discussions which had pointedly not included Hearne; the main body of women and all the children had just been detached; and Matonabbee was assuming more and more authority.

Hearne kept his own counsel but concluded, somewhat tardily it must be admitted, that the real purpose of Matonabbee's cooperation, to date, had been to lead a mass murder party against the Eskimos rather than any desire to help the Hudson's Bay Company, or Hearne, find Anián or locate the copper mines.

The 1795 edition of the Hearne journals say that Matonabbee neither proposed nor desired such a raid but was forced into it by pressure from his comrades. This defense may be questioned. Chipewyans and Eskimos were bitter foes and Matonabbee was a Chipewyan first, Company man second. Furthermore, there is little in the record to support the thesis that the big Chipewyan could be influenced by any such pressure.

CHAPTER FIFTEEN

Hearne Finds the Coppermine

SAMUEL HEARNE was in a delicate position. He was determined to find the copper deposits and prove or disprove the existence of a northwest passage but his conscience demanded he attempt to divert the attack against the Eskimos.

Hearne had only one card from the deck played by the Chipewyans and that was that when the raiding party was eventually organized "only sixty volunteers would go with us"—a fact which might, or might not, indicate that there was no great enthusiasm for the murder venture. Those who had refused to go said, somewhat equivocally, that they had no "goods to squander away among their countrymen as Matonabbee and those of my party did." Just perhaps the real reason was that no one actually wanted to kill anyone.

The card was worth playing and Hearne played it—and lost. The Chipewyans said he was "acuated by cowardice" and he, knowing the fate of the expedition and his own life depended on his retaining his leadership, dropped his appeal for peace and said, "I did not care if they rendered the name and race of Esquimaux extinct," and that if he or his immediate party were endangered the Chipewyans would find whether or not he was a coward.

This was no idle boast. Samuel Hearne was still the gentle, considerate commander-explorer; he would always prefer to give in rather than say no; but he would not be pushed beyond the line he thought it wise to hold. Maturity had brought an inconspicuous wisdom, especially in the ways of the Chipewyans, and Hearne set about participating in the preparations for the attack. This action was "received with great satisfaction." "When I came to consider seriously, I saw . . . it was the highest folly for an individual like me, and in my situation, to attempt to turn the current of a national prejudice. . . ."

It was near the first of June but the weather was so bad that the hoped-for dash against the Eskimos on the Coppermine was more of a crawl. It was the middle of the month before Hearne registered their location as 67° 30′ north, (an error in latitude) where Matonabbee proposed "the women . . . should wait our return from the Coppermine River."

When the weather finally cleared the Indians were in a fever of speed. Hardly waiting to gulp down a morning meal they rushed off, north and west: past Lake Aylmer, close by the shoulder of Clinton-Colden; skirting east of Lac de Gras and Lac du Sauvage; working furiously across

Courtesy Geological Survey of Canada, Ottawa

Coppermine River Where it Leaves Lac de Gras

Pellat and arriving at Contwoyto Lake, 110° west and 65° 30′ north—eighty miles in four days.[1]

The land between Clinton-Colden and Contwoyto might be termed a plateau, the elevation remaining more or less constant at 1,200 to 1,500 feet. It is marked with countless lakes ranging from seasonal potholes to major bodies such as Aylmer or Contwoyto, each several hundred miles in circumference.

While the Indians were crossing this plateau Hearne had little time for anything but the task of keeping up, but, even so, it was obvious to the leg-weary Englishman that the area in which Anián might exist was rapidly dwindling. The second Coppermine expedition had moved as far north as the Aberdeen Lake region, 64° 30′. Hearne was now at Contwoyto, seventy miles farther north and at least three hundred miles farther west.

The myth of Anián would soon be resolved, provided Samuel Hearne survived the raid against the Eskimos.

Somewhere along the more than one hundred miles between Clinton-Colden and Contwoyto Hearne took a reading which he recorded as 68° 46′ north, but this is assuredly wrong for the mouth of the Coppermine River itself is well south of any such latitude.

Somewhere, too, along these miles Hearne and

---

[1] Sir John Franklin, the Arctic explorer, said he talked with a very old man who, as a boy, was with Hearne and that the name Rum Lake was given to Contwoyto at that time in honor of Hearne's having given rum to the Indians there.

Courtesy Canadian Wildlife Service, Ottawa, Canada

Caribou Trails, Contwoyto Lake

Matonabbee had been joined by a band of Copper Indians, or Red Knives, who were helping ferry the warriors over such lakes as the condition of the ice demanded.

Matonabbee knew most of the Coppers personally and through this relationship they promised to help Hearne in the last stages of the expedition.

While the ceremonial pipe was smoked there was much talk concerning a Company settlement among the Red Knives. Hearne knew this was only talk and tried to minimize the idea as much as possible without interrupting the enthusiasm.

He questioned the Coppers about the country ahead, probing for clues to Anián, but the one bit of information he got of any value was that the sea at the mouths of the rivers is never ice free.

In return, he furnished the Red Knives with some considerable amusement. They went over him with embarrassing detail and finally announced that he was a human being but a very poor specimen. His hair resembled the "stained hair of a buffaloe's tail," and his eyes, "being light," were like "those of a gull"; the whiteness of his skin only reminded them of "meat which had been sodden in water till all the blood was extracted." But with all these poor opinions they carefully preserved loose hairs from Hearne's comb, probably as proof to their grandchildren they had once seen a strange sample of man.[2]

---

[2] Some bands of Coppers had been to Hudson Bay but Hearne infers this particular group had never before seen a white man. See E. E. Rich, *Hudson's Bay Company, 1670-1870* [Hudson's Bay Record Society Publications, Vols. 21-23] (London, 1959), II, 47.

Despite the good relations between the Chipewyans and Coppers, thieving got out of bounds. Seizing the Red Knife women, or their furs, was taken for granted and neither Hearne nor Matonabbee tried to control it. Hearne was much puzzled over Chipewyan enthusiasm for Copper women since he said he could see no difference. And there was none—it was only that Samuel Hearne could not understand the age-old urge of the male to seek a fairer breast on another couch.

The theft of Copper bows and arrows was a much more serious matter. There were no nearby trees suitable for making replacements and since the Red Knives did not have Company goods they relied on the ancient weapons.

Notwithstanding these several difficulties, Matonabbee sent his brother with a few inches of Hearne's precious tobacco to as many nearby bands as possible, telling them of the purposes of the third Coppermine expedition and, if the truth were known, probably urging them to join in the raid against the Eskimos.

It was time now, Matonabbee said, to make the "final" separation of the women and children from the raiding party. There had already been more than one of these "last" separations but somehow exceptions always managed to creep in and, at this juncture, there were still a considerable number of Chipewyan girls, plus some Copper families, with the men.

They were camped at "Congecathawachaga," probably the modern Kathawachaga Lake, or the river connecting it and Contwoyto Lake. Meat was plentiful but sun drying enough to last the women a year, if aired occasionally to control mold, took several days and it was July 1 before the warriors, strictly devoid of female company at last, were ready to go. Then at the very moment of leaving a heavy sleet storm stopped all activity until nine o'clock next day, after which they walked only ten miles before stopping to sleep.

July 3 broke dull gray and leaden skied. Before a hasty breakfast could put the war party in motion their world turned into a howling, drifting white in which it was quite impossible to see, speak to each other, or travel.

Indian war parties carried no tents, of course, and each man, including Samuel Hearne, could only select a large rock, crouch in the lee thereof, and smoke, munch dried deer, or nod and dream. As hour piled on hour it became apparent that the storm was no passing shower and Hearne, his Chipewyans and their Red Knife companions sat on their heels, moved from one tiresome position to another no less so, damned their luck, and waited. Waited for twenty-four hours.

It's a lonesome track that great men leave and Samuel Hearne was never more lonely than during the hours he lay huddled beside a rock somewhere beyond Contwoyto, profoundly disturbed by his role in a war party he was powerless to stop. The Chipewyans and Coppers could dream of the glories of war and the pleasures of rapine;

Hearne could only question his decision to remain with the war party. Like greater and much lesser men, his choice was not of good and evil —he must elect one of two wrongs: aid in the murder of an innocent people, as gentle as himself, or give up the search for Anián, see scorn in the eyes of his Indian friends, and be deserted and left completely alone more than eight hundred air miles from any hope of human help. No civilized man had even an inkling of where he was in that vast land behind Hudson Bay. To go on meant the screams of war, and blood, and lust; to turn back meant a third defeat and certain personal death—staggering, hopelessly lost, in ever dimmer circles until ——— No, no, he would not do that! He would not be denied now! If he had no faith in Chipewyan gods or owned his own he must still keep faith with Matonabbee —massacre or no—but he could not kill an unarmed foe—yet Anián must be found, or proved a myth ——— Still, it was not right that babes at breast should die because of an ancient hate—but Anián and a "name for himself" might be just beyond the swirling snow ——— Was there no compromise?

Perhaps! But Samuel Hearne never found it. Before he could solve his personal crisis, the winds stopped while the snow continued lazily to earth and twenty-four hours after the storm started the battered warriors stood up, stretched their cramped legs and backs, and faced into the cold.

Once in motion they walked twenty-seven miles

northwest, "fourteen of which were on what the Indians call the Stony Mountains," a terrain so rough they were compelled to "crawl on our hands and knees" even where "there is a very visible path the whole way across these mountains."

Along this path were several large, flat, table-like rocks on which were numerous pebbles, placed there by the Indians as they crossed and recrossed the trail, each pebble representing a good-luck token.

Desertions from the war party were now taking place, several braves saying the trouble of crossing the "stony mountains" was not commensurate with the pleasure of attacking the Eskimos.

And all the while the wet summer snow came down. Came in such huge flakes they were all "in danger of being smothered in our caves."

For five days Hearne and his Indians shivered inside their wet leather clothes; for five nights, lighted by the midsummer Arctic sun, they crawled behind whatever shelter they could find in that treeless waste to rest a few hours before they hurried on. Hurried across the now unidentifiable Musk-ox Lake on the ice; killed and made "shoe soles" of an old animal too lean to eat; lay down another night in the slush atop the sodden moss and rocks and tried to sleep.

July 8! A willow grove, a fire, a hot meal! The sun shone! Hearne and his companions stripped off their clothes, basked in the warmth and felt "more comfortable than we had done since we had left the women."

Now the weather became as intolerably hot as it had been cold, and the giant northern mosquitoes swarmed with "stings almost insufferable." Everyone was on edge and when the Chipewyans met the Indian, Oule Eye, and his family and they tried to rob Hearne's companions even after smoking the peace pipe, Hearne lost his patience and said, ". . . had any of their women been worth notice they would most assuredly have been pressed into our service . . . my companions [took] what dry provisions they chose from our unsociable strangers."

Very carefully Hearne avoided mention of the anxiety he must have suffered during these days. Aware of his own limitations in the science of observation, he knew he was always partially lost; the hope of finding Anián was waning; and was Matonabbee really seeking the copper mines or was he secretly stalking the Eskimos? After all these months would the third Coppermine expedition end only as an extended version of the first two ventures—but with the memory of a massacre to cloud his days and damn his sleep?

Matonabbee claimed they were near the Coppermine River, but were they? Could he be trusted in the final analysis? Chawchinahaw and Conne-e-quese had talked true until the very end, when each had betrayed him. Was Matonabbee doing otherwise as he led Hearne and the now almost naked warriors fifteen miles to a small stream some forty miles from salt water?

Hearne could not know how close he was to the

storied Coppermine, or how near he was to the end of the many centuries' search for Anián. He must wait a little longer. Wait until the Indians killed a deer and had a feast of "beeatee": blood, shredded fat, tender flesh, heart and lungs "torn into small shivers" and put back into the stomach and roasted over the fire. Wait until they had walked down the tiny tributary westward to a fringe of trees which seemed the most likely site of a larger stream.

Would it be the Coppermine?

Could it be Anián?

The journals of great explorers reveal they rarely dramatize the moment of their success. Alexander Mackenzie buried the first east-west crossing of North America in a discussion of the filth under Indian houses; Cortez submerged the discovery of the ancient City of Mexico in a welter of military trivia.

And so Samuel Hearne, after a feast of "beeatee," tramped ten miles more and came "to that long wished for spot, the Coppermine River."

Perhaps such modesty is the reason Hearne has been neglected as a great explorer. He is always just out of sight behind his accomplishments. He passes over his deeds as if to mention them were bad manners. And historians have somehow succumbed to this humility—seeing the modesty and missing the deeds.

Here is a solitary, twenty-six-year-old white man, daily risking his life in the search for Anián and the copper deposits, completely at the mercy of uncivilized Indians, months of time from any possible aid, with no food supply beyond today, but who, in the moment of his success merely records his arrival at "the long wished for spot."

Hearne almost certainly reached the Coppermine River at Sandstone Rapids, 150 miles, more or less, from Congecathawachaga. Naturally, the Coppermine was a disappointment. Hearne had been led to believe the river would easily accommodate Company ships, and at the most sanguine of all hopes, might, indeed, be Anián. Instead, it would scarcely float an Indian canoe, while a succession of rapids effectively blocked even those craft from being used extensively.

Nevertheless, the river must be charted and described, and Hearne began his work at once. He and Matonabbee turned northward down the Coppermine, each man keeping his thoughts to himself. It would not do to let the Indian know how inconsequential was his vaunted river. It would not do to let the Englishman know that all further exploration must await the massacre.

Each man was goaded by his own private question, a whole civilization apart: Where were Anián and the ore beds? Where were the Eskimos? For the moment neither man was interested in, or sympathetic to, the other. Matonabbee was stalking an immemorial foe—Samuel Hearne was stubbornly surveying a river.

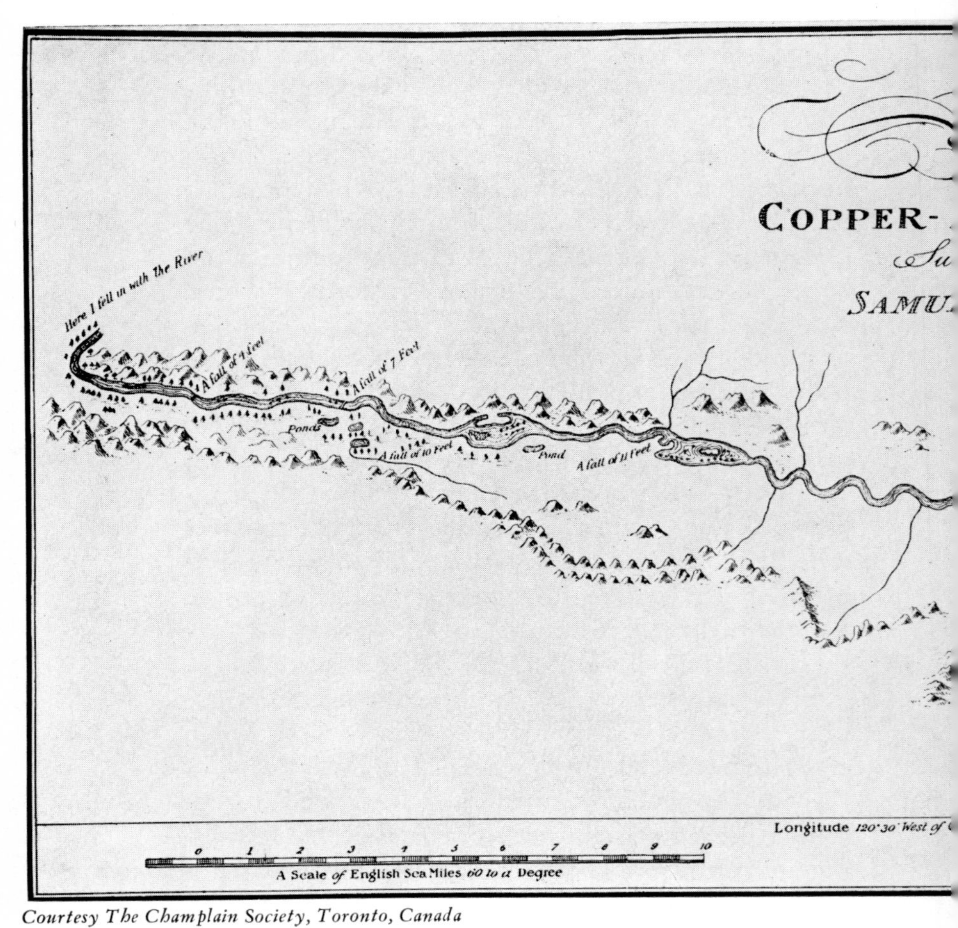

Courtesy The Champlain Society, Toronto, Canada

HEARNE'S "A PLAN O

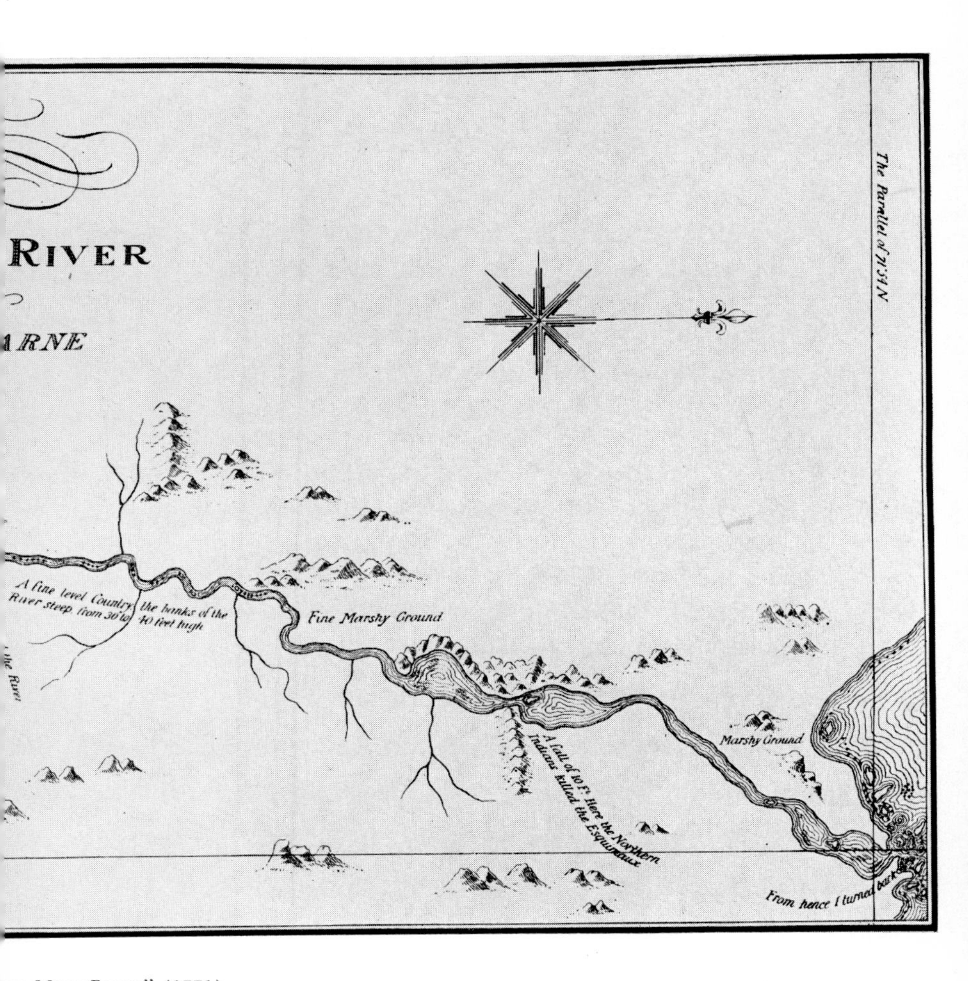

ER-MINE RIVER" (1771)

C H A P T E R   S I X T E E N

Bloody Falls

JULY 15, 1771. The last starved tree gave way to the cold and only bare rock and tundra led on to the sea. Hearne surveyed a useless river and Matonabbee's scouts returned saying that twelve miles downstream were five tents of Eskimos, so placed as to be easily surprised.

The Indians paid no more "attention to my survey" but began planning their raid. The Eskimos were on the west side of the river and Matonabbee's warriors on the east, so they crossed over, got out the wooden shields, mixed their crude paints and smeared the shields "with images of imaginary beings, which, according to their silly notions, are the inhabitants of the different elements, Earth, Sea, Air, etc. . . ." Some had the sun, some the moon, some birds or imaginary animals. Still others used unidentifiable patterns which could have had meaning only for the painter and may have been purely decorative without any occult significance.

Since the warriors were limited to the two natural colors at hand, red and black, and they were in a great hurry besides, the results were anything but artistic. Hearne took one look at the display and said they were "worse than our country sign painters in England"—no compliment to either group, it would seem.

With these simple preparations the party began a stealthy approach. No talking now, no following the river; take the back way even if it means slithering knee deep through the icy marshes; down to the river now and again for a quick reconnoiter—and long enough for Hearne to see it was no more navigable than before. Matonabbee was the acknowledged leader here—no disputes—military law; orders were obeyed silently and willingly, everyone sharing with his comrades in a true "war psychology" pattern. There was no way to stop the massacre now; only Providence could save the sleeping Eskimos. Hearne fought off the mental anguish and slogged along with the rest, as helpless to stop his little war as millions like him, before and after, have been helpless to turn the tides of theirs, and like them, hating every minute of it.

Only two hundred yards more; barely breathing now; no crunching a lingering piece of ice; no clanking of equipment; down on bellies and watch the tents; be sure; take no chances; they must not escape or be permitted to fight back.

Hearne was invited to drop behind but he refused, saying that to do so would place him in a dangerous and unwarranted position since any escaping Eskimo would be justified in attacking him and he would be cut off. The Indians agreed to his company even though he made it clear he would have nothing to do with killing. They gave him a "spear, another lent a broad bayonet for my protection, but at this time I could not be provided with a target (shield); nor did I want to be encumbered with such an unnecessary piece of lumber."

Perhaps in his own way, Hearne, too, had painted a protective "spirit" on his own mental shield. And he was justified to trust his destiny. This was not to be the first blood he had seen. Hood and the Royal Navy spilled blood too. He had come unscathed through European war. He had trudged home, defeated but alive, from two northern expeditions. Why should he feel his date with the Scythe was on the Coppermine?

Time now for the last-minute rites; paint faces black and red; strip off all clothes so as to be swift and sure; tie the hair close to the head or cut it off so it will offer no leverage or get in the eyes: "fearing I might have occassion to run with the rest, I thought it advisable to pull off my stockings and cap, and tie my hair as close as possible." Quietly now; a few more yards; one hour past midnight, July 17, 1771.

Now!

". . . in a few seconds the horrible scene commenced; it was shocking beyond description; the poor unhappy victims were surprised in the midst of their sleep, and had neither time nor power to make any resistance; men, women, and children, in all upward of twenty, ran out of their tents stark naked, and endeavored to make their escape; but the Indians having possession of all

Courtesy National Museum of Canada, Ottawa

Bloody Falls Gorge, Very Near to the Site of the Massacre

the landside, to no place could they fly for shelter."

A girl, perhaps eighteen or nineteen, was speared at Hearne's feet; she grabbed his legs and two more spears pinned her to the ground where she was "twining round them like an eel"; Hearne pleaded for her life but was denied and in turn laid down an ultimatum—kill quickly or he would. A bloody spear was yanked out and thrust again "through her breast near the heart," but the love of life is powerful and she tried to ward off this "friendly blow."

Following the custom of generations, the Eskimo bodies were desecrated in savage fashion as if the blood of the killing were not enough. The Chipewyans were "particularly [brutish] in their curiosity in examining, and the remarks they made, on the formation of the women; which they pretended to say differed materially from their own." Hearne said there were plenty of opportunities to notice any differences but that he was too sick with it all to do so and said that "had there actually been as much difference between them as there is said to be between the Hottentots and those of Europe, it would not have been in my power to mark the distinction."[1]

Though no stranger to bloodshed it was difficult for Hearne to hold back the tears at Bloody Falls. He said that even in later years he wept freely at the memory.

[1] This may refer to a story credited to Captain James Cook that in Hottentot women the vagina is covered by a flap of skin absent in other races. See also R. G. Thwaites, *Travels in the Interior of North America*, II, 257n.

Courtesy Geological Survey of Canada, Ottawa

Bloody Falls from the Air

Across the river from the massacre were seven other tents of Eskimos but the Chipewyans had left their canoes upriver and contented themselves, for the moment, by firing their guns at the Eskimos, who, completely ignorant of the nature of the noise, ran out to pick up the lead and see what was "sent them." Very shortly a bullet thudded into an Eskimo leg, at which they all took fright, jumped into their own canoes and paddled to shoal water where they stood about, knee deep in water, and discussed these surprising developments.

The Chipewyans then looted the tents on their side of the Coppermine. They piled the copper utensils, hatchets, and knives in a pile, clashed their spears in unison and chanted "Tima, tima," an Eskimo word meaning "what cheer" or, "good fun."

When this activity palled the Chipewyans went to get their canoes. On the way they came upon an old, half-blind woman, fishing at the foot of a falls, whom they killed and went on. When they arrived back at the seven tents they found some of the Eskimos had returned to salvage their treasures. One old man, too intent on saving his things, was unable to escape again and "I verily believe not less than twenty had a hand in his death, as his whole body was like a cullender."

The Eskimos had stone kettles as well as copper[2] ones and the Indians took great delight in break-

[2] Two small bits of iron and a type of bead never sold by the Company led Hearne to believe these Eskimos may have been in contact with the Danes on Davis Strait.

ing these. Also in throwing their tents and tent poles into the river, the latter being a grievous loss because of the scarcity of trees.

When the Chipewyans could do no more damage or think of any way to capture or kill the escaped Eskimos "we sat down" and "made a good meal of fresh salmon."[3]

Their blood thirst quenched and their bellies full of fish, the Indians informed Hearne they were again ready to explore—with due consideration for their purification rites.

After such massacres as Bloody Falls the Chipewyans considered themselves unclean, both physically and spiritually. Those actually involved in the letting of blood were prohibited from preparing food in any manner until the purification rites were completed. Until then the guilty were not allowed to eat the head, entrails, or blood of any animal and all food must be eaten raw, dried in the sun, or broiled—never cooked in water.

At mealtime each Indian smeared the lower half of his face with red earth. He used only one dish and one pipe throughout the rites and these were discarded in a ceremonial fire at the conclusion of the period. Except that only the pipestems were thrown away—the bowls were too valuable.

---

[3] Chipewyan-Eskimo war was common. In 1756 the Indians massacred more than forty Eskimos almost in sight of the Company sloop at Knapp's Bay. Hearne said that the Eskimos retaliated with enthusiasm whenever they could but that for the most part they relied on their remote camps, often on islands, for protection. Eskimo-Indian enmity reflected on Company men who for many years dared not go among the Eskimo unarmed. Gradually the Company coaxed the Eskimos into the trading posts and these contacts with both whites and Chipewyans eventually led to reasonably peaceful relations.

All very well to follow the ancient rituals but no need to be impractical and destroy items as difficult to replace as pipe bowls!

Thus the purification rites were obviously very simple but they might stretch over several weeks for they were not considered finished until the arrival of the new winter, although just how that exact date was determined is obscure.

In the present case two Indians had not shed blood and to them fell the task of preparing all the meals until they reached the women again. Hearne was well pleased as otherwise he would have had to prepare his own food, "which would have been no less fatiguing . . . than humiliating and vexatious"—the English officer bubbling to the surface in that reaction!

And so, with the smell of blood and the screams of butchered Eskimos besetting his senses, Samuel Hearne resumed the search for Anián.

CHAPTER SEVENTEEN

And There Is No Anian

OCTOBER 12, 1492! July 18, 1771! Almost three centuries, and men had searched thousands of leagues of coastline and hundreds of thousands of square miles inland for a passage from the Atlantic to the Pacific.

The French had canoed and tramped two thousand miles from the Great Lakes to the Gulf and found no east-west waterway.

They and the English had, with equal diligence, searched from the Atlantic to the Great Lakes, thence at right angles north to the Churchill, but in all that vast expanse there was no Anián. Every foot of North America from Churchill south in a straight line to the Gulf had been explored without finding any passage between the oceans.

If Anián existed at all it had to be between Fort Prince of Wales and the Arctic.

And Samuel Hearne was at Bloody Falls, only eight miles from the northern sea.

He records no high drama now. There is no flag waving, no inscribing for posterity any sense of self importance, no recording his disappointment—only his sense of history.

He knew! He was intensely aware of his accomplishment and of the role he played.

Eight miles more! Then the sea was actually in sight! Open bits of water were visible between the land and the unbroken ice to the north.

Not much hope now. But, orders and good explorership demand that he go on to the end.

Plod on to the Arctic. Plod on and settle for all time that there is no Anián!

". . . and. . . it has put a final end to all dispute concerning a North West Passage through Hudson's Bay."

Thus simply was the ghost of Anián laid.

The third Coppermine expedition reached Arctic salt water at low tide. Seals were playing on the offshore ice. "At the mouth of the river the sea is full of islands and shoals. . . ." The weather was clear and Hearne studied the location until about 1:00 A.M., July 18, when a fog rolled in accompanied by rain. This preliminary survey convinced him the river and its mouth were useless for trading purposes and he decided not to wait for clearing weather to make more extensive observations. He believed his readings were accurate enough to place Bloody Falls and the mouth of the Coppermine within twenty miles of their true location, and with that decision he raised "a mark" and took possession for the Great Company.

As might be expected, there were skeptics who doubted that Samuel Hearne had reached the Arctic.[1]

---

[1] For later-day skepticism see Jeannette Mirsky, *To the Arctic! The Story of Northern Exploration from Earliest Times to the Present* (Rev.

Courtesy National Museum of Canada, Ottawa

Granite Cliffs and Hills Bordering Tree River, Coronation Gulf

Sir John Richardson, the English Arctic explorer, disbelieved on the evidence that the tides do not fluctuate ten or twelve feet as Hearne said and the latter was indeed in error on that point.

Perhaps because of business rivalries the North West Company and Alexander Mackenzie refused to accept Hearne's work and Mackenzie brazenly took credit for the demise of Anián when he arrived at the mouth of the Mackenzie River, 1789, eighteen years after Hearne had reached the Arctic.

The British Admiralty, blind to the accomplishment of anyone outside the commissioned circles, sent George Vancouver along the Pacific coast seeking a Northwest Passage in 1792.

But such jealousies could not efface the facts. Samuel Hearne was the first white man to reach the American Arctic by land, 278 years after Columbus. The evidence in his favor is overwhelming.

A half century after 1771, Sir John Franklin, equipped with every physical asset known to science, entered the identical wastes Hearne had crossed, discovered little new and returned to England a national hero. Why is the lone Englishman who did it first virtually unknown except to professional historians?

Nevertheless, Franklin performed a real service to the memory of Samuel Hearne for he verified

---

and expanded ed.; New York: Alfred A. Knopf, 1948), p. 113n; also Vilhjalmur Stefansson, *Great Adventures and Explorations* (New York: The Dial Press, 1947), p. 515.

Courtesy Geological Survey of Canada, Ottawa

Caribou, South of Richardson Bay, near the Mouth of the Coppermine River

the findings of 1771. "Several human skulls which bore the marks of violence, and many bones were strewed about the encampment, and as the spot exactly answers the description, given by Mr. Hearne, of the place where the Chipewyans who accompanied him perpetrated the dreadful massacre of the Esquimaux, we had no doubt of this being the place. This rapid is a sort of shelving cascade, about three hundred yards in length, having a descent of from ten to fifteen feet. It is bounded on each side by high walls of red sandstone, upon which rests a series of lofty green hills."[2]

Hearne placed Bloody Falls eight miles from the sea, almost a perfect measurement; he correctly described the tree line at this latitude; his recording of the nature and heights of the riverbanks agree with those of Sir John Franklin and are accurate.

And, not least by any means, what motive would Hearne have for falsifying his report? To reach the sea and find no Northwest Passage, no navigable stream, no great copper deposits were disappointments which certainly would have been better served by holding out the opposite idea, namely, that he had not yet reached salt water and perhaps Anián and the mines might yet be found.

In truth, Hearne put an effective end to several

---

[2] Samuel Hearne, *A Journey from Prince of Wales's Fort in Hudson's Bay to the Northern Ocean in the Years 1769, 1770, 1771, and 1772;* new edition with introduction, notes, and illustrations by J. B. Tyrrell (Toronto: Champlain Society, 1911), pp. 186-87n.

cherished dreams: There is no Strait of Anián; the Coppermine River is useless as a navigable stream; and the copper deposits, when finally found, were neither where the Indians said they were, nor did they appear as valuable as the Company had hoped.

To insist that these truths were falsehoods told by Hearne to promote his own greatness violates common sense.

C H A P T E R   E I G H T E E N

The Arctic Copper Mines

SAMUEL HEARNE was the first white man to reach the American Arctic, lay the myth of Anián, and discover the Coppermine River. But he had not yet found where the Red Knives and Eskimos got their metal. This he must do.

But first he was obliged to get some sleep. It was 6:00 A.M., July 18, and the last rest Hearne had had was on the fifteenth. He lay down where he was and slept for five or six hours.

After waking, a meal of raw musk-ox was "intolerable, as it happened to be an old beast," but he ate and turned south-southwest.

Eating raw musk-ox or when traveling along a wet trail, Hearne was forever asking the Indians what legends or beliefs were associated with the day's locale. Thus, he soon had a tally of Eskimo customs, cooking utensils, household wares, the flora and fauna, and, in detail, the Red Knife legend of the mines.

The original discoverer of the ore, they said, was a strong-willed woman who led her men to the mines each summer to collect their annual supply of metal. As she was the only woman on these long trips the men became over attentive and took liberties which angered her. In retaliation she sat down on the mine and vowed she would stay there until she sank into the earth, taking the copper with her.

The following year the men reached the site with great difficulty. They found the woman alive but half buried. The year after that she had disappeared and only fragments of ore were left.

The Coppers believed each of these fragments resembled some animal. The one Hearne eventually found looked like a rabbit, they said, but these fantasies had no particular significance to the Indians, any more than the "pictures" our children see in the clouds have to them.

Thirty miles from the mouth of the Coppermine River, probably along the modern Burnt Creek, Samuel Hearne came upon one edge of the great Canadian ore beds.

These mines actually exist, of course, although not in the position or condition the Company had been led to believe. As Hearne saw them they were little more than a "jumble of rocks and gravel, which had been rent many ways by an earthquake," with a small knee-deep river running through the center of the deposit.

Sir John Franklin visited them in July of 1821 and his colleague, John Richardson, also reported on the beds. Others have followed at long intervals. The whole story has not yet been told but we know that the deposits are widespread, extending east of the Coppermine nearly two hundred miles.

The Indians usually picked their bits of metal

from the rubble at the foot of the sheerer mountains, some of which rise to a height of two thousand feet. Pieces of the ore often weighed five or ten pounds and several have been found too heavy for a man to lift. The one Hearne carried back to Fort Prince of Wales, and which is now in the British Museum, weighs four pounds.

No thorough survey has ever been made of the total accumulation of copper. Estimates of its worth range from "not worth the cost of extraction" to the opposite—that the deposit may equal or exceed that on Lake Superior.[1]

Between 1913 and 1954, hundreds of claims were filed and allowed to lapse. Nevertheless, in August alone, 1955, over one hundred new claims were filed by a single company.

Hearne, himself, made no attempt to search beyond the immediate river area and never pretended to any extensive investigation. With some justice, perhaps, he has been sharply criticized for this failure. However, he was totally untrained in mineralogy and he had fulfilled the letter of his orders. He had found the Coppermine River, ascertained the location of the ore deposits near its mouth, and proved the nonexistence of a Northwest Passage through the continent. Winter would close in before he could have accomplished much more.

Most important of all, he must remain with the Chipewyans if he were ever to see the Churchill

---

[1] See J. B. Tyrrell, *The Coppermine Country* (Toronto, 1912), p. 29.

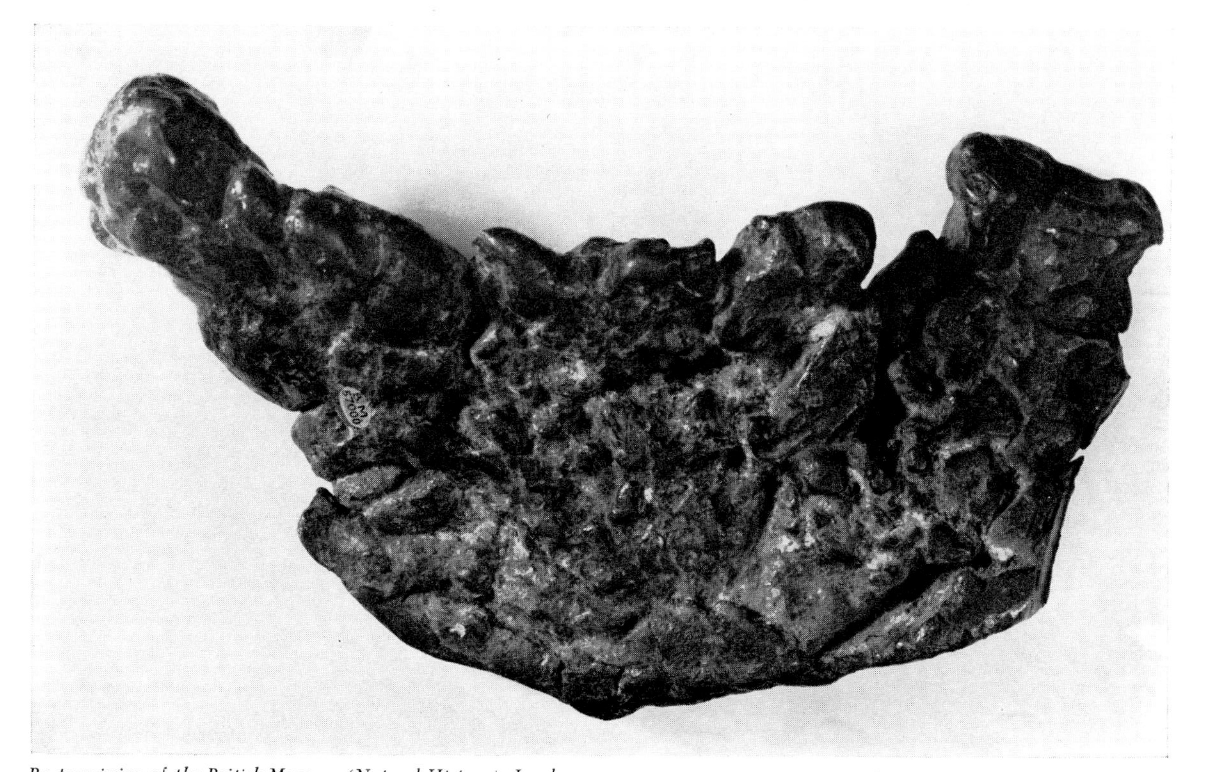

By permission of the British Museum (Natural History), London

The Lump of Copper, now in the British Museum, Which Hearne Picked Up on the Coppermine and Carried All the Way Back to Fort Prince of Wales.

again and make any report at all. And the Chipewyans certainly had no intention of spending the winter on the Arctic coast away from their women.

With these decisions Hearne turned south with Matonabbee and headed home, although it eventually turned out to be a route very different from the one he expected.

CHAPTER NINETEEN

The Discovery of Great Slave Lake

SNOWSTORMS delayed the return journey and it was the third week in July before the expedition was a hundred miles away from the Coppermine.

On the outward trip Matonabbee had sent his brother with a small party to acquaint the Coppers of the advent of the war band, after which he was to rejoin Hearne. This crew had been unable to return to the expedition before Bloody Falls and now came wearily into camp at three o'clock in the morning of July 22. They had not slept since finding Matonabbee's direction markers one hundred miles away on the back trail!

Hearne, sleeping when the Indians arrived, arose, heard their report, and walked with them another forty-two miles before "we put up about the middle of the Stony Mountains."

A tramp of 142 miles without sleep. These Chipewyans were men!

July 22, 1771, was hot and sultry and the sun, bouncing off the patches of late snow, burned and blinded, but Hearne searched on. If there were no fabulous mines and Anián only a myth, there might yet be something the Great Company could use—a new tribe to contact or a land rich in soft northern furs. So tramp on.

And Matonabbee was anxious. Only two wives near. Five more, here or there, out beneath the stars or roasting stomachs under a tree. Time to find them.

Forty-five miles today!

It was 1:00 A.M., July 24, 1771. Eat, rest an hour, hurry on. Congecathawachaga is in sight down at the edge of the horizon. Perhaps those really are Chipewyan smokes and not a hope-mirage. One hundred and sixty miles and seven days from the hates of Bloody Falls!

Five hours more! Congecathawachaga! But anticipation turns bitter in the mouth. Only an old man, one of Matonabbee's several fathers-in-law, sits by a lonely fire.

No women. No boys and girls to ask questions and stand wide-eyed before the returning warriors. "All our women had got set across the river before the Copper Indians left that part."

Once before Hearne mentioned the women and children in *his* house, and now, "our women." Does that mean that he had taken at last a native girl as something more than a servant? Perhaps. One can almost wish (with a proper sense of guilt and due obesience to our present mores) that the man who laid the ghost of Anián was one with all that robust galaxy who boasted and brawled, loved and labored, cheated and lied, lived their lives and gave them, to trace the rivers and mountains of a whole continent and leave it ready for the plow and sod houses, barbed wire and traffic signs.

"Our women." They have indeed been here, the moss is on fire! Hurry! We can catch them yet tonight!

Eleven o'clock P.M.!

They were here too, but they have wandered on.

Ten miles more!

Two o'clock A.M.! The first women!

Contwoyto Lake and time to rest.

Indeed, it was fast becoming a race between native passion and Hearne's stamina. The "unmerciful rate" had cut moose-hide footgear to shreds; the feet swelled, became numb, and were bumped blindly against rocks. Nails festered and dropped off, raw flesh absorbed sharp sand, and Hearne's bloody footprints marked the insensate dash from Bloody Falls to Contwoyto. Even the Chipewyans complained but their feet were not "the twentieth part in so bad a state as mine, . . . quite honeycombed by the dirt and gravel eating into raw flesh."

Hearne warmed water, washed his feet, put "spirits of wine" on the swollen parts, "Turner's cerate" on the open sores, and went to bed. Next morning he was so much improved he said he ceased to worry. But he had had sufficient cause. The Chipewyans were in no mood to lessen their "unmerciful rate" and he must either keep up or be stranded, completely alone, one thousand trail miles from the Churchill.

While Hearne was treating his feet the Indian

women were giving their men ceremonial headbands decorated with porcupine quills and moose hair which each man wore until he tossed them into a special fire concluding his purification. Following which, there was, said Hearne, much kissing of wives and caressing of children.

After the reunion with the women the expedition loafed along at a leisurely eight or nine miles per day until they arrived at a rendezvous with more of the families on the last day of July, probably on some lake between Contwoyto and Point lakes.

Matonabbee's immediate family and some of Hearne's crew were not yet present, however. More smokes were visible toward the east and since Matonabbee believed these must be from the tents of his remaining wives he sent a small detachment after them. They returned on the fifth of August with the missing wives plus forty additional tents!

A sudden accretion of probably four hundred souls!

Among these latter was the man Matonabbee had so savagely stabbed on the outward journey. The young husband at once led his wife to Matonabbee's tent and set her down beside the big chief. She was in tears and moaned, "see'd dinne, see'd dinne," my husband, my husband, over and over. Matonabbee pretended no attention but when he could tolerate her moans no longer he told her that if she thought that much of her husband she should never have left him (as if she had had a choice) and to return to him. With sham reluctance she did so.

Shortly after this episode an outbreak of intestinal disturbances immobilized the expedition. For these disorders the medicine men used either conjuring or a unique treatment of "blowing into the anus, or into the parts adjacent, till their eyes are almost starting from their heads: and this operation is performed indifferently on all, without regard either to age or sex."

"The accumulation of so large a quantity of wind is at times apt to occassion some extraordinary emotions, which are not easily suppressed by a sick person; and as there is no vent for it but by the channel through which it was conveyed thither, it sometimes occasions an odd scene between the doctor and his patient."

A flippant remark by Hearne harvested immediate resentment from both patient and doctor.

When conjuring was the remedy the medicine man attached a cord to a cherished object and swallowed it, retrieving it later by pulling on the cord. This was done, said the practical Chipewyans, because the item would be too difficult to digest and too valuable to lose—and besides, the "medicine" lay in the act of swallowing, not in the destruction of the article.

Hearne said, "I must confess that it appeared to me to be a very nice piece of deception, especially as it was performed by a man quite naked."

After the illness abated the Chipewyans began drifting apart in small bands, some in one direction, some in another. By the second week only twelve tents remained with Hearne. No one was in a hurry as the expedition moved southwest seven or eight miles per day.

Thus, leisurely, Hearne discovered Point Lake, 65° 30′ north and 113° west, then turned almost at right angles southeastward until he reached the tree line again early in September.

On this leg of the journey one of the women was abandoned to "perish above ground." Chipewyan custom provided that persons thus deserted be given a little food and water, "firing" materials if available, and covered with robes. The others went on, believing it were better to abandon one than to imperil all. In the present case the old woman staggered to her feet, struggled through early snow and sleet, and caught up with her band three times before she fell behind at last, to die alone.

October came in "roughly" with much snow and wind. One night a gale wrecked the entire camp. Tents were blown down, poles broken, and, as a sort of defiant gesture the storm again tossed Hearne's quadrant to the frozen ground and broke it. Hearne, displaying a bit of unusual temper, seized the damaged instrument, broke it into smaller pieces and gave them to the Indians who immediately smashed them into still smaller fragments to be used as shot.

The third Coppermine expedition was making no pretense of retracing the outward trip. No white man had ever before traveled the miles

Courtesy Geological Survey of Canada, Ottawa

SECOND PORTAGE, RAE RIVER

Matonabbee was laying out for Samuel Hearne. If Anián was now only a myth, that did not preclude that around the next snowdrift might lay a great and hitherto unknown geographic fact. And so Hearne explored on, gambling that on the morrow he might "make a name for himself" and "benefit mankind."

In the meantime Chipewyan life followed its normal pattern: several more tents broke away to hunt beaver and moose; Matonabbee imagined another insult to his dignity and threatened to leave, and this time Hearne told him to go ahead, albeit such conduct was unworthy of him; the Indians wanted to stop and fish but Hearne demurred, saying it was far too cold to sit on the ice dangling a hook; they reached "Methy" Lake (perhaps the modern Cook Lake); they "French fried" the spruce partridge, as we call it, dumb, dark meated, and pungent with the flavor of spruce needles, but a not undeserving dish for all of that; they fried deer skin in like manner and enjoyed a meal "exceedingly good."

Hearne stood by an evening fire and watched a naked medicine man "swallow" a board longer than his back and twice as wide as his mouth, aided, he said, by the "cloud spirits," and, unable to detect any deception, Hearne reported, "I never had so thick a cloud thrown before my eyes before or since." Hearne saw his paralytic servant take the blowing and sucking cure and leave his bed and walk and talk, then change from a happy, friendly person into a mean and sullen one—a

Courtesy Geological Survey of Canada, Ottawa

Boulders by an Unnamed Lake near Yellowknife River

change of personality not unknown to modern medicine; he pleased Matonabbee by pretending to kill one of the Chipewyan's enemies by remote control, only to find later that the man had indeed died, if from quite another cause, and Hearne rested on his laurels and refused to perform again.

The party labored on and discovered, Christmas Eve, 1771, Great Slave Lake, tenth largest in the world: 2,000 feet deep, 300 miles long, 11,000 square miles of inland sea, its southern edge green with forest, its northern arms, fancied by the Indians to resemble female breasts and called by them Lake of the Breasts, stretching toward the tundra.

Once again the discovery of a great geographic fact is buried so thoroughly in a modest journal that if one does not look sharp the notation will be missed, ". . . we shaped our course more to the Southward, and on the twenty-fourth, arrived at the North side of the great Athapuscow Lake."

Beyond the above notation Hearne made no special note of his discovery. This is perhaps understandable. He was a modest man and since leaving Fort Prince of Wales he had seen, walked over, paddled across, or fished in literally thousands of lakes, and "Athapuscow," as he called it, was just one more lake, larger than all the others but without other significance at the moment.

Nevertheless, Samuel Hearne was the discoverer of Great Slave Lake, and the Matonabbee Point and Hearne Channel of modern maps are paltry tributes to a great Indian and a great explorer.

CHAPTER TWENTY

The Return to the Churchill

SAMUEL HEARNE spent a lonesome Christmas on Great Slave Lake, then crossed it via the modern Simpson Islands and entered bison country where the great beasts, huge as they were, could outrun an Indian on snowshoes even when the animal's belly dragged in the snow. "I . . . once had the vanity to think . . . I could have kept pace with them; but though I was at that time celebrated for being particularly fleet of foot in snowshoes, I soon found that I was no match for the buffaloes," said Hearne.

The Chipewyans "celebrated" New Year's Eve by plundering a small family whose home was in an oasis of green out on the Barren Grounds near the Thelon River, not far from its juncture with the Dubawnt.

The animals and birds came regularly to the oasis and the little band led a semi-stabilized existence there, even learning to preserve and store some food supplies.

Because of their drastic need for more wood they had come at least four hundred miles for enough birch bark to make two canoes and enough fungus to use as tinder for the ensuing year.

Hearne was most interested in their story but

was seething over the treatment of their women, whom the Chipewyans had seized. ". . . this last act . . . displeased me more than all their former actions, because it was committed on a set of harmless creatures."

A few days later Hearne and Matonabbee followed a strange snowshoe track ending at a little hut in which sat, quite alone, a young Dogrib woman. She had been taken prisoner in the summer of 1770; seen her baby killed by the Athapascans; served as a slave; escaped; got lost; built a shelter; and for the past seven months had lived alone.

Snared small game kept her in good supply. She had a fishnet of willow bark; she had a knife fashioned from an old hoop; she had turned an arrowhead into an awl; she made fire by knocking two sulphurous stones against each other; she was, in fact, a very resourceful girl, a most desirable package!

She was, said Hearne, "one of the finest women, of a real Indian, that I have seen in any part of North America." Her rabbit-skin clothes showed "great taste, and exhibited no little variety of ornament . . . the whole of her garb [had] a very pleasing, though rather romantic appearance."

Every man in camp schemed to own the young Dogrib. She was won and lost a dozen times that evening and we should very much like to know if Samuel Hearne entered the wrestling matches or not!

Naturally Matonabbee wanted to get in the con-

Courtesy Canadian Wildlife Service, Ottawa, Canada

CARIBOU RESTING AT GHOST LAKE, MACKENZIE DISTRICT, SPRING MIGRATION, 1949

Many hundreds were outside the camera range

test and would have done so except that one of his wives taunted him, saying that he already had more wives than "he could properly attend." For this insult Matonabbee beat her until she eventually died from the effects. The Chipewyan code permitted such discipline and the killing carried no social stigma.

All these digressions were exciting enough but they were not conducive to efficient exploration. The third Coppermine expedition was almost at a standstill just south of Great Slave Lake. Furthermore, the relation of Matonabbee to Hearne was somewhat uncertain. Matonabbee had fulfilled his promise to guide Hearne to the Coppermine and could argue he had no further obligations to please Hearne. From Bloody Falls to the present location the expedition had been steadily drifting southward while Fort Prince of Wales was hundreds of miles to the east.

Whether this item ever came to a head between Hearne and Matonabbee we do not know but as the pace of the expedition became slower and slower, Hearne, for once, interfered with Matonabbee's trail orders and called a council in mid-January at which the Indians agreed to set traplines, collect a supply of pelts, and be at Fort Prince of Wales in time for the annual ship. Accordingly, the expedition worked up the Slave River for approximately forty miles and then turned almost due east toward the fort.

All we know of the next month is that Hearne was finally going home. His daily locations are quite impossible to identify in many instances. His watch had stopped at Great Slave Lake and he no longer had either quadrant or watch to determine location or directions. But we know that he was going generally east for he occasionally mentioned recognizable landmarks and he eventually picked up his outgoing trail.

During March the expedition, now augmented to two hundred persons, left the "fine level country of the Athapuscows" and entered the "stony mountains" which served as the western boundary of the Chipewyan domain.

It was again a busy time for the Indians: collecting birch rind for canoes, tent poles for use now but later to serve as snowshoe frames; fishing in Hill Island Lake, 150 miles east of the southern shore of Great Slave Lake; fighting the tremendous gales when it was impossible to walk upright in the open and dangerous to do so even in the shelter of the trees.

But there was time for fun, too: time to race the moose to the death over the crusted snow. Sometimes a virile old fellow would lead his Chipewyan tormentor forty-eight hours before he turned at bay to meet the Indian knife, the only weapon permitted in the game. And it was considered purely a sport for the race raised the body temperature of the moose to a "violent fever" and the beast rarely had more than a quart of free blood, said the Indians, the rest having dispersed into the flesh, "which in that state, must be ten times worse tasted, than the spleen or milt of a bacon hog." "Though I was a swift runner in those days I never accompanied the Indians in one of these chaces," said Hearne. No wonder!

One day in April the "villains belonging to my crew . . . robbed . . . [another band of strangers] of almost every useful article," then dragged the young women a little distance from their tents and "not only ravished them, but otherwise ill-treated them, and that in so barbarous a manner, as to endanger the lives of one or two of them."

Hearne, despite a previous resolve never to interfere again in Chipewyan ways, remonstrated against these actions and was told that if any of his female relatives had been there they would have received like treatment. For some reason the Chipewyans were in a nasty mood.

May Day was "exceedingly fine and pleasant" but a sudden snowstorm followed by another northern gale caught the expedition "on top of a high barren hill" far from any trees and nothing to do but turn backs to the storm and wait while the wind grew stronger and forced everyone to lie down, when, "long before morning we were in a puddle of water, occasioned by the heat of our bodies melting the snow." Following the storm the weather veered from one extreme to another and they must "wade above the knees through swamps of mud, water and wet snow," which froze on their leather stockings and threatened to freeze their feet and legs.

When the expedition reached Wholdaia Lake, only seventy miles west of Kasba Lake, discovered

Courtesy Geological Survey of Canada, Ottawa

GEOMETRIC CRACK PATTERN IN THE MUSKEG

It is caused by action of the ice on small rocks and fine soil

on the outward journey, Hearne and his companions encountered the most tragic famine of all three expeditions.

There had been no deer for ten days and four small ones on the following day furnished only a taste for the two hundred Indians. In desperation individuals and small groups struck off by themselves, hoping to flush game but they returned as hungry as when they left. Many were too weak to carry their goods and cached them.

Death was very present.

Starved bellies swelled, eyes deepened in their sockets and lost luster, minds clouded, and women and children stumbled along, numbly waiting. ". . . several died for want. It is a meloncholy truth, and a disgrace to the little humanity of which those people are possessed, . . . that in times of want the poor women always come off short; and when real distress approaches, many of them are permitted to starve, when the males are amply provided for."

Ten days later, "our numbers were greatly lessened" and three deer "served us for two or three meals."

Two weeks before a like number of animals had furnished only a taste. How many had starved? No one knows. A few old folks and children had been sent to the Barren Grounds. A few had drifted off, seeking food. A few were with Hearne.

The remainder had starved.

Relatively speaking, the third Coppermine expedition was almost home. They skirted the end

Courtesy Canadian Wildlife Service, Ottawa, Canada

MUSK-OX

of Ennadai Lake, crossed the Kazan River. Another storm made it impossible to travel or pitch tents and they sat for three days with their tents over their heads but with nothing to eat until the wind died and the wild geese took wing when "The only inconvenience we now felt were the frequent showers of heavy rain, but the intervals between . . . being very warm . . . and bright, that difficulty was easily overcome, . . . as the belly was plentifully supplied with excellent victuals."

After Wholdaia Lake, 60° 45′ north and 104° west, the expedition was roughly following the outward trail except that everyone must walk around the larger lakes because the canoes they carried were too slight for such as Kasba, Ennadai, or Nueltin.

June 18 they reached the Egg River again and Matonabbee suggested that Hearne send a fast courier to apprise Norton of their arrival.

Eight days later Hearne reached the Seal River but another gale prevented crossing at the moment. "In the afternoon the weather grow more moderate" and all were ferried over except one Red Knife Indian whose goods were already across. The Chipewyans wished to abandon the Copper and keep his goods, thus adding another case in point to the Red Knife belief that it was unhealthy to visit Fort Prince of Wales.

Matonabbee risked the ridicule of his fellows and rescued the Copper, restored his goods, and, following a short visit at the fort, piloted the lone man all the way back to his own people, about five hundred miles away from the Churchill. These Chipewyans were, indeed, unpredictable!

After crossing the Seal the expedition resumed the trail and was soon met by the returning courier with tobacco and "some other articles which I desired."

Samuel Hearne was sometimes most aggravating! Besides tobacco what did he want most after all the months away from civilization? Hard liquor? No, he used it very little, none at all for long periods of time. Civilized food? Hardly, he was too thoroughly converted to native dishes. Ammunition? Not likely; he was too near home. Clothes? Just perhaps, especially if he wished to dress for a conspicuous entrance into the Company fort.

What *did* he want? What did he want so badly he could not wait the last few miles? A tantalizing question with an answer we shall never know.

We do know that with all his modesty Samuel Hearne was now determined to receive his earned salute. He was only ten miles from Fort Prince of Wales but he chose to camp overnight on the "Goose-hunting Islands" and make his entry next morning, June 30, 1772, when there was a better chance of having Moses Norton in full control of his faculties and the fort's personnel on hand to give him the welcome and honor due.

"Next morning I arrived in good health at Prince of Wales' Fort, after having been absent eighteen months and twenty three days on this last expedition; but from my first setting out with Captain Chawchinahaw, it was two years seven months and twenty four days.

"Though my discoveries are not likely to prove of any material advantage to the Nation at large, or indeed to the Hudson's Bay Company, yet I have the pleasure to think that I have fully complied with the orders of my Masters, and that it has put a final end to all disputes concerning a North West Passage through Hudson's Bay."

Readers who demand that a biography end on the note of highest adventure should lay this volume aside at this point. Hereafter Samuel Hearne never seriously endangered his life, beyond the limits experienced by all frontiersmen; never approached another Bloody Falls; never discovered another Arctic Ocean or Great Slave Lake.

But for those who want to follow a man's trail to the end—these must read the record of another twenty years as Hearne lived them. Such readers will not forget that it was an era of exploitation and revolution in which many men spent an adventurous youth and a less dramatic maturity. A New World was still being conquered and partitioned. France was losing her share of North America but her Little Corsican was studying military strategy and dreaming of his sweep across Europe. The mobs of Paris were simmering; the Orient and South Africa were sulking under British colonialism; and the traders of Boston and the farmers of Vermont were spawning a new nation.

Samuel Hearne could not escape either the exploitations or the revolutions. The remaining chapters of this volume are a summary of his participation therein.

CHAPTER TWENTY-ONE

Hearne Defends His Expedition

SAMUEL HEARNE entered Fort Prince of Wales in the forenoon of June 30, 1772, concluding the third Coppermine expedition. For the next fourteen months we have very little data. He was appointed mate on the *Charlotte,* under Magnus Johnston, master. Hearne, Johnston, and a dozen men went to Sloop Cove, cleared away the moorage, and laid up the ship. After the first of October Hearne was occupied in and around the post, including such uninspiring tasks as shooting partridges for the winter larder.

Moses Norton's journal says he sent Hearne and five men to the cove again May 19, 1773, to get the *Charlotte* ready for her "Voyage to the North on the Trade."[1] Johnston and Hearne went as far north as Knapp's Bay and Whale Cove. They returned to the Churchill August 22 and the next day Johnston was ordered to "Mak the Brigg *Charllotte* in propper trim Fore Sea, In order to Go to York Fort."[2] A week later they sailed with Hearne and Robert Longmoor as passengers.

---

[1] Published by permission of the Governor and Committee of the Hudson's Bay Company.

[2] Published by permission of the Governor and Committee of the Hudson's Bay Company.

From York Hearne may have gone farther south along the bay because he drew maps of Albany, Moose, and Slude rivers and although they are dated 1774 some authorities think he drew them during the fourteen months.[3]

We do know that he sent an official report, with notes and charts, to the Company because their reply, dated May 12, 1773, said:

MR. SAMUEL HEARNE,

SIR,—Your letter of the 28th August last gave us the agreeable pleasure to hear of your safe return to our Factory. Your Journal, and the two charts you sent sufficiently convince us of your very judicious remarks.

We have maturely considered your great assiduity in the various accidents which occurred in your several Journies. We hereby return you our grateful thanks; and to manifest our obligation we have consented to allow you a gratuity of ———[4] for those services.

Among the scientific gentlemen of London, however, Hearne's accomplishment was received with very much less than enthusiasm. He had hoped that the third Coppermine expedition would lessen the criticism of "Dobbs, Ellis, Robson and American Traveller" regarding Company policy toward exploration and expansion but instead the critics now attacked Hearne. They said he took

---

[3] See Samuel Hearne, *A Journey from Prince of Wales's Fort in Hudson's Bay to the Northern Ocean in the Years 1769, 1770, 1771, and 1772*; new edition with introduction, notes, and illustrations by J. B. Tyrrell (Toronto: Champlain Society, 1911), p. 5.

[4] Beckles Willson says the amount was £200 and this estimate was probably not far wrong as the total of wages due Hearne plus the gratuity amounted to £272. 16. 6. This data courtesy of the Governor and Committee of the Hudson's Bay Company.

too few readings of latitude and longitude and that what he gave were inaccurate. And it is true that Hearne's readings were sometimes three or four degrees too far north but Sir Francis Drake erred six degrees estimating his position on the Northwest Coast and George Vancouver missed the Columbia River. No one called them inefficient. To belittle Hearne's work because he made mistakes in latitude was pure peevishness.

The critics said the sun could not possibly have been in sight all night where and when Hearne said it was; why did he not give some detail about the instruments he used; there could have been no plant life near the mouth of the Coppermine because there is none on Greenland in the same latitude; the Indians couldn't range over such vast distances as Hearne implied and the Chipewyan stories must have referred to rivers and mines entering or bordering on Hudson Bay. And why didn't he give botanical data for the western portion of his supposed track?

To all these complaints Hearne offered simple, straightforward answers: on the second expedition he used a Hadley quadrant made by Daniel Scatlif of Wapping, and on the third expedition he used a thirty-year-old Elton quadrant.

The sun was indeed visible whether anyone believed it or not.

Any geographer or scientist as great as Alexander Dalrymple, soon to be hydrographer to the Admiralty, should know that latitude regulated plant life only to a certain limit.

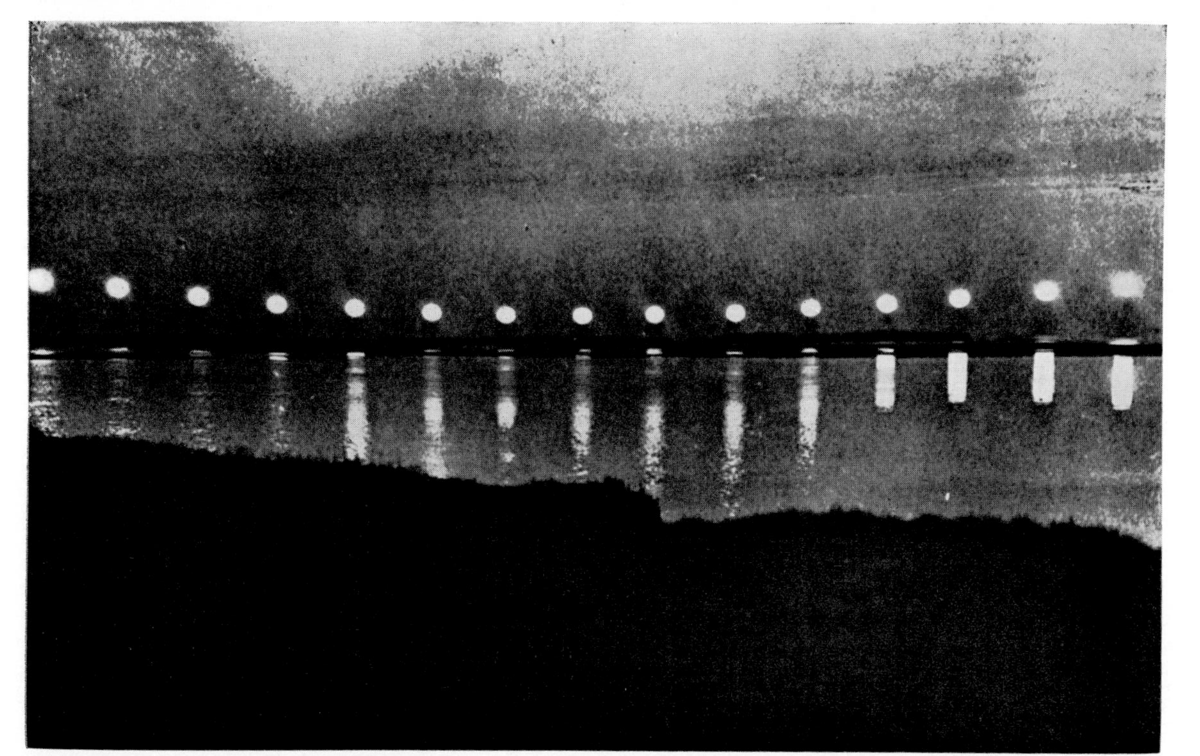

Courtesy Hudson's Bay Company, Winnipeg, Canada

Hearne's Critics Said the Sun Could Not Have Been Visible All Night When and Where He Said It Was

This multiple-exposure photograph, taken at the mouth of the Coppermine, clearly depicts the setting and rising of the Arctic sun in midsummer.

He understood English bewilderment regarding the great distances traveled by the Indians but the facts were as he stated.

And the reason for having no botanical information for certain sections of his travel was very simple: "I was invariably confined to stony hills and barren plains all Summer, and before we approached the woods in the Fall of the year, the ground was always covered with snow to a considerable depth; so that I never had an opportunity of seeing any of the small plants and shrubs to the Westward."

Then, referring to the criticism of Ellis, Hearne said, "As to a passage through the continent of America by way of Hudson's Bay, it has so long been exploded, notwithstanding what Mr. Ellis has urged in its favour, and the place it has found in the visionary Map of the American Traveler, that any comment on it would be quite unnecessary. My latitude only will be sufficient proof that no such passage is in existence."[5]

After other events and much later, Hearne closed his debate with his critics by saying, "As further proof of the Company's being perfectly satisfied with my conduct while on that Journey, the Committee unanimously appointed me Chief of Prince of Wales's Fort in the summer of 1775; and Mr. Bibye Lake, who was then Governor, and several others of the Committee, honoured me with a regular correspondence as long as they lived."

[5] Hearne is speaking of the Henry Ellis referred to in chap. 4.

And that is all we positively know of Hearne's activities following his return from the Arctic until he was sent to "Basquia."

CHAPTER TWENTY-TWO

The First Century of the Hudson's Bay Company

SAMUEL HEARNE had been sent to the Arctic for two basic reasons: the criticisms of Arthur Dobbs and his clique; and because the Company was in financial trouble.

To detail the years of the first century of the Company would be to divert this volume from the story of Samuel Hearne to a history of the Company. Nevertheless, a broad survey of the hundred years must be presented lest we miss the significance of Hearne's work after he returned from the Coppermine.

They were fantastic grants of power and territory that Charles II gave the "Gentlemen Adventurers" in 1670. Roughly speaking, Company land was all the realm draining into Hudson Bay—almost one fourth of North America! And over that immense region the Company held sovereign rights. They built forts and settlements; they held a monopoly of all legal trade; they owned every known, or unknown, natural resource; they granted military commissions; they made war and peace; they wrote laws and inflicted punishments, even to the life or death of their subjects.

In return the Company was expected to seek

Courtesy Canadian Wildlife Service, Ottawa, Canada

Caribou Skull and Antlers at Foot of Tyrrell Falls

the Northwest Passage; explore their domain; collect furs, minerals, and "other considerable commodities"—and make a profit.

But they did not hold that domain unchallenged. France, too, claimed sovereignty over the same lands and sent military expeditions against Company posts at the mouths of the Moose, Albany, Severn, and Nelson rivers. And this warfare was waged largely irrespective of the war-peace status of the mother countries. The French won most of the battles and lost all the wars.

Beginning with the Treaty of Utrecht, 1713, France was steadily compelled to recognize British sovereignty over more and more northern realm until, with the Treaty of Paris, 1763, she relinquished all claims to the lands draining into Hudson Bay, indeed to all of North America.

Despite these events the first century of Company life was characterized more by inertia than by energy. Perhaps it could plead extenuating circumstances.

It was an uneasy century. The feudal age was making its last efforts to maintain its privileges; modern science was only beginning to stir; present-day commercialism was unborn; illiteracy and superstition ruled the lives of the masses and it was a rare Company employee who read or wrote; bigotry and intolerance were common and men were still ruled by masters, not by laws. To indict the Company for these same shortcomings is to be unrealistic.

Besides, there were other events to divert the

attention of the gentlemen in London. England and France had engaged in a series of long and costly wars and the final eclipse of France in North America brought new English responsibilities on the St. Lawrence at the very time other colonies along the Atlantic seaboard were becoming restless.

The mobs of Paris were starving; Voltaire, Rousseau, and Diderot were upsetting the smug content of the nobles and clergy and arousing the masses; revolts flared and were put down with savage ruthlessness; Charles II, Anne, George I and George II were all gone, and George III was trying valiantly to follow his mother's advice and "be a King," only to lose his mind and the best of his kingdom in the attempt; Captain Cook sent shivers of patriotism up English spines as he carried British supremacy from Alaska to Botony Bay. Indeed, it was a restless century.

Furthermore, London was a relatively small city, a bare half million people in 1760, and consequently there was a very small group of really powerful men operating both internal and external affairs through the century. They constituted a sort of closed corporation and their influence was out of proportion to their numbers. Some of them were household words: Prince Rupert, the Duke of York, Lord Churchill, Sir Bibye Lake, William Pitt, George Grenville, Samuel Johnson. But there were others, less known outside the inner circles perhaps, but just as powerful.

Sir Joseph Banks, mentioned above, was such a one. His name rarely appears in a general history;

encyclopedias list his contributions to the botanical sciences; and Company histories ignore him. But Banks had a versatile mind and money enough to indulge it. He went with Cook to Botony Bay; he journeyed to Iceland; he corresponded with the great throughout the world; his letters of recommendation were passports to every learned society and most of the courts of Europe; the directors of the East India Company sought his advice and he was one of the few Englishmen who genuinely liked George III, with whom he spent many hours walking in the Royal gardens discussing plants.[1]

Sir Joseph collected power as he did plants and by the time he became president of the Royal Society, six years after Hearne returned from the Arctic, he was, perhaps, the most powerful man in London. His home on Soho Square was the unofficial headquarters of every scientist of repute; and in time he became the confidential adviser without portfolio to a succession of British governments.

But Sir Joseph was not interested in Hudson Bay. If he was concerned with the Strait of Anián or inland exploration or Company profits it has escaped the attention of our time and his latest biographer indexes none of them. His influence was so great, however, that it exercised a negative pressure on the affairs he ignored and we cannot help but wonder what would have happened at York or on the Churchill or on the Barren

---

[1] Hector Charles Cameron, *Sir Joseph Banks* (London: The Batchworth Press, 1952), pp. 262, 280.

Courtesy Geological Survey of Canada, Ottawa

COPPER ESKIMO WOMAN MENDING CLOTHES

Caribou hides have sometimes given way to canvas for tents

Grounds if he had turned his attention to them as he did to the settlement of Australia and the development of Spanish Merino sheep and the plants in Kew Gardens.

The Treaty of Paris, 1763, eliminated French authority in North America but it did not stop the inroads of individual Frenchmen, stranded by the several treaties in the American wilderness, nor did it check the combinations of Jacobite Scotsmen from Montreal or Quebec who delighted in attacking the Company.

The French trader had an affinity for the Indians and frontier life which the Englishman could neither duplicate nor understand. The Frenchman could enter the earthy pleasures of the natives without his tongue in his cheek; he could cheat the Indians with their own methods and retain their respect; he could eat their food, help scalp their enemies, and captivate their women and affect no condescension at any time. And the end result was that long before 1763 he had penetrated far behind Company lines and was in a fair way to bankrupt it by intercepting the richest furs before they could be taken to the posts on Hudson Bay.

Some of these French ventures were nothing more than unorganized peddling. Others set out to challenge the Crown and Company on a continental scale.

The Vérendrye family had traded (and searched for Anián) far into the west twenty years before the Treaty of Paris. Their Fort St. Pierre on

Rainy Lake, Fort St. Charles on Lake of the Woods, Fort Bourbon at the mouth of the Winnipeg River, Fort La Reine on the Assiniboine, Fort Dauphin on Lake Manitoba, and Forts Pasquia and Des Prairies on the Saskatchewan had all been built before the fall of Quebec.

As long as there were profits, however, the gentlemen in London paid scant attention to this competition although there were isolated cases of English competitive trade in the interior. Forty years before Vérendrye one Henry Kelsey, age eighteen, left Hudson Bay, went to the Assiniboine country, wandered to the buffalo plains and circled back to York Factory, 1691. But there was no follow-up action.

Indeed, there were a good many derelictions of Company responsibility during the first century. No London official had ever visited Hudson Bay[2] and their ignorance of the American frontier was both tragic and ludicrous. As late as 1784 they sent 150 copies of *The Country Clergyman's Advice to Parishioners* to be distributed among their subjects!

To the already reviewed criticisms of Arthur Dobbs might be added the remark of Edward Umfreville, Company writer at Fort Prince of Wales, to the effect that the Indians were often mistreated at the Hudson Bay posts and "This is

[2] Robert E. Pinkerton, *Hudson's Bay Company* (New York: Henry Holt and Company, 1931), p. 119.

one of the reasons why the trade of York Factory has so materially declined. . . ."[3]

For almost an even century the Company had made little effort to extend trade away from salt water and even less to explore the interior. Hearne's accomplishment was an exception to Company policy. A whole generation passed before Brunswick House on Moose River, Henly House on the Albany, Split Lake Fort on the Nelson, and Flamborough Factory on the Hayes were built, none of which was beyond two hundred miles from Hudson Bay and not really inland at all.

Fifteen years later, on the very eve of the Seven Years' War, Anthony Henday (Hendoy, Hendry) asked[4] and received permission to go inland from York.

Henday was an Isle of Wight man who had found the American wilderness a convenient asylum from a smuggling conviction. Little more is known about his early years. Like Hearne, he traveled with the Indians. When he arrived at the French posts at Pasquia (Basquia, The Pas) he was welcomed with much courtesy by the two Frenchmen on duty. After a short visit he crossed over to the Blackfeet and wintered about midway between the modern Calgary and Edmonton. Here he collected a cargo of excellent pelts and

[3] Edward Umfreville, *Present State of the Hudson's Bay Company* (London, 1790), p. 68.

[4] W. Stewart Wallace, *The Pedlars from Quebec* (Toronto: The Ryerson Press, 1954), says that Henday was sent inland, thereby inferring that the Company took the initiative. The question seems moot.

with high spirits started for York in the spring of 1755. He stopped again at the French posts and again was received with courtesy—but with a difference. The French boldly told him he was trespassing and that he was to be arrested and sent to France. They would retain his pelts.

Henday laughed at their threats but the "Pedlars," as the English called the French Canadians, had the last word—they had brandy! And when Henday finally reached York the Pedlars had his choice furs, the Indians had brandy, and Henday had a few coarse furs for a year's work.

Henday told his employers the Indians preferred to trade with the Canadians; that their merchandise was now as good or better than Company stock and was freighted direct to the natives, thus saving them the weary trip to salt water and return. Furthermore, "The French speak several [Indian] languages to perfection. They have the advantage of us in every shape; and if they had Brazile tobacco, . . . [they] would entirely cut off our trade."[5] Officials at York did not take kindly to such news. They gave Henday a paltry twenty pounds and denied him permission to make a second trip. He quit. And the Great Company settled back to enjoy its "monopoly" and watch its dividends shrink.

As soon as the Treaty of Paris removed French power in North America, Scotch traders, representing the very essence of individualism, moved

[5] Pinkerton, *op. cit.*, p. 90.

into the vacancy to exploit the western fur country. As ancient enemies of the English these new pedlars delighted in hiring the stranded French trappers and, with them, attacking the Company on its own ground.

Alexander Henry, the elder, moved into Michilimackinac even before the treaty and Thomas Corry (Curry) and James Finlay were on the Saskatchewan in 1766. By the time Hearne got back from the Arctic the pedlars had launched a full-scale invasion. In 1772 one François reached Finlay's house on the Saskatchewan and Peter Pangman and Joseph Fulton were at Fort Dauphin.

Mathew Cocking, Company factor, said François was an "ignorant Frenchman, seemingly above sixty years of age," and had been "thirty years upon this business." If true, he well may have been with Vérendrye.

These pedlars had more than courage—they had a delightful impertinence. A few months after he arrived at Fort Dauphin, Peter Pangman showed up at York with a valuable catch and Ferdinand Jacobs reported, "We had one Peter Pangman, a petty pedler, down here to spy out the Market. With advice of the Council, I seized the furrs; gave him a good supply of goods to carry him back again & notice to him and another pedler to move off the Company's land."

But Pangman did more than "spy out the Market." He asked Jacobs to ship the Pangman pelts to market on Company boats and thereby relieve Pangman of the long canoe haul to Montreal!

If Peter Pangman was a "petty pedler," the three Frobisher brothers (Benjamin, Thomas, and Joseph) were not. Benjamin remained in Montreal and Thomas and Joseph assailed the Company. They had tried to get beyond Michilimackinac in 1764 but the recent wars had upset Indian relations and their hostility defeated the brothers. Nine years later conditions had improved and Thomas and Joseph reached Fort Dauphin and wintered there.[6] Thomas built a post on Pine Island Lake, about ten miles east of the future Cumberland House of the Hudson's Bay Company.

Alexander Henry, mentioned above, extended his interest to the prairies also, and either by design or happenstance, he and the Frobishers joined forces in 1774 and started for the Churchill River with only a one-meal food supply. This was a near-fatal mistake for when they reached the Churchill the Athabaska Indians failed to arrive and the traders changed their plans and headed up the river for Lake Athabaska, still without a food supply.

Eight days later they met some Chipewyans going to Fort Prince of Wales and stopped for a friendly chat and comradely drink. It would never do to overlook such an opportunity to outdo the Company. "On the third morning, this little fair was closed; and on making up our packs, we found that we had purchased twelve thousand

[6] There is a possibility that one or both of the brothers had gone to the Churchill River two years earlier. See Pinkerton, *Hudson's Bay Company*, p. 132.

beaver skins, besides large numbers of otter and marten," said Henry.

But there was no food and before the winter was over, one and perhaps more of their men starved to death and rumors of cannibalism reached England.

In the meantime the Henry-Frobisher combination met one Louis Primo and induced him to leave his temporary attachment to the Company and work for them. They sent him to build Fort La Traite on the Churchill in which to store the excess of their season's catch and from which they hoped to reach the Athabaska country. In the spring, however, starvation forced Joseph Frobisher back to the Saskatchewan. Later, he and Alexander Henry went to Grand Portage while Thomas built another house on Lake Isle a la Crosse, well on the way to the Athabaska region.

This early combination of the Frobishers and Henry is often considered the genesis of the formal North West Company which eventually forced the Hudson's Bay Company to merge with it several years after the death of Hearne.

Nor did the Company make any very serious attempts to curb these many challenges to its authority and profits. Once, to be sure, the Company tried coaxing the lesser invaders to desert to the English for higher wages and some of them did. But they could, and also did, desert a second time. Louis Primo, above, one of the more prominent of the interlopers, had defected to the Company. They sent him inland where he collected

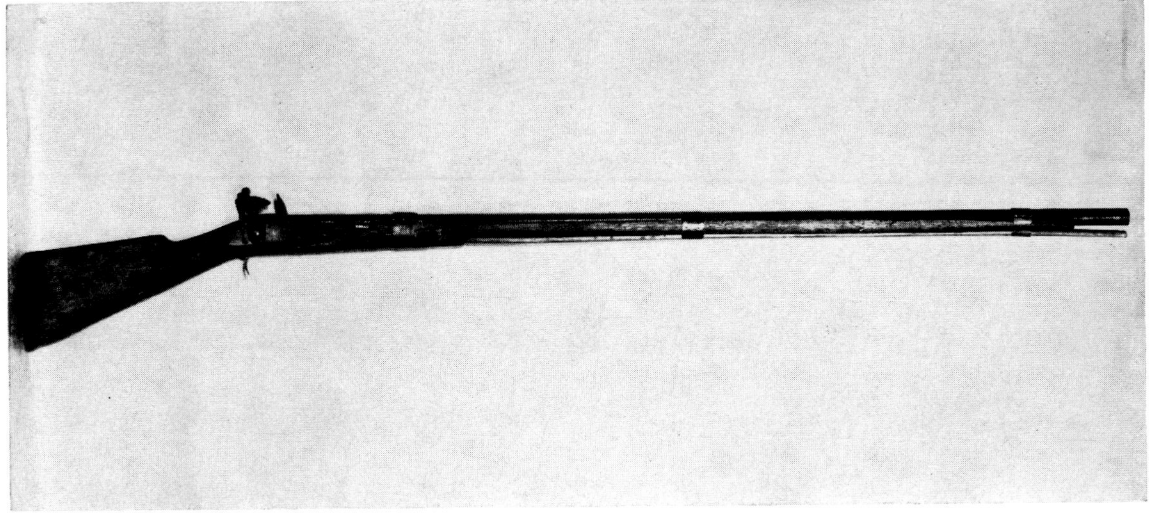

Courtesy The Royal Ontario Museum of Archaeology, Toronto, Canada

HUDSON'S BAY COMPANY TRADE GUN

With an .87 bore, it was sold to the Indians and Eskimos. Under normal conditions Company officers carried a gun with approximately twice this bore.

a valuable cargo in the Saskatchewan area and then met Mathew Cocking somewhere inland from York Factory. Primo brazenly told Cocking he had no intention of honoring his contract with the Company but was going to run away with their pelts to Montreal. And he did.

More or less garbled accounts of all such pedlar activities reached the bay and resulted in some desultory talk about moving inland to meet the competition but it seems to have never been more than talk. Certainly there is no present evidence that the Company considered doing anything about it and it is extremely doubtful if Andrew Graham, factor at York, expected anything to come of it when he wrote to the Committee in London partially as follows:

YORK FACTORY August 26th, 1772

HONOURABLE GENTLEMEN. . .

The Situation of your Affairs in the Country is very unpromising, I have not been Indolent, I have gained certain Information of what is doing inland, & I think it my Duty to lay before you the success of my Enquiry. Your Trade at York Fort and Severn is greatly diminished . . . being intercepted by the Canadian Pedlars who are yearly Gaining fresh Influence over them [the natives] by supplying them with Goods Inland . . . every Inducement to visit Company's Factorys is forgot, & prime furrs are picked out & traded, the refuse is . . . brought down to us. . ."

Graham went on to tell of the individual pedlars:

Thomas Corry . . . Messrs. Blandeau . . . George McBeath . . . Tod . . . John Erskine . . . & another French Gent^{n}.

Name unknown . . . not less than 500 packs of Furrs annually . . . sev[l]. tribes unknown at your Factorys have left their former Country, & drawn nigher the Canadian Settlements for the conveniency of Trade . . . this Information entirely agrees with the report of Bat & Primo [Company employees] who were coming down hither with 160 Canoes, but were met in the River de Pane by other Indians who told them that the Canadians were at the Cedar Lake, had Plenty of Goods & Spirituous Liquors, upon which they wheeled off to go thither notwithstanding all the Arguments of our Men to persuade them to the contrary.

The Indians that did come down never offered to deny having traded their prime Furrs with Canadians . . . & I overheard them say to each other "Purchase only this or that Articles as for the rest we can get them Yonder."

It appears to me . . . nothing will do but the making of a Settlement Inland . . . to supply . . . Ammunition Tobacco & Brandy, . . . without the latter the Indians would not resort to Your House if they could procure it elsewhere.

[The] Master of the Undertaking must be a Young, lively Person, that will continue some Years in your Service, I know no Person that would Answer so well as Mess[rs]. Hearne at Churchill & Mr. Hutchins at York Fort.

Graham added that he had sent Mathew Cocking, who by now had been as far as the Saskatchewan once or twice before, to the west to sort fact from fiction regarding the pedlars. The flag on Cocking's journal said, "Being the journal of a journey by Mr. Mathew Cocking . . . in order to take a view of the inland country, and to promote the Hudson's Bay Company interest, whose trade is diminishing by the Canadians yearly intercepting natives on their way to the settlements, 1772-1773."

And Cocking learned! "It surprises me," he said, "to perceive what a warm side the natives hath to the French Canadians."[7] He talked to the Indians and "The Natives all promise faithfully to go down to the [Company] Forts next year & not to trade with the Pedlars: but they are such notorious liars there is no believing them."

Not very good news to bring to Andrew Graham but there it was. And there could be no optimism about Company profits either.

Even allowing for the secrecy which the Company maintained regarding its affairs, enough is known to indicate wild fluctuations of income over the first century. The total original capital had been £10,000. Twenty years later profits were so high it seemed best to split the stock, three for one. In 1720 even this inflated stock was again split three for one plus 10 per cent. From 1670 to 1737 Company profits were 10 per cent or better on the outstanding stock.

Charles I had proscribed any material except beaver fur for men's hats and the beginnings of the English Industrial Revolution gave British goods a marked advantage over their French rivals. The future looked bright, indeed, for the "Gentlemen Adventurers."

For a pound of cheap tobacco they bought a

---

[7] E. E. Rich, *Hudson's Bay Company, 1670-1870* [Hudson's Bay Record Society Publications, Vols. 21-23] (London, 1959), II, 36, denies Cocking made such a statement.

prime pelt; for a cheaper "looking glass" and a comb they received two beaver; for a gun so poorly made it might explode at the first shot they charged twelve pelts.

Profits were very, very satisfactory.

Too satisfactory, in fact. For in the hope of seizing such an opulence the French attacked the Company posts and the independents invaded Company realm with the result that defense expenses plus the loss of pelts taken by others so sharply reduced income that Company solvency was threatened by the time Hearne returned from the Arctic.

Pedlar competition, a smallpox epidemic, Company hesitancy and the wars caused customs value to fluctuate between £5,000 and £38,000, and profits naturally reflected these volumes. No dividends were declared between 1782 and 1786, and other single years were omitted.

Debate over culpability for these reverses—and the remedies which should or should not have applied—has never ceased. Every new history of the Great Company presents an old or new blame or solution.

In any event, Company finances in the 1770's caused even the unimaginative Committee in London to concede that times had changed and something must be done or the Hudson's Bay Company would collapse.

Finally, then, the Committee looked at Andrew Graham's letter; checked the Company bank balance; clucked their annoyance at what they saw;

and told Ferdinand Jacobs, Chief factor at York, and Moses Norton at Fort Prince of Wales, to act immediately: send Samuel Hearne to establish a post "at or near Basquia," six hundred miles southwest of York in the very heart of pedlar land. Mathew Cocking was to help Hearne.

The spring mail of 1773 brought this decision and with it the usual impossible orders for work to be done in a wilderness as if that wilderness had paved streets, a call box on every corner, and Big Ben striking the hour.

Hearne and Cocking were to go to the interior in the summer of 1773, establish a permanent post, build canoes during the winter, and bring out the first load of furs in the summer of 1774. Hearne was to take latitude and longitude readings, record the names of all rivers and lakes, and make a survey of the pedlars.

To fulfill such orders was an impossibility. A glance at the map will disclose literally thousands of lakes, ponds, and rivers, most of them unnamed, except locally, even today. As for making a comprehensive study of the Canadians, Hearne would do well if he could keep his eye on them when they were his next-door neighbors, for these ubiquitous interlopers swarmed and squirmed over the fur land in such a complicated manner they were sometimes in competition with their own partners. Hearne could hope to do no more than get a general idea of their activities and Mathew Cocking had already delivered that data to Graham.

However, there is no evidence that Hearne challenged his orders. As a good explorer he had accepted impractical instructions for the Coppermine expeditions and quietly disregarded the sections he considered unrealistic. So, now, he entered heartily into his new assignment, reserving for his own judgment which of his latest orders to obey.

Governors Norton and Jacobs believed the new post could best be launched from York and, as we have seen, Samuel Hearne and Robert Longmoor arrived at York the last of August, 1773, pursuant to organizing the first major inland venture of the Great Company.

It had taken the Hudson's Bay Company a full century to begin the work of exploring their domain toward the Arctic and it was fitting that Samuel Hearne should also be assigned the task of establishing the Company's first real interior post.

CHAPTER TWENTY-THREE

Cumberland House Rescues the Great Company

IT WAS too late in the season of 1773 to arrange transportation for an inland trade venture and it was decided Hearne should spend the winter at York and leave for the interior in the spring of 1774. During the winter he would organize his expedition and attend to personal business.[1] He would go and come to Fort Prince of Wales and the Severn post, consulting Andrew Graham and Edward Umfreville, among others.

Graham, who had previously believed pedlar competition would die if the Company but remained firm on its coastal sites, had reversed his opinion and now favored inland posts. Even the rich Blackfeet pelts, currently going to the pedlars via the Saskatchewan and the Assiniboins, might be acquired by the Company if inland centers were properly located.

Hearne, therefore, had a certain positive cooperation from Company officials—Norton, Jacobs, Graham, Cocking, and others. This was important, for these men often competed savagely to make their own records look good and, had they chosen, could have seriously hindered Hearne.

---

[1] Among his personal affairs Hearne asked that a sum of money be transferred to his mother, who had remarried and was now Mrs. Dianna Paine, this simple fact being one of the few clues we have to her personal life.

As it was he had trouble: two of the great north canoes ordered for the inland trade had not arrived; and Jacobs and Graham argued over the loading schedule, food allowances, and size of packages, quite forgetting that Samuel Hearne had been farther inland than they and knew the Indians as well or better.

But Hearne's major difficulty came in the recruitment of his labor crew. London had suggested using a dozen or more Orkney men in addition to such veterans as Primo, Batt, Cocking, or Longmoor. It was hoped, too, that several of the pedlar employees would desert to the Company flag.

It was the Orkney men who proved justifiably stubborn. Many of them had left families on the islands and they wished their wages paid in cash there. The Company refused. Wages would be given only in goods at the Company posts on Hudson Bay where private trade was most harshly punished. Thus, excess goods were virtually useless to the men and the policy, in effect, gave the Company the Orkney services for little better than board, lodging, and clothes—a state of employment difficult to distinguish from certain forms of slavery.

Hearne complained that the "Orkney men are the quietest servants and the best adapted for this Country that can be procured; yet they are the slyest set of men under the Sun; and their universal propensity for smuggling, and Clandestin dealings of every kind, added to their Clannish attachment to each other, puts it out of the power of any one English man to detect them."[2]

Nevertheless, Hearne recruited them, albeit he had to promise a small increase in wages, after which he suggested to London that hereafter employees be required to serve inland if ordered to do so.

In the meantime he chose and catalogued supplies; readied a roster of his employees for the home office; made Isaac Batt and Mathew Cocking responsible for his chief freight; and ordered still other contingents to travel west with such Indians as came to the bay and were returning to their homes.

Hearne, himself, would precede these various parties and make such initial decisions as would facilitate the total undertaking.

And Samuel Hearne applied for the governorship of Fort Prince of Wales, should a vacancy occur.

> June 23, 1774. Fine pleasant Weather, in the Morning, self, Andrew Garret, and Robt Longoar [Longmoor] sot out from the Fort accompan'd by Me-sin-e-kish-ac an upland leading Indian, and 3 of his crew, also two of the home Indians, we were all in 5 canoes and tho deep laden we had but about 180 lbs Brazil Tobaco 130 lb's Powder 200^{wt} of Shott & Ball 6 Gall^{ns} Brandy, 6 D^{o} White Waters and some trifling articles of Trading goods. . . .

Hearne also had carpenter tools and "2 Pecks

---

[2] E. E. Rich, *Hudson's Bay Company, 1670-1870* [Hudson's Bay Record Society publications, Vols. 21-23] (London, 1959), II, 128.

of Oatmeal and 12 lb of Bisquett"—not much of a food supply but beyond tidewater the rivers were too shallow for even this amount and he was forced to send part of his cargo back to the factory.

On this journey Hearne was not exploring except in so far as he was surveying a practical route to "Basquia." He went up the Hayes and Fox rivers; overland to the Nelson River; and then to Grass River. He was on Paint Lake July 15, on Setting Lake two days later; thence up the Grass some thirty-five miles and on through Reed and Cranberry lakes to Cranberry Portage, which separates the northeast-flowing rivers from those draining southwest and south. He paddled through "Athapuscow" and Goose lakes to the mouth of Goose River on the Sturgeon-Weir River, where he found nine tents of families belonging to his crew.

Tobacco was passed and the men settled down to talk—the burden of which was that the Hudson's Bay Company was too late; the Canadians were too well established; they were very generous, never accepting any pay for "Knives, Steels, Worms, Flints, awls Needles & Paint," and charged prices far below the Company for other articles of better quality.

Hearne was surprised and disturbed. It "gave me no little uneasiness to see so many fine fellows of Indians and their Families not only cloth'd with the Canadians goods finely ornamented, but ware also furnished with every other Necessary artical and seem'd not to be in want of anything."

After these disquieting talks Hearne moved down the Sturgeon-Weir River to Sturgeon Landing and learned of the Frobisher activities noted above.

Everything seemed to be going wrong. Rival traders were ahead of him; one site suggested by the Indians for the new post proved unsuitable because of lack of fuel; Batt and Cocking had not arrived; there was no game and food was gone, forcing the crew to eat a berry "which when eaten in so large a quantity as to stop hunger are such an astringent quality that me and my 2 men ware much disorder'd by them, at the same time hunger oblig'd us to have recourse to still greater quantity let the Consiquence Prove as it may."

Just before starvation forced Hearne to retreat, ten canoes of Indians paddled by with a supply of dried meat.

With hunger assuaged for the moment, Hearne moved to the Saskatchewan River and on down to Basquia, or The Pas, as we know it.

The Pas is a famous name in western Canadian history. Indians and whites had used the site for a long time. The banks of the river on the up side were low and muddy while below they faded off into indefinite marsh teeming with waterfowl.

Such men as Kelsey, Vérendrye, Henday, William Pink from York, Mathew Cocking, and others had been there before 1774.

Hearne found a lone chimney and the rotting remains of cabins but he was not impressed with The Pas as a site for a permanent Company post.

Returning to Carrot River he met Magnus

Slater and William Flatt with one of his freight divisions from York. They brought tobacco, a four-foot gun and assorted trade goods, and from them Hearne learned that Robert Flatt, with another cargo, had been plundered and abandoned by his Indians at the mouth of the Saskatchewan River. Hearne felt there was nothing he could do to rescue Flatt and he resumed searching for a location.

Sixty miles beyond The Pas and just east of the present-day Cumberland House, "I determin'd to build the house, at least for the insewing winter, at a Part Call'd Pine Island Lake . . . it is the general opinion of those Indians that that Part will be more commodious for Drawing the Indians then Basquia, it laying in the Middle between three Tribes."

Now every day was crowded.

The Hudson's Bay Company's Cumberland House, as the post was named, was to be no temporary shelter; it was to last as long as the foreseeable future. A log tent with a "floar with Round loggs" must serve until squared timbers for the "Proper house," thirty-eight by twenty-six feet, were hewn out and put together. Indian bands came and went; trading for pelts began; and the food supply fluctuated according to Indian willingness to sell their meat.

On October 9, the Frobishers, William Holmes, François, and Charles Paterson landed with seven canoes—and Robert Flatt. François and Paterson had come upon Flatt, rescued him, brought him

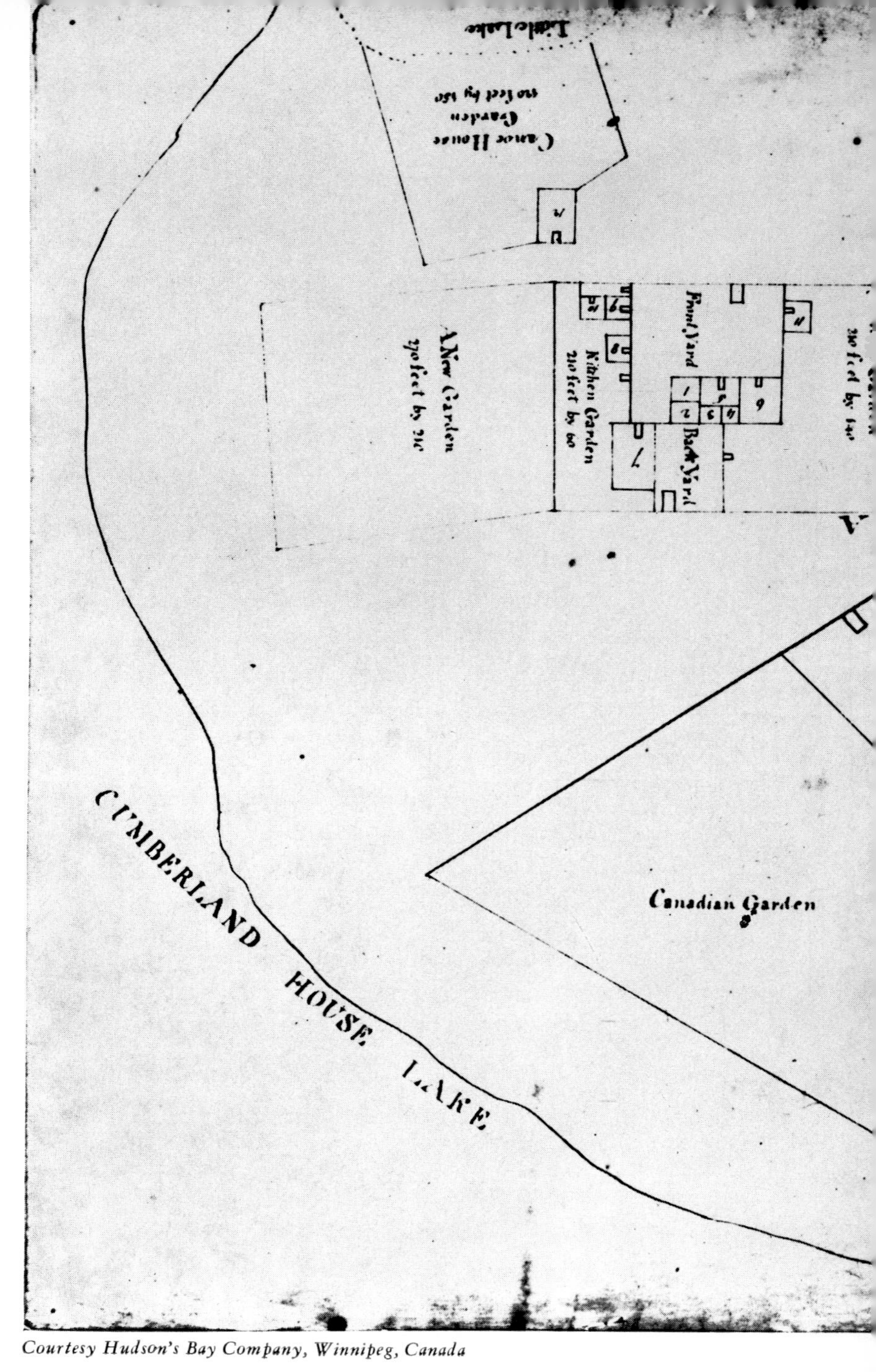

Courtesy Hudson's Bay Company, Winnipeg, Canada

PLAT OF THE GROUNDS AT CUMBER

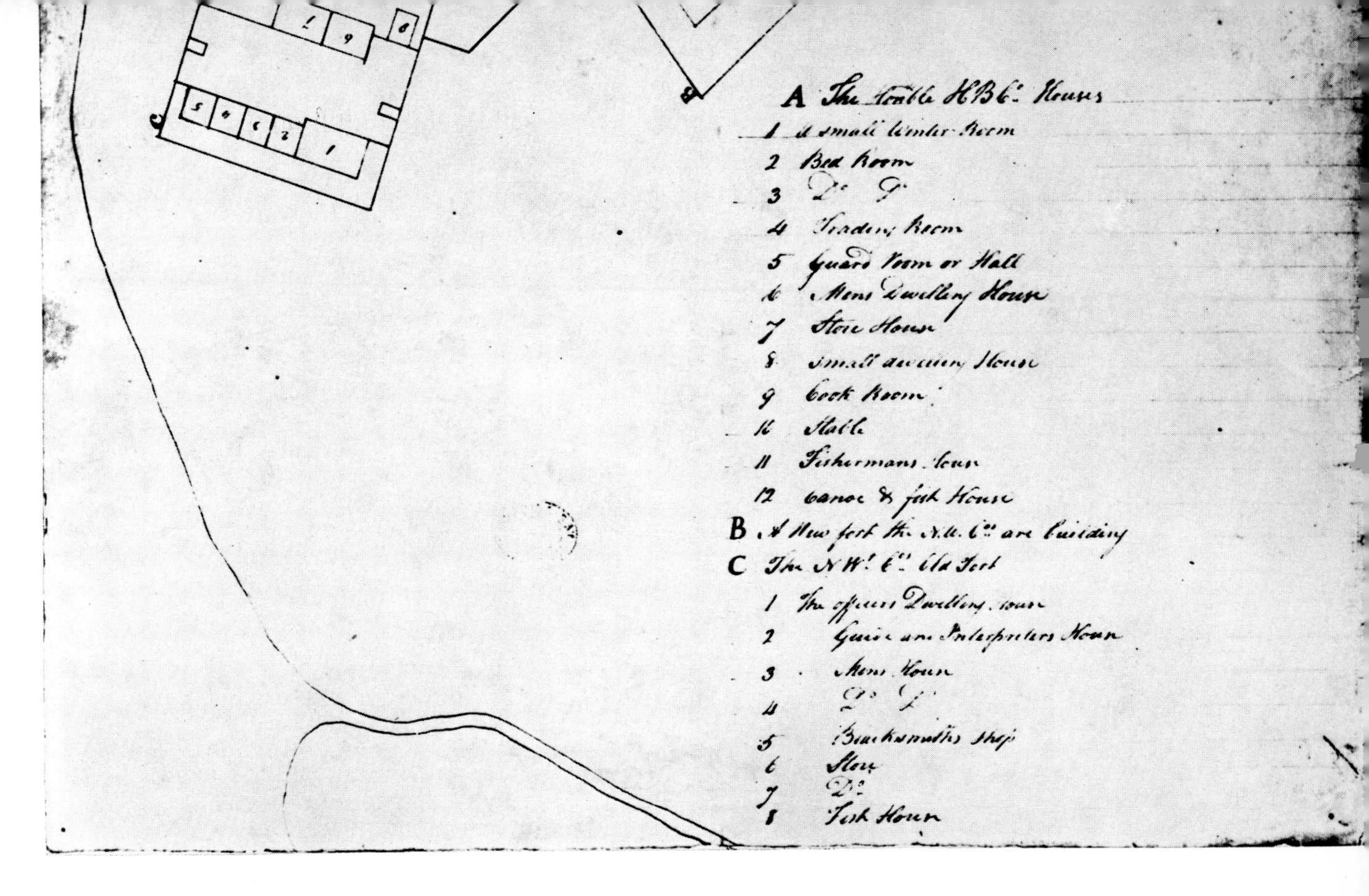

USE AT THE TIME OF HEARNE'S REGIME

to Hearne, and now generously refused any reimbursement, even for the clothes they had supplied Flatt. In addition, they invited Hearne to "sup with them which as they ware so near I did not think any harm in accepting of."

As far as we know, this was Hearne's first meeting with the pedlars; his first glimpse of their goods; and probably his first acquaintance with their freight canoes made of birch bark little thicker than a piece of paper: twenty-four feet long, four to five feet wide, twenty inches deep, and manned by four canoemen, each dressed as gaudily as circumstances and his purse would permit. Despite their fragility the canoes carried sixty to seventy packs of goods plus ten weeks' provisions—in all, approximately four thousand pounds.

Hearne was impressed.

The visiting pedlars moved on and late on the evening of October 17, seven more canoes arrived from York bearing congratulations on the establishing of Cumberland House. They hoped that Cocking had finally got through (which he had not); they unloaded thirty-five gallons of brandy, over two hundred pounds of tobacco, and a quadrant.

By late October Pine Island Lake was frozen over and all the Indians were gone "Except 2 or 3 Women who Stays to Make, Mend, Knitt snowshoes && for us dureing the Winter."

A starving Indian family across the lake was given emergency food; in mid-December one of the Frobishers, very near starvation, applied for help and Hearne gave him the same as for his own men, "being but two Scanty meals p[r] Day."

And the holidays came and went with little attention. The journal entry for Christmas: "Sunday the 25th Ditto Weather."; for New Year's: "Sunday the 1st of January, 1775. Fine clear Weather."

All but three or four of Hearne's men were scattered over a wide area searching for game in the bitter cold. Those remaining at the post complained and blamed Hearne for their hunger. All he could say was that he had no more than they.

"Robert Longmoor having ben a hunting came home at Night with both his big Toes much froze. . . . I lay'd [his] Toes open which are froze to the Bone . . . [and applied the] inner Rind of the Larch Tree Root which is generally us[d] among the Natives to stop or Prevent a Mortification."

Despite the hunger and cold, Hearne, suddenly stern and demanding, compelled his men to work twelve-hour shifts and they rightly complained that this was longer than they worked at York. But Hearne was determined that Cumberland House should not fail and he drove them on without respite. This harsh leadership succeeded. The post was firmly established, many pelts were collected, and when the ice was gone and the rivers high enough to float heavy-laden canoes, May 29, 1775, "I this day about Noon embark'd for the Fort [York] in Company with 32 canoes of Indians, 17 of which are to accompany me to the Fort."[3]

The new post was left in charge of Andrew Garret (Garrioch in some accounts) and "Mag^{n} Slater & Wm Flatt also stays with him."

Hearne arrived at "York Fort about 6 in the evening of the 24" of June and presented his report: He had seen the work of the Frobishers, François, Paterson, Holmes, Pangman, William Bruce, Barthelemi Blondeau, and James Tate, to mention a few; the Canadians would trade at the nearest post; they did tent-to-tent trading and the Company must do the same; birch-bark canoes were the only satisfactory ones but were difficult to acquire; the Company should have more inland factories and it should resolve the difference in prices and qualities of goods between it and the Canadians.

The Company was not immediately convinced of the wisdom of these judgments.

Hearne remained at York only from June 24 until July, when he started for Cumberland House again.

On this second journey he tested the practibility of another route: up the Nelson River, through Gull and Split lakes, to the mouth of Grass River, to Cranberry Portage, Goose Lake and Goose River, and southwest to Cumberland House via the modern Namew Lake.

---

[3] Hearne is reported to have said that had he been given a satisfactory subcommander he would have surveyed possible sites for subsidiary posts to supplement Cumberland House. See Rich, *The Hudson's Bay Company, 1670-1870*, II, 64.

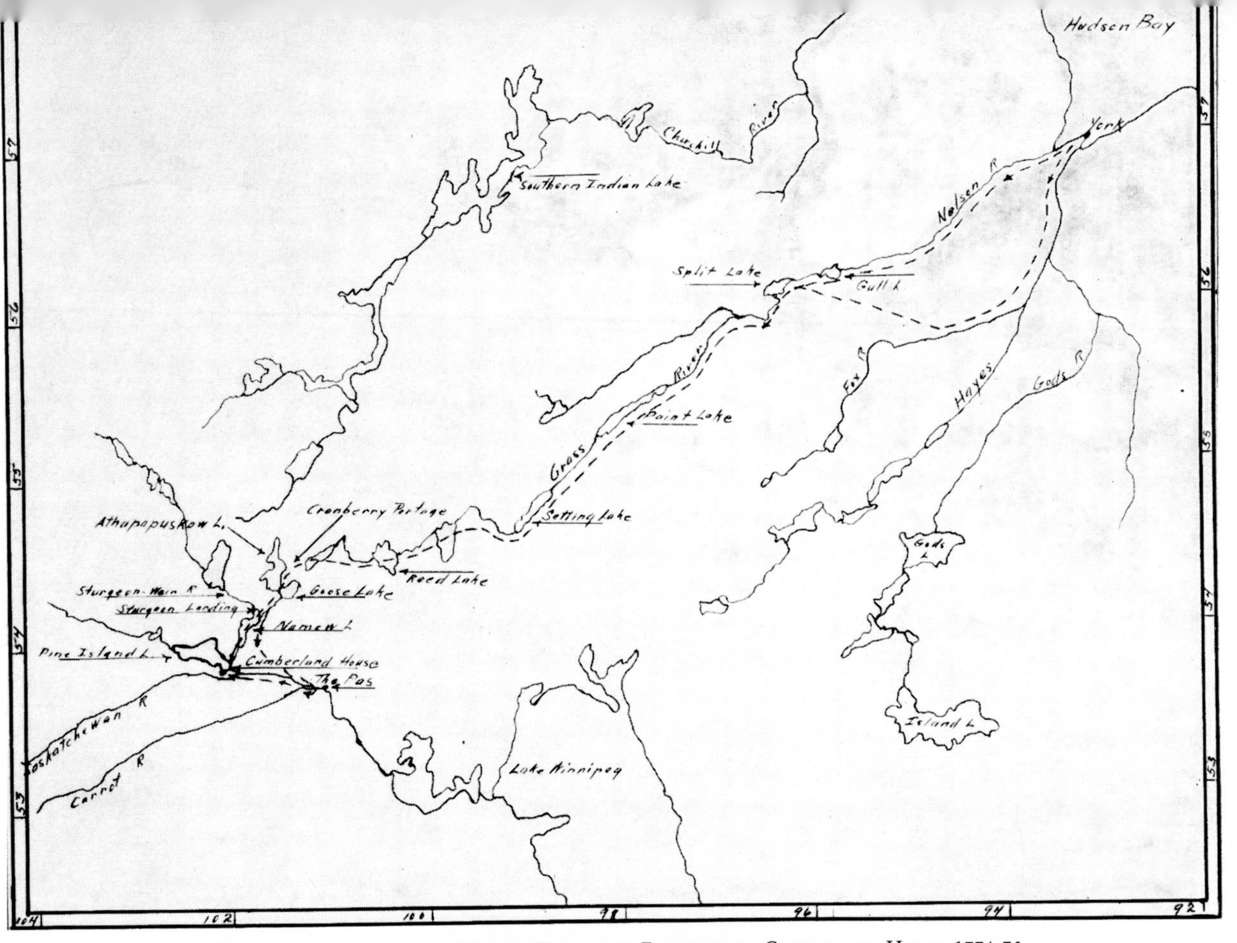

The Approximate Routes Used by Hearne in Establishing Cumberland House, 1774-75

There was little of interest on the way except trouble with the Indians who broke into the liquor "Kaggs" when Hearne was out of sight, got drunk, tried to abandon the freight, got caught, and then demanded still more liquor.

A scuffle ensued but "we being all sober and they much intoxicated" no "affensive Weapons" were needed—"only gave them a little old English Play, which had so good an effect that we soon drubbed them into seeming good humour again, tho some of them ware a little sulky."

Hearne was at Cumberland House in time for breakfast August 19, and resumed command until October when Cocking finally arrived fresh from York with the following letter:

York Fort August 25th 1775

Mr Samuel Hearne
Sir

The Committee of the Honourable Hudson's Bay Company having appointed you chief of Prince of Wales's Fort, and desired us to inform you of their intentions with the utmost dispatch and appoint a Proper person to succeed you at Your Settlement Inland, we have in obediance to these orders sent Mr Cocking to succeed you, to whome you will please deliver the said Settlement, together with all the Trading goods, Stores, Provisions & Furs now in your possession, taking a Receipt for the same. Inclosed you will Receive their Hounors Letter and all others, but in your own breast it remains either to touch here, or proceed directly to your Command. Mr Marten who succeeds Mr Jacobs at York Fort will esteem it as a perticular favour if when time will Permitt, you will point out to him your sentiments of the most prudent methods to be pursued to bring to Perfection the plan you have with such credit to yourself hitherto executed

Courtesy Hudson's Bay Company, Winnipeg, Canada

CUMBERLAND HOUSE, 1875

From the *Canadian Illustrated News*

Wishing you a happy and speedy passage down, we Remain

SIR

Your Sincear Friends
FERDINAND JACOBS
HUMPHREY MARTEN

Naturally Hearne was much pleased and began preparations to leave at once. Two days later he took the Grass River route for York, accompanied by the crew that brought Cocking out.

It was late in the season and they traveled whenever possible regardless of the time of day or night. On Paint Lake the ice was already so thick they had to break their way through and when they reached the Nelson River via Gull Lake it was so much frozen they abandoned their canoes sixteen miles from York.

The weather detained Hearne there until after New Year's, when he left for the Churchill where he arrived January 22, 1776.

Thus Hearne pioneered in the movement that marked the turning point in the career of the Hudson's Bay Company.[4]

Samuel Hearne bridged a transition period in the story of the Hudson's Bay Company. He entered the service when it was characterized by inertia, lack of vision and temerity. He furnishes the first known example of that loyalty which much later was to become the Company's chief glory. He pioneered in the ultimate extension of trade into the heart of Rupert's Land. . . .[5]

---

[4] M. Catherine White, *David Thompson's Journals Relating to Montana and Adjacent Regions* (Missoula: Montana State University Press, 1950), p. xi.

[5] Robert E. Pinkerton, *Hudson's Bay Company* (New York: Henry Holt and Company, 1931), p. 106.

> The Company's success . . . sprang in no small degree from the timely foundation of Cumberland House in 1774. Had this step not been taken when it was taken, the Company's chance of surviving . . . would have been greatly reduced.[6]

To this extent then, the Great Company itself may be said to be Samuel Hearne's monument.

---

[6] R. Glover, *Cumberland House, The Beaver* (Winnipeg), December, 1951, p. 4.

CHAPTER TWENTY-FOUR

Hearne Becomes Governor of Fort Prince of Wales

SAMUEL HEARNE accepted his new charge with only a sampling of his predecessor's invoice and became governor of Fort Prince of Wales, January 22, 1776, eight months after the beginning of the American Revolution split the British empire in North America into two warring parts, a fact which was one day to play an historic role in the reputation of Hearne.

As new governor Hearne received fresh instructions from the home office: he was to continue preceding policies especially as they applied to the whaling industry; he was to keep the various tribes at peace "as the principal means of the Company availing themselves of the Trade of that extensive Country"; and he was to push "all Inland Discoveries as the surest means of promoting Our Trade and the Public Interest."

Such instructions did not quite meet all the needs as Hearne found them. The Canadians were cutting ever deeper into Company business and the Hudson's Bay men were forced farther and farther up the streams to get above their rivals. These lengthening supply lines brought the obvious difficulties and others not so readily apparent, e.g., as the men moved farther away from the coast they came in contact with new place names and new tribes. In consequence, each report to London, via the Churchill or York, was a hodgepodge of terms almost unintelligible to the central office.

Faced with a hopeless task of administration unless this difficulty was resolved the Committee wrote to William Wales asking for three surveyors to explore and draw maps of the Company's inland domain.

Only one man, Philip Turnor,[1] who had done other work around Hudson Bay, was finally chosen for this immense task, May 6, 1778 — a trenchant bit of evidence regarding London's failure to understand the size of interior North America despite all that Samuel Hearne had done to enlighten them.

In fact, Hearne had already covered much of the ground Turnor was to survey but Hearne's word was constantly challenged by Dalrymple, hydrographer for the Crown. And the issue was eventually further clouded by a map of the west drawn by Peter Pond.

Pond had entered the west, 1775, and wintered on Lake Dauphin. He spent two seasons near the mouth of the Sturgeon River; he crossed the Methy range to the Athabaska country, 1778, and built a post some forty miles south of Lake Athabaska. He had moved north to the lake; traded on Peace River and perhaps got to Great Slave Lake. He spent the winter of 1787-88 with Alexander Mac-

---

[1] Sometimes Turner in early Canadian references. See, *Index and Dictionary of Canadian History* (Toronto, 1911), p. 389.

kenzie at Athabaska and then about 1790 was forced from the fur business because of implications in two murders, although his guilt or innocence was never proved.[2]

None of this would have been important except that Pond, using an erroneous formula for estimating distances, had drawn a map of the fur country on which he showed Lake Athabaska much too close to the Pacific. When this map was used in conjunction with Captain Cook's charts of the Northwest Coast, Lake Athabaska appeared to be only one hundred miles from the Pacific Ocean, an acute difference with the reports of Hearne.

Dalrymple sided with Pond. It was this impasse which is generally conceded to be the basis for Turnor's assignment.[3] He was to settle the location of Athabaska, among many things, and vindicate either Dalrymple or Hearne.

The subsequent work of Philip Turnor, extending from Hudson Bay to Athabaska, Great Slave Lake, and Peace River, and continuing well beyond Hearne's rule on the Churchill, has no place in this volume except to note that, in general, he supported Hearne's reports and charts.

During the years Turnor was surveying, Hearne carried on routine business. He believed that "By proper attention to cleanliness and keeping the people at reasonable exercise" he had defeated the

---

[2] W. Stewart Wallace, *The Pedlars from Quebec* (Toronto: The Ryerson Press, 1954), pp. 19-20.

[3] David Thompson, *David Thompson's Narrative of His Explorations in Western America, 1784-1812;* edited by J. B. Tyrrell (Toronto: Champlain Society, 1916), p. 28.

Courtesy Geological Survey of Canada, Ottawa

DIVIDE BETWEEN MACKENZIE AND COPPERMINE RIVERS

scourge of scurvy, although his own health was so precarious he contemplated resigning his command. He continued his predecessor's policy and sold lumps of sugar, grains of coffee, pepper, cloves, tea, nutmeg, or ginger to the Indians as potents against the evil eye, bears, barrenness, or difficult labor.

And he devised a skiff to replace the birch-bark canoes. They were to be prefabricated in London, be light enough for two men to carry, and sturdy enough to bear a ton of freight. The inland men and certain other governors objected but the home office backed Hearne and the first skiffs were shipped to Hudson Bay in 1777. From them may have evolved the famous York boats which eventually did supplant the great canoes.[4]

Trade surged up and down, with more declines than advances, and the Committee tended to blame Hearne. He countered with a renewal of his recommendation that common wages be raised to improve morale and that more inland factories be established up the "Theiscatchiwan River, near Messrs. Patterson, Homes, Pangman &c also that valuable Branch of Trade so intersepted by Joseph Forbersher to the westward of Churchill River. . . ."[5]

Hearne disputed with Humphrey Marten at York as to which post certain Indians should bring

[4] See R. Glover, *Cumberland House, The Beaver* (Winnipeg), December, 1951, p. 7.

[5] *Cumberland and Hudson House Journals,* Series I (London: Hudson's Bay Record Society, 1951), p. xxxi-xxxii.

Courtesy Hudson's Bay Company, Winnipeg, Canada

A Famous "York Boat"

These boats delivered many fortunes in furs to Company posts on Hudson Bay

their furs; he raised a few turnips and planted a few peas; Matonabbee drifted into the fort now and again and one day exacted an outrageous tribute of 7 lieutenant coats, 15 common coats, 18 hats, 8 guns, 140 pounds of powder and shot, some hatchets, ice chisels, files, knives, tobacco, yardage, blankets, combs, mirrors, stockings, handkerchiefs and 400 "Beaver worth" of additional goods—all as the price of abstaining from trade with the pedlars!

In 1781 the Company suggested that the annual sloop be sent to the head of Chesterfield Inlet but Hearne said there were far too few Indians there to make it worthwhile and that the time lost would prevent the sloop from completing the regular tour, thus losing money on both counts.

Then someone in London thought that since Captain Cook had reported sea otter on the Pacific coast Hearne should hunt them in Hudson Bay, and again it was his ill fortune to disagree with his superiors because there were no sea otter in the bay.

These constant differences of opinion might ultimately have undermined Company confidence in Hearne but before that situation could develop the American Revolution had exploded from an isolated riot into an international war. France and Spain, ancient enemies of England, saw their opportunity to settle old scores and entered the lists with a relish, and just before the defeat of England, the French admiral, Count de La Perouse, as an ally of the revolting colonies, sailed into Hudson Bay, purportedly flying false English colors.

C H A P T E R   T W E N T Y - F I V E

Hearne Surrenders Fort Prince of Wales

ON FEBRUARY 6, 1778, France signed two treaties with the rebelling colonies in the New World which, in effect, permitted France to help them as openly as she had been doing surreptitiously. Pursuant to these agreements, Jean François de Galaup, Count de La Perouse was dispatched in 1782 to capture the British forts in Hudson Bay, with special emphasis on York and Fort Prince of Wales.

La Perouse had three ships: the *Sceptre,* 74 guns; the *Astarte,* 36 guns; and the *Engageante,* also with 36 guns. In addition La Perouse carried four field pieces, two mortars, and three hundred bomb shells.

La Perouse arrived on Hudson Bay in full strength and anchored four miles north of Fort Prince of Wales. The following day he sent a boat to sound the river. The third day he landed four hundred men on the mile-long spit leading to the fort.

Samuel Hearne opened the gates and surrendered.[1]

---

[1] Some reports say Hearne negotiated for terms and won some concessions. La Perouse said, "The governor and garrison surrendered at discretion." See *Cumberland and Hudson House Journals,* Series I (London: Hudson's Bay Record Society, 1951), p. lxxxvii.

La Perouse loaded his booty on board, burned what he could of the fort, took Hearne prisoner, repeated his foray at York, taking Governor Humphrey Marten prisoner, and sailed for Hudson Strait September 2.[2]

La Perouse was towing the Fort Severn sloop which he had captured at York. On September 10 he was off Cape Resolution where he allowed Hearne, Marten, and thirty-one other prisoners to take the sloop and sail for England. They arrived at Stromness, Orkney Islands, October 15.[3]

Three days later Hearne wrote a letter to the Company which was read before the Governor and Committee a month later.[4] Existing Company records do not indicate the contents of the letter but logic would certainly argue that Hearne made a report on and defense of his surrender.

Shortly after Hearne sent his report to London the sloop sailed from Stromness for the Thames, "Having a Proper pass from Monsieur Laperouse,"[5] presumably to clear the French blockade of the North Sea. When the sloop arrived in England is not known.

"It will be seen from the above . . . that neither Samuel Hearne nor Humphrey Marten . . . were taken to France as prisoners."[6]

---

[2] H.B.C. Arch. B. 239/a/81. Published by permission of the Governor and Committee of the Hudson's Bay Company.

[3] H.B.C. Arch. E. 2/12, H.B.C. Arch. C. 1/386. By permission.

[4] H.B.C. Arch. A. 1/142, p. 54. By permission.

[5] H.B.C. Arch. C. 1/386. By permission.

[6] R. A. Reynolds, Secretary, Hudson's Bay Company, Beaver House, Great Trinity Lane, London, July 29, 1955.

Contradictions appear to exist in Company records since reputable scholars sometimes present widely differing views to the above.[7]

Hearne's whereabouts and his actions after his return to England are not clear. He seems to have been in London for John Deseret, Company Secretary, wrote to Hearne, presumably at a London address, on November 28, 1782, and requested his opinions regarding rebuilding Fort Prince of Wales.[8, 9]

One more positive item is recorded: On January 7, 1783, the Company wrote to the Royal Government and asked it to honor an agreement Hearne and Marten had made with La Perouse calling for the English to release as many French prisoners as La Perouse had done off Cape Resolution.[10] Whether the Crown honored this request is not evident.

These are the known facts regarding the surrender of Fort Prince of Wales.

---

[7] One authority suggests that the Company ransomed Hearne and other prisoners, while another scholar insists that Hearne was taken to France as a prisoner. See Captain James Knight, *The Founding of Churchill, being the Journal of* [the author], *Governor-in-chief in Hudson Bay;* with a historical introduction and notes by James F. Kinney (Toronto: J. M. Dent & Sons, 1932), p. 107. See also E. E. Rich, *The Hudson's Bay Company, 1670-1870* (3 vols.; New York: The Macmillan Company, 1961), II, 83-88.

[8] H.B.C. Arch. A. 5/2, fo. 80. By permission.

[9] This letter to Hearne has sometimes been invested with a flavor of mystery and reputedly addressed to Hearne at Gosport, England. See Samuel Hearne, *Journals of Samuel Hearne and Philip Turnor;* edited with introduction and notes by J. B. Tyrrell (Toronto: Champlain Society, 1934), pp. 30-31.

[10] H.B.C. Arch. A. 5/2 fo. 83 d. By permission.

Hearne never attempted publicly to defend his actions, although others were free to criticize.

David Thompson said, years later:

> Hearne . . . allowed the french boat to sound the River . . . without firing a . . . shot; [thus] Admiral De la Peyrouse judged what kind of Commander . . . he had to contend with; . . . he landed four hundred men, who marched on the Fort. . . . The men in the Fort begged . . . Hearne to . . . mow . . . the French with . . . grape shot [but] he refused; [and] surrendered at discretion.
>
> Mr. Hearne was . . . looked upon with compt by the french [and] . . . as soon as the Hudson's Bay Company could do without his services they dismissed him for cowardice.[11]

Beckles Willson used such terms as "panic stricken," "craven" and the "Governor's cowardice" and John Townsend, Company employee, said, "our fort would have outlasted their ammunition."[12]

Sir Edmund Walker, ex-president of the Champlain Society, said, "Hearne, mightier with the pen than with the sword . . . ingloriously dies out of history."[13]

With these judgments we must disagree. To follow Hearne in the Seven Years' War, then to Bloody Falls and the Arctic and Great Slave Lake and Cumberland House and back to Fort Prince

---

[11] J. B. Tyrrell, ed., *David Thompson's Narrative of His Explorations in Western America, 1784-1812* (Toronto: Champlain Society, 1916), pp. 9-11.

[12] Beckles Willson, *The Great Company* (New York: Dodd, Mead & Co., 1906), p. 323.

[13] Samuel Hearne, *A Journey from Prince of Wales's Fort in Hudson's Bay to the Northern Ocean in the Years 1769, 1770, 1771, and 1772;* new edition with introduction, notes, and illustrations by J. B. Tyrrell (Toronto: Champlain Society, 1911), p. vii.

of Wales and accuse him of being a coward is an absurdity.

What, then, were his reasons? We do not know, but we may make such deductions as the known facts permit:

La Perouse was in sight with three ships and 146 guns; Hearne had 40 guns; La Perouse had more than 400 men; Hearne had 39. Hearne had repeatedly demonstrated that he held a profound regard for human life and that he was under the influence of the French intellectuals, especially Voltaire. David Thompson, the apprentice who later became world-famous as a surveyor and explorer, witnessed that on one occasion Hearne took Voltaire's *Dictionary* and said, ". . . here is my belief, and I have no other."[14, 15] It is possible, therefore, that Hearne, believing his forces hopelessly outnumbered and outgunned, agreed with the philosophers and considered the lives of thirty-nine men more valuable than bundles of fur.

"Resistance would have made good reading today, and would have been folly at the time."[16]

Nor could La Perouse have viewed Hearne with contempt. The Count treated his prisoner with the greatest kindness, permitted him to take his personal belongings on board the flagship, *La*

---

[14] J. B. Tyrrell, ed., *David Thompson's Narrative of His Explorations in Western America, 1784-1812* (Toronto: Champlain Society, 1916), p. 11.

[15] Samuel Hearne may have been an athiest but there are numerous respectful references to the Diety throughout his journals, especially the 1795 edition. See also the Dublin edition, 1796, p. 127n.

[16] Robert E. Pinkerton, *Hudson's Bay Company* (New York: Henry Holt and Company, 1931), p. 109.

Sceptre, and, once away from Hudson Bay, read Hearne's journals and extracted a promise from Hearne that he would edit and publish them as soon as he was free to do so.[17]

Such acts are not motivated by contempt.

Nor will Mr. Thompson's, ". . . as soon as the . . . Company could do without his services they dismissed him for cowardice," stand the test of accuracy for no sooner had peace been declared than the Company sent Hearne back to the bay to reestablish Fort Prince of Wales and remain as governor although they had readily available such men as Jefferson, Cocking, Isham, and Longmoor, whom they could have named to the Churchill post—as indeed they did when Hearne's health made it imperative that he retire.

It appears, then, we are forced to accept two facts: Hearne's exact and total reason for surrendering the great stone fort are unknown to date, and, he must have had such reasons that when he presented them to the Company they accepted them as adequate and sent him back to Hudson Bay to repair the damage as best he could and carry on for the Company.

---

[17] The New York Historical Society records contain a note stating that Albert Gallatin met La Perouse at Machias, Maine, where La Perouse told Gallatin that he had specified Hearne's journals were to be published as a condition of the latter's release. See Edward Weber Allen, *The Vanishing Frenchman, the Mysterious Disappearance of Laperouse* (Rutland, Vermont: Charles E. Tuttle Company, 1959), pp. 153-55.

CHAPTER TWENTY-SIX

Hearne Retires to London

THE Treaty of Paris, 1783, ended the American Revolution and Samuel Hearne was back on the Churchill River the same year, September 14. He carried orders to choose a site for a new Fort Prince of Wales at the "most convenient Situation above Cockolds Point near or upon the place where the Old Wooden Factory stood," five miles up the river from the stone fort. Eleven days later he wrote, "We have erected the house on the very spot where the old wood Fort stood"—the spot James Knight had chosen more than sixty years before.

But affairs at the new fort did not go too well. The bitter ghosts of war and defeat seemed to hang about the northern post.

Fear of plundering French soldiers had driven Mary Norton, twenty-year-old daughter of Moses Norton, into the wilderness where she froze to death; Matonabbee came to the fort, found Hearne captured and the fort disabled, and knotted a rope about his neck and hanged himself, leaving his wives and children to starve outside the mighty stone walls; and there was not enough wood for fires and the men must move about constantly to stay alive. "I have known men to stand at the saw for only 20 minutes when their face & hands has been froze so they have been obligh'd to Retire to the Surgeon to have Such Cur'd or Cutt off &.," said James Isham, speaking of the Hudson Bay climate in general.[1]

By 1785 the Committee in London was said to be openly criticizing Hearne: Trade was still falling off and the profit ratio was down—it was his fault; he was too free with his gifts to the Indians—most certainly his fault; the general management of the industry on the bay was wrong—indubitably his fault.

But as we have seen, deterioration in the profit structure was well advanced even before the capture of Fort Prince of Wales. Only two years after Hearne had built Cumberland House the pedlars were boldly buying and selling on the very headwaters of the Churchill, and while the Company countered with Hudson House and another post far up the Saskatchewan River, the Canadians simply moved to the Peace River and north down the Mackenzie and the Company continued to lose valuable pelts day after day.

Sometime in the spring of 1780 one of the pedlars had been killed by the Indians and the resultant ill will forced all traders from a lucrative field.

In 1781 smallpox killed three fourths of the Chipewyans and before the shock of these losses

[1] E. E. Rich, ed., *James Isham's Observations on Hudson's Bay, 1743, and Notes and Observations on the Book entitled "A Voyage to Hudsons Bay in the Dobbs Galley, 1749"* (Toronto: Champlain Society, 1949), p. 67.

could be absorbed La Perouse had seized Fort Prince of Wales and York Factory.

"These disasters paralyzed the energies of the Hudson's Bay Company. . . ."[2]

Now, too, there were other factors contributing to the crisis. There was a general commotion among Company employees, a sense of ill-being, bred by the cold and long winter nights and nurtured by such autocrats as Humphrey Marten, who, since his release by La Perouse, had "become so rough and overbearing that life under him must have been anything but agreeable."[3] He beat the Indians without cause or mercy and they left the fort seething with hate; William Tomison, Chief Inland, resigned his command rather than do business with Marten and only reconsidered when London recalled Marten. This might have helped except that in a clumsy attempt to remedy all matters at once the Company shuffled personnel until no one was satisfied.

Obviously Samuel Hearne was not to blame for this chain of misfortunes but as a Company governor he must bear his share of executive wrath, guilty or no.

Hearne could be held responsible only for his lavish gifts to the Indians but even there he must outgive the pedlars or there would be no trade

[2] J. B. Tyrrell, ed., *David Thompson's Narrative of His Explorations in Western America, 1784-1812* (Toronto: Champlain Society, 1916), p. xxxv.

[3] *Ibid.*, p. xxvii.

Courtesy Hudson's Bay Company, Winnipeg, Canada

CUMBERLAND HOUSE, 1955

at all and the Company would need neither post nor governor on the Churchill.

Hearne received these criticisms as he always accepted censure: he defended himself with a simple statement of his case. It was a "duty incumbent on himself in vindication of his conduct to assert . . . that after nineteen years hard servitude in a variety of Stations and places of trust, he can with the strictest Truth and Boldest Confidence Assert" that he had always held the interests of the Company paramount. He would let history give the verdict on his management as he had on his explorations.

In 1786 Hearne pleaded ill health for the second time to the Committee and was finally permitted to turn over his accounts and his authority to William Jefferson and retire to London, 1787.

For five short years he lived in warmth amid the civilized amenities he had renounced half a lifetime before.

Very little is known regarding these five years. Between his retirement and 1789, when his account with the Company was closed, he drew approximately £600 as back wages, premiums, and dividends on Company holdings. Rumor says that bad loans caused him financial reverses but, like so many other statements made about him, this cannot be verified.

Regardless of the above, Hearne certainly worked on his journals, possibly in conjunction with Bishop John Douglas of Salisbury, who edited the first Hearne edition. Diocesan records presently available, however, appear to carry no reference to the Bishop's work.[4]

Another tale has it that Samuel Hearne became a member of the Bucks Club and if he did join the "famous and noble Order of Bucks"[5] he was entering very racy society. The Bucks have been described as a "spurious offshoot of the Freemasons,"[6] but they were primarily a drinking club. There were thirteen lodges of Bucks in London in 1770 and they had been meeting regularly at least since 1739. They met in taverns—the old Globe, the Thatched House on St. James Street, and the like.

The Bucks made no pretensions of unctiousness. They came together to drink, tell bawdy tales, get slightly or mightily drunk, and, as the night wore on, they would leave the seclusion of the dim, pungent old tavern and sally forth to the streets of London to make an unholy nuisance of themselves.

It cost a pretty penny to belong and attend meetings. Engraved invitations to their formal parties were common and a rule, or at least a positive custom, forbad a Buck to wear the same waistcoat more than once to the club. The quality of the liquor they drank and the crystal they smashed after every toast were presumably equal to their clothes.

---

[4] Diocesan Registry, Salisbury, Wilts, England, February 5, 1958.

[5] *Notes and Queries*, Series 9, IV, London, 1849, p. 333.

[6] *Ibid.*

It is almost impossible to imagine Samuel Hearne in such a company. On the American frontier where intense drinking was taken for granted he was almost a teetotaler; on a continent where sex was taken raw and unabashed he remained either celebate or so circumspect that no positive evidence whatever has come to light concerning his relations with women.

If Hearne joined the Bucks, why? What had they to offer that he wanted or enjoyed? He was nearing the end of his life and they were a young man's crowd. Hearne would surely have felt out of place among them. He was ill with a dropsical condition and could not have been very pleased staying out all night drinking huge quantities of liquor which he had so studiously avoided for forty years.

And yet—it would have been completely in keeping with the contradictions of the man to lead a singularly moral and abstemious life on the frontier and then join the Georgian rakes when he retired.

Be all that as it may, Hearne could not have been very happy during his retirement for day by day he must watch the dropsical swellings in his feet and legs point unerringly to the end which came in November, 1792.

"Though my discoveries are not likely to prove of any material advantage to the Nation at large, or indeed to the Hudson's Bay Company, yet I have the pleasure to think that I have fully complied with the orders of my Masters, and that it

Courtesy Canadian Wildlife Service, Ottawa, Canada

Indian Platform Cache

Note the notched pole ladder

has put a final end to all disputes concerning a North West Passage through Hudson's Bay."

Samuel Hearne had indeed put an end to any reason for a further search for a passage through North America.

There is no Anián.

But what else had he done? Historians have been strangely blind to his other achievements.

Samuel Hearne's work is best appreciated when compared with more celebrated names: Lewis and Clark, supported by forty-five trained and specially equipped men, departed from an established town and ended their journey on a coast already known to hundreds of mariners—they had crossed a continent and verified an assumed fact, that it could be crossed. Samuel Hearne traveled a similar distance through an unknown, frozen wilderness, without white companionship, and ended his trip on a shore never before visited by a civilized man.

Alexander Mackenzie traced a great river to the Arctic but did so only by a ruthless exploitation of the Indians along his way. Hearne reached the Arctic first, if by a lesser stream, and left a host of native friends.

Hearne drew the first extended map of the interior of northern Canada on which he placed Great Slave Lake, tenth largest in the world, and Dubawnt, among the earth's greatest fifty. He first delineated the rivers and topography of a region so vast that much of it is still uncharted.

His natural history of the vanished Chipewyans has never been surpassed, can never be recaptured.

Courtesy Canadian Wildlife Service, Ottawa, Canada

A STONE CACHE ON THE BARREN GROUNDS

His description of the great Barren Grounds is still authority.

His prefabricated freight skiffs led to a system of cargo movement equaled only by the birch-bark canoes and Mississippi flatboats.

The trappers' rendezvous at Pierre's Hole, Jackson Hole and the Popo Aggie have long passed into history, but Cumberland House saved the Great Company from failure and is rounding out a second full century of trading service.

Sacajawea guided Lewis and Clark for a few miles and is known in every hamlet of America. Matonabbee performed a greater service over more miles and for a longer time.

The Strait of Anián, Samuel Hearne, and Matonabbee! They do not deserve the near oblivion with which our century has surrounded them. One was a truly great chimera, one was a great and gentle man, one was a grand barbarian.

Courtesy Canadian Wildlife Service, Ottawa, Canada

Drying Caribou Meat on the Barren Grounds

Appendixes

J. B. TYRRELL

Joseph Burr Tyrrell was born in Weston, Ontario, 1858. By profession he was an engineer turned explorer and historian. He was attached to the Geological Survey of Canada and served with G. M. Dawson when he explored the Canadian Rockies in 1883. During the next ten years Mr. Tyrrell explored extensively in western and northern Canada. In 1893, he and his brother, Mr. J. W. Tyrrell, set out on a 3,200-mile canoe trip across the Barren Grounds from Lake Athabasca to Chesterfield Inlet. The next year he was again on the Barren Grounds and crossed and recrossed the area for a total of thousands of miles. On one excursion alone he traveled 750 miles by snowshoe.

For these services he was awarded the Back Premium by the Royal Geographical Society. In addition to the Back award Mr. Tyrrell was the recipient of almost every important honor in the field of exploration and engineering offered by Canada and the British Crown.

Mr. Tyrrell practiced as a mining engineer in the Klondike between 1898 and 1905, then moved to Toronto where he spent much time editing the journals of Samuel Hearne, Philip Turnor, and *Documents Relating to the Early History of Hudson Bay.* He wrote *David Thompson, Explorer,* and edited and wrote extensively in the field of Canadian history.

ROBERT LONGMOOR

Robert Longmoor entered the service of the Hudson's Bay Company in 1771 at York Factory. Samuel Hearne said, "He possesses a very essential qualification, which is, that of being universally beloved by the natives."[1]

Longmoor helped establish Cumberland House in 1774; lived at least part of 1775 with the Indians; went up the Saskatchewan River with James Spence and Malcolm Ross in 1776, and made a trip to the buffalo country the following year. He returned to the Saskatchewan River in 1778; helped William Tomison establish Hudson House in 1779; and was master there for two separate terms: 1780-81 and 1783-85. He built Manchester House; was second in command at Fort Prince of Wales; and in 1792 went to England. He returned to Hudson Bay as superintendent at York. For four years he was master at the Swan River post and between 1800 and 1804 was sent inland from York Factory. After this he

---

[1] J. B. Tyrrell, *David Thompson's Narrative of His Exploration in Western America 1784-1812* (Toronto: Champlain Society, 1916), p. xxviii.

was second in command at Island House on the Saskatchewan but was back at York the next year. Then for two years he was at Island House again, 1808-10.

At the end of this stint Longmoor retired and went to Europe but the New World held too strong a lure and he was back on a farm near Montreal in 1812.

MATHEW COCKING

Mathew Cocking first went to work for the Hudson's Bay Company as a "writer" at York Factory, 1765. Five years later he was second in command.

Twelve days after Hearne left for The Pas, Cocking, accompanied by James Lisk, also left York and about the same time Isaac Batt and Charles Isham started on the same mission, namely, to carry additional supplies and generally reinforce Hearne's efforts. The two parties started separately but contacted each other and traveled together for a short time, then separated again.

Cocking went up the Hayes River, through Knee and Oxford lakes, across a portage, over Playgreen Lake, past Norway House to Lake Winnipeg, then up the Saskatchewan River to Cedar Lake where he again came upon Batt and Isham, who had been deserted by their Indians.

This reunion posed a problem in ethics for Cocking. He could not take Batt and Isham with him for lack of room in his canoes; his own Indians would go no farther up the Saskatchewan; he had an obligation to support Hearne but he could not leave Batt and Isham to starve. His decision was to stay with Batt and let Hearne solve his problems alone.

In effect this decision created a sort of splinter expedition without any official sanction, with no orders and no program of operation, except that the Company wanted pelts. With that in mind the Cocking forces moved over to Lake Winnipegosis, Red Deer River and Red Deer Lake; found an old post built by the trader, Blondeau, about 1772; decided to move on to Swan River, then to the Assiniboine and so on until they had made a great circle around the Porcupine Mountains.

Cocking apparently disliked this area for he went back to God's Lake for the winter, where he was visited by Blondeau.

After the weather opened up Cocking started west again; picked up a rumor that "Franceway" had taken two Indian girls to Montreal to be sold as slaves; reached Red Deer River again; drifted along the shore of Winnipegosis and then to the mouth of the Saskatchewan. He met "Franceway," who was actually headed for the Grand Portage with 170 packs of fur at 90 pounds per pack, a sizable fortune. Cocking then started for York without making any further attempt to locate or help Hearne.

From Cumberland House Cocking moved up

the ladder of Company authority, becoming governor at Severn and finally master at York.

He died in 1799.

THE CARIBOU

The North American caribou was mentioned in Purchas' *Pilgrimes*, 1625, but Samuel Hearne was the first European to give a detailed description.

The caribou are divided into four main species and several subspecies but popular nomenclature tends to classify them only as woodland caribou or Barren Ground caribou.

The caribou are generally clove brown but with shadings of whites and grays according to individuals and seasons. They reach a height of four feet, have sturdy legs and splayed hoofs for better traction over the snow.

The bulls carry a fine spread of antlers and the cows a smaller version of the same, but no two sets on either sex are ever exactly alike, often the right and left branches differing. The antlers, as much as three feet long and seeming to overbalance the animal, grow at different rates and at different times. During the rut (which takes place on the Barren Grounds in late October and forms the second of two annual migrations) the bull's antlers are hard, clean, and polished while the velvet is still hanging in untidy strips from the cows. After the rut the bulls shed their antlers and as food becomes scarce they eat their cast-off finery. By the following August a new set is in full velvet but they are far from solid. When a bull trots by, the rack springs in and out with each step and the new antlers appear to be sensitive and tender. The bull will frequently turn his head, scratch the rack gently with a rear hoof, and then lower his head carefully among the low-growing shrubs where he feeds.

The caribou have a keen sense of smell, moderate hearing, and a deep sense of curiosity. When in large bands they will allow humans to approach so closely as to separate the herd into two parts, each part gazing intently at the interlopers.

They are fleet creatures and have been clocked at fifty miles per hour. On their annual migrations, which may be followed easily by the long parallel grooves worn in the tundra by the passage, they average twenty to forty miles per day.

They are a gregarious animal traveling in great bands of 100,000 or more and range west of Hudson Bay to the mountains and north to the Arctic. David Thompson, North West Company explorer and contemporary of Samuel Hearne, records that he once saw a band of migrating caribou 100 yards wide and 180 *miles* long, which he estimated as containing more than 3,500,000 animals.[1]

Fear of humans or the wish to avoid human habitations has nothing to do with their migration routes. They frequently go between the buildings of such settlements as Fort Chipewyan and Churchill; 75,000 of the animals annually cross

[1] J. B. Tyrrell, *David Thompson's Narrative of His Explorations in Western America* (Toronto: Champlain Society, 1916), p. 101.

the Hudson Bay Railway and they have been known to hold up airfield activities as their instincts followed trails older than the white man and his machines.

The animals prefer to cross rivers at falls or rapids, apparently attracted by the sound of rushing water. It was at these crossings where the Indians and Eskimos killed thousands of the caribou for the purpose of getting their annual supply of sinews, furs, and hides. Caribou thongs used by the Arctic explorer, Captain Back, in 1833 were still usable when found more than a century later.

The extremely low temperatures on the Barren Grounds, –45° to –60° F., accompanied by an average of three and one-half feet of snow, force the caribou into the spruce forests for protection. While the herds tend to remain in their own general areas, making their summer migrations to the farthest north and their rut migrations to a shallower penetration of the Barren Grounds, they do not invariably return to the exact feeding ground of the preceding year. They use the same locality for several seasons, then choose a different one many miles away for the next several years.

There is no established leader of a band; they are docile and rarely fight. Even during the rut the bulls engage only in sham battles, are seldom hurt, and serve the cows impartially. The cows care for their calves over a long period and have been seen to suckle a calf so large that when it rose from a semi-kneeling position it raised the hind legs of the cow off the ground.

For sake of the annual count made by the Canadian Wildlife Service the modern herds are named: The Great Bear, Hanbury, Athabasca, Churchill, Radium, Yellow Knife, Aberdeen Lake, and so on. The bands still roam the Barren Grounds but not in their original numbers. No one factor has been responsible for the decline. Disease has taken some; the wolves, bear, and golden eagle have pulled down a few; whaling fleets have used as much as 300,000 pounds of meat per winter; modern firearms have given the natives greater killing power; and the increase of human population on, or near, the caribou ranges have all contributed to the decline.

Nevertheless, the caribou still constitute an impressive item in the economy of the Canadian North. As late as 1954 approximately 20,000 people, both native and white, were dependent to a greater or less extent on the caribou for food and winter clothes and the present annual utilization of caribou is estimated at 100,000 head. There are large areas where human life would be quite impossible to maintain without the caribou.[1]

SOME ADDITIONAL NOTES

1

The flesh of the common black bear was palatable

[1] A. W. F. Banfield, *Preliminary Investigation of the Barren Ground Caribou*, Wild Life Management Bulletin, Series I, 10-B, pp. 67, 70; Series 10-A, pp. 36-37 (Ottawa, 1954).

as long as their diet was berries but before these were ripe the bears ate "May flies" (*Ephemeridae*) which were washed up on the lake shores. These insects were sometimes "lying in putrid masses to the depth of two or three feet." This diet then made bear meat unfit to eat, said Hearne.

2

The Southern Indians often took the cubs of the black bears and made pets of them. "And one of the Company servants, whose name is Isaac Batt, . . . absolutely forced one of his wives, who had recently lost her infant, to suckle a young bear," said Hearne.

3

The otter was a playful animal and one of his favorite sports was to get on a high ridge of snow, "bend their forefeet backward, and slide down the side of it, sometimes to the distance of twenty yards," said Hearne.

4

The whooping crane "visits Hudson's Bay in the Spring, though not in great numbers. They are generally seen only in pairs, and that not very often." Both Indians and whites considered them good eating and the "wing bones of this bird are so long and large, that I have known them made into flutes with tolerable success," said Hearne.

5

The meals the Bay men ate were often Gargantuan. One Indian and one Englishman once consumed a piece of bacon, some dumplings, six partridges and two geese at one sitting. (*James Isham's Observations*, p. lxviii.)

6

The Indians often performed crude surgery on themselves and on each other. "They frequently cutt their own fingers of[f] and make a good Cure." (*James Isham's Observations*, p. 96.)

7

Beckles Willson says that after Hearne returned from the Coppermine he went to England and related his experiences in a paper read before the Committee. The present writer has been unable to verify this voyage and doubts that it took place. (Beckles Willson, *The Great Company*, p. 307.)

8

The Committee in London once thought that Cumberland House could be reached easier from Fort Prince of Wales than from York, despite Hearne's finding to the contrary. They sent Malcolm Ross to try it out.

In a letter dated August 6, 1786, Hearne wrote to Joseph Colen at York that "Malcolm Ross's experiences in the interior parts of the country will I hope, render him perfect master of the business he is going about."

Ross had extreme difficulty reaching Cumberland because of the shallow waters of the upper Churchill River and Colen told Hearne about it. Hearne replied, "I am sorry to hear of the difficulties Malcolm Ross had to encounter with, tho' from my own knowledge no less could be expected; this little river a little distance from here is inaccessible for anything much larger than a light canoe." (*David Thompson's Narrative,* p. xxxvi.)

9

Warburton Pike, a big-game hunter especially interested in musk-ox, hunted the Barren Grounds and published his experiences in 1892. Pike said that Hearne's technique was still the best: trust the Indians. They were difficult to control but knew how to survive on the Barren Grounds.

10

John Meares, American fur trade and international schemer, was also smitten with the myth of Anián. Writing to his captain, William Douglas, he said, "In your Journal mention is made of prodigious Sounds which Inclines you to imagine a N.W. passage may exist. Such a thing is not impossible as I can by no means give credit to Mr. Hearn's track which at once removes what the whole world esteems an inseparable Obstacle to the reality of such a Passage. . . . We have the greatest reason to imagine that both the Charts and Journals of Admiral de Font are fictitious [nevertheless there is the possibility] remaining of such a noble discovery being made yet."

The above appears to be contradictory but Meares is presumably trying to say that if Hearne's route is correct it effectively removes all possibility of a Northwest Passage.

11

Southwest of York Factory was the "Muskrat country," controlled largely by the Canadians. In 1780 Hearne wrote, "The Canadians have found means to intercept some of my best Northern Leaders. However, I still live in hopes of getting a few [furs] from that quarter." And Hearne, or someone else, was successful in capturing the "Muskrat" trade, for by the early 1800's the bulk of the trade was going to the Company. (*David Thompson's Narrative*, p. xxxiii.)

12

While Hearne was serving aboard the Company sloop he became interested in the Eskimos and had his duties permitted would doubtless have made a careful study of their life, as he did of the Chipewyans. As it was he left the following tantalizing fragments of notes and observations:

A description of the Eskimo sealskin bags, supposedly filled with unfreezable "Pure train oil," but which often contained partially decayed fish or game. Due to the lack of flies this food was often still edible after a year, however.

An observation that although the Eskimo knew how to heat copper and spent long hours gathering moss "for firing," he ate his food raw and made no effort to use fire for warmth.

An observation that the Eskimos drank only cold water but had learned to drink ale or brandy and water mixed.

A recipe for a favorite Eskimo dish: raw deer liver mixed with the partially digested contents of the stomach, with preference given to the most digested part.

The Eskimos were fond of maggots; did not like European food but could learn to eat it.

The musk-ox in herds of 80-100 were widely distributed over the north, often coming to the coast and at least once to within nine miles of Fort Prince of Wales. The Eskimos used the long hairs from the fore parts of the animals to make mosquito nets.

An observation that he could discern no established governmental system among the Eskimo although there seemed to be a rudimentary "elder statesman" idea of giving and accepting advice.

13

Thomas Pennant, whom Hearne called "my respected friend," in the acknowledgments in his *Arctic Zoology* (London, 1792), paid Hearne the following tribute:

> To Mr. Samuel Hearne, the great explorer by land of the *Icy Sea,* I cannot but send my most particular thanks, for his liberal communication of my zoological remarks, made by him on the bold and fatiguing adventure he undertook from Hudson's Bay to the *ne plus ultra* of the north on that side.

14

Despite the short summers some gardens were grown at the Company posts on Hudson Bay. Humphrey Marten once remarked that although his garden was not as good as at Moose Factory, nevertheless, it produced "20 pounds" of potatoes and "several messes of green pease and Beans, and about ten bushels of Turnips." On June 6, 1779, he wrote to Hearne that "all our gardens are sowed." (*Cumberland House Journals and Inland Journals*, Series 2 [London: Hudson's Bay Record Society, 1952], p. xxxiii.)

Index

Y

Z